AFRICAN CAPITALISM

AFRICAN CAPITALISM

A Case Study in Nigerian Entrepreneurship

E. WAYNE NAFZIGER

HOOVER INSTITUTION PRESS • 1977

The Hoover Institution on War, Revolution and Peace, founded at Stanford University in 1919 by the late President Herbert Hoover, is an interdisciplinary research center for advanced study on domestic and international affairs in the twentieth century. The views expressed in its publications are entirely those of the authors and do not necessarily reflect the views of the staff, officers, or Board of Overseers of the Hoover Institution.

Hoover Institution Publication 169

International Standard Book Number: 0-8179-6691-9
Library of Congress Catalog Card Number: 76-48484
Printed in the United States of America

To Mother and Dad

who raised questions about capitalism

Contents

Tables

Illustrations

Acknowledgments

This work originated as a doctoral dissertation at the University of Illinois, under the guidance of John F. Due. Research during my association with the Economic Development Institute, University of Nigeria, Enugu, was facilitated by the Director, Carl K. Eicher. Funds were provided by the Midwest Universities Consortium for International Activities (for the field study); the H.B. Earhart Foundation; the Graduate School of International Studies, University of Denver; the Social Science Foundation; and Kansas State University. Royden Dangerfield, Paul L. Kelley, Edgar S. Bagley, William Stamey, Shirley Olson, Vernon Larson, and David W. Norman helped arrange time, resources, and facilities for the project; Lorraine Douglas typed the first draft and the final manuscript; and Karen McCulloh proofread the final copy. Entrepreneurs, civil servants and other officials spent hours being interviewed. Stanley W. Steinkamp, Ralph W. Cummings, Jr., Robert W. Gillespie, Sayre P. Schatz, Peter Kilby, W. Robert Stevens, Franklin Van Buer, John R. Harris, Mary P. Rowe, Maurice Amoye, H.M.A. Onitiri, T.I. Torti, Archibald Callaway, Lawrence A. Rupley and many others have also contributed to the study. My wife, Elfrieda, whom I met in Nigeria, shared her insights about the country, edited and criticized the manuscript, tolerated inconveniences and disruptions, and assumed responsibilities for tasks so as to leave me more time for research. I am deeply grateful to all who have helped, but I am solely responsible for errors and weaknesses.

Portions of "The Political Economy of Disintegration in Nigeria," *The Journal of Modern African Studies (JMAS)*, XI, No. 4 (1968), 505-36, and "Inter-regional Economic Relations in the Nigerian Footwear Industry," *JMAS*, VI, No. 4 (1968), 531-42, published by Cambridge University Press; "The Relationship Between Education and Entrepreneurship in Nigeria," *Journal of Developing Areas*, IV, No. 3 (April 1970), 349-59; "The Effect of the Nigerian Extended Family on Entrepreneurial Activity," *Economic Development and Cultural Change*, XVIII, No. 1 (October 1969), 25-33, published by the University of Chicago Press; and "The Market for Nigerian Entrepreneurs," in *South of the Sahara: Development in African Economies*, ed. by Sayre P. Schatz (Philadelphia: Temple University Press, 1972), pp. 61-78; were reprinted by permission.

E.W.N.

Department of Economics
Kansas State University
June 1976

Tinibu Square, Lagos

Shehu,
maker of
leather goods,
Zaria

Mallam Sanusi, Maiduguri Shoe Firm

Finishing machine for smoothing the outsole, Maiduguri Shoe Firm

Leather tannery,
Zaria

Ogbete Market, Enugu

Chapter 1

Introduction: The Study of Entrepreneurship

The Role of the Entrepreneur in Economic Development

The rate of economic growth is dependent upon the growth in the factors of production and the rate of technical change. Recently some economists have shifted the emphasis away from the increase of physical capital to the expansion of high-level manpower, such as entrepreneurship, as the major determinant of economic development. In part, this shift in emphasis towards entrepreneurship resulted from empirical studies suggesting that increases in the supply of capital explain no more than a fraction of growth in income per capita or in productivity per man. Robert Solow, for example, indicated on the basis of U.S. data from 1909-49 that "gross output per man-hour doubled over the interval, with 87½ percent of the increase attributable to technical change and the remaining 12½ percent to increase in the use of capital."[1]

However, the residual factor in growth, identified as "technical change," needs to be explained. Joseph A. Schumpeter, perhaps the major contributor to the theory of economic development in the first half of this century, attributed novel ways of doing things (i.e. innovations responsible for technical change) to the entrepreneur.[2] In fact, Arthur H. Cole, in his Presiden-

---

1. Robert Solow, "Technical Change and the Aggregate Production Function," *Review of Economics and Statistics*, XXXIX (August 1957), 320.

2. "Economic Theory and Entrepreneurial History," in *Change and the Entrepreneur: Postulates and Patterns for Entrepreneurial History*, Harvard University Research Center in Entrepreneurial History (Cambridge, Mass.: Harvard University Press, 1949), pp. 73-7.

tial Address to the Economic History Association in 1946, even argued that "To study the 'entrepreneur' is to study the central figure in modern economic history, and, to my way of thinking, the central figure in economics."[3]

Empirical studies such as Solow's are not inconsistent with the contention that increases in productivity stem mainly from improvements in the combination, organization and coordination of inputs, attributable by most definitions to the entrepreneur, rather than to growth in the quantity of inputs. The exact contribution of the entrepreneur cannot, however, be gauged, given problems of measurement and conceptualization, but its undoubted importance makes it worthy of study.

Economists have increasingly maintained that the major obstacle to the economic development of less developed countries is not so much a shortage of capital as a lack of absorptive capacity, resulting in part from the shortage of skill and knowledge needed to mobilize, organize, and coordinate capital and other resources of production. The crucial role of entrepreneurship, the productive resource which coordinates and organizes the others, is indicated by the following observation of W. Arthur Lewis:

> To lend money to entrepreneurs who lack managerial capacity is merely to throw it down the drain. . . . The main deficiency of local enterprise is not capital but knowledge and experience.[4]

Although all other resources of production tend to be substitutable for one another, entrepreneurship is a complementary factor. The more capital, labor, and natural resources a firm has, the more entrepreneurial resources are needed to combine these productive factors. Organizational and entrepreneurial skills are considered to be crucial bottlenecks in less developed economies, regardless of whether production is centered in the public or private sector, and thus the question of the need for entrepreneurship is free of ideological overtones.

---

3. "An Approach to the Study of Entrepreneurship: A Tribute to Edwin F. Gay," in *Explorations in Enterprise*, ed. by Hugh G.J. Aitken (Cambridge, Mass.: Harvard University Press, 1965), p. 37.

4. "Aspects of Industrialization," *Nigerian Trade Journal*, II, No. 4 (October-December 1954), 11-12.

The Significance of Entrepreneurship for Nigerian Economic Growth

Capital was at one time considered the crucial bottleneck in Nigerian economic growth, but this emphasis has now changed. On the basis of a study of the record of Nigerian Federal Loans Board loan recipients, Sayre P. Schatz contends that the alleged shortage of capital in Nigeria is an illusion. "Instead of a large number of viable projects vainly seeking capital," Schatz maintains, "the situation has been one of capital vainly seeking viable private projects."[5]

Several economists, in rejecting the idea of capital as a limiting factor in Nigerian economic development, have pointed to entrepreneurial, managerial, and organizational skills as the scarce factor. Professor Wolfgang F. Stolper, Head of the Economic Planning Unit in the Nigerian Federal Ministry of Economic Development during the preparation of the 1962-68 National Development Plan, views skilled manpower as the strategic factor in Plan success. Stolper writes:

> [With regard to the Plan,] I have personally not the slightest doubt that the money will be forthcoming, but that the real limitations will be neither capital nor foreign aid but manpower. . . . The limitation is linked very intimately with the shortage of executive manpower.[6]

The authors of the Third National Development Plan, 1975-80 state that "manpower or executive capacity remains a bottleneck to the development of the nation. . . . Management or entrepreneurship as a resource is generally in scarce supply in the Nigerian economy."[7]

The Study of Indigenous Manufacturing Entrepreneurs

This study focuses on manufacturing (or industrial) entre-

---

5. *Development Bank Lending in Nigeria* (London: Oxford University Press, 1964), p. 97.

6. "The Main Features of the 1962-68 National Plan," *Nigerian Journal of Economic and Social Studies*, IV, No. 2 (July 1962), 90.

7. Nigeria, Ministry of Economic Development, *Third National Development Plan, 1975-80*, I (Lagos: Central Planning Office, 1975), 48, 64.

preneurs. Cross-sectional and longitudinal studies indicate a positive correlation between per capita gross national product (GNP) and the percentage of GNP originating in the manufacturing sector, although the implication of this correlation need not be that an increase in the relative size of the industrial sector is a cause of higher GNP per capita.[8] However, the literature sets forth several reasons why countries aspiring to rapid economic development might want to place a high priority upon industrialization. First, because industrial goods have a higher income elasticity of demand (percentage change in the amount of goods demanded/percentage change in income) than agricultural commodities, the expansion of industry offers more scope for the growth of output. Second, industry is more likely to have substantial backward linkages (stimulus of demand for the outputs of other sectors needed as inputs for the manufacturing activity) and forward linkages (inducement of attempts to utilize the outputs from the manufacturing activity as inputs in other sectors) than agriculture and other sectors. Third, manufacturing is more likely to give rise to external economies (benefits which accrue to some unit in the economy other than the producing firm), such as the training of skilled labor, or the lowering of the prices of inputs to other industries. Fourth, manufacturing is more likely to be characterized by economies of large-scale production, or increasing returns to scale. Fifth, manufacturing offers more potential for increases in output as a result of technological improvement. This may especially be the case in underdeveloped countries, which can often make use of a backlog of previously unutilized technology. Sixth, diversification from less dependence on agriculture to more production in manufacturing can reduce the economic costs associated with a vulnerable economy highly dependent upon the export of only a few primary commodities. Finally, entrepreneurs and capitalists in the manufacturing sector may have a higher propensity to save than those in other sectors.

In the early years of post-Independence development planning in Nigeria, the highest priority was placed upon the growth of the manufacturing sector through the substitution of domestic

---

8. Colin Clark, *The Conditions of Economic Progress* (London: Macmillan, 1951), pp. 350-439; Simon Kuznets, "Industrial Distribution of National Product and Labor Force," *Economic Development and Cultural Change* (Supplement), V, No. 4 (July 1957), 5-19; and Jacob Viner, *International Trade and Economic Development* (Glencoe, Ill.: Free Press, 1952), pp. 62-73.

production for imports.[9] In recent years, Nigerian leaders, like their counterparts in other underdeveloped countries, have realized that the early emphasis upon industrialization was excessive. The issue is not one of industrial development *versus* agricultural development, but the interaction between the two sectors and the contribution that each can make to the other.[10]

A detailed evaluation of the arguments, cited previously, for putting a high priority upon the manufacturing sector is beyond the scope of this study. It is obviously not essential to maintain that industry be given top priority and encouraged at the expense of other sectors, in order to argue its importance for study. Moreover, industrial growth does offer a number of dynamic benefits important for bringing about structural change associated with rapid economic development. Finally, in Nigeria itself as in most developing countries, industrial development is still given a high priority by planners[11] although attention is returning to the agricultural sector.

The entrepreneurs studied here are Nigerian. A number of scholars and political leaders in less developed countries have become increasingly concerned that the growth of their economies has been dependent on decisions made by foreigners on the basis of the development and expansion of the metropolitan economies. Typically, in poor countries, foreign capital and entrepreneurship have dominated industry more than any other sector except mining. In 1965, foreign private ownership in Nigeria comprised 62 percent of total ownership and 85 percent of total

---

9. Nigeria, Ministry of Economic Development, *National Development Plan, 1962-68* (Lagos, n.d.), p. 8; Nigeria, Ministry of Information, *Statement on Industrial Policy*, Sessional Paper No. 6 (Lagos, 1964), p. 1; Nigeria, Ministry of Finance (Festus Sam Okotie-Eboh, Federal Minister of Finance), *The Six Budget Speeches, 1958-1963*, presented to the Federal House of Representatives (Lagos, n.d.), pp. 6, 185-6; and Nigeria, Ministry of Economic Development, *Guideposts for Second National Development Plan* (Lagos, June 1966), p. 7.

10. Gerald M. Meier, *Leading Issues in Economic Development: Studies in International Poverty* (Stanford: Oxford University Press, 1970), p. 391.

11. Nigeria, Ministry of Information, *Second National Development Plan, 1970-74* (Lagos, 1971), pp. 281-2; and Nigeria, Ministry of Economic Development, *Guidelines for the Third National Development Plan, 1975-80* (Lagos, n.d.), p. 17.

private ownership in manufacturing establishments with over ten employees.[12]

Since Independence - and in fact even in the last few years of the British era - the Nigerian government has paid lip service to the importance of policies to accelerate the Nigerianization of capital and high-level manpower in industry. A decree in mid-1971, which increased the number of industries reserved for Nigerians, raised the requirements for indigenous equity participation in a number of enterprises. Tightened quotas for foreign business personnel were in response to the frustration of a part of the Nigerian political leadership to the slow progress of indigenization resulting from previous efforts. It is in the context of the difficulties encountered by policies for Nigerianization that the need for a study of indigenous entrepreneurship becomes clearer.

The Entrepreneur in Orthodox Economic Analysis

Before presenting the concepts and design of this study, and the analysis of Nigerian entrepreneurs, I shall provide an outline of the relevant literature on entrepreneurship, especially in economics. It is important not only as a background to the concepts and questions considered in the study, but also as an indication of the range of scholarship. In the following three sections, I want to fill a gap in the literature by sketching the concept of the entrepreneur in the history of orthodox economic theory, in Marxian economic thought, and in contemporary economic analysis.[13]

The treatise of the French writer, Richard Cantillon, fre-

---

12. Nigeria, Office of Statistics, *Industrial Survey of Nigeria, 1964 and 1965* (Lagos, 1968), pp. 32, 34, 37. I elaborate on this point in chapter 2 (see especially table 2.8).

13. The important contributions of Max Weber, Everett E. Hagen, Bert F. Hoselitz and David C. McClelland, which however do not belong in a discussion of the entrepreneur in the history of economic analysis, are discussed in E. Wayne Nafziger, "The Mennonite Ethic in the Weberian Framework," *Explorations in Entrepreneurial History/Second Series*, II, No. 1 (Spring-Summer 1965), 187-204; John R. Harris, "Industrial Entrepreneurship in Nigeria," (Ph.D. dissertation, Northwestern University, 1967), pp. 40-53; and Peter Kilby, ed., *Entrepreneurship and Economic Development* (New York: Free Press, 1971), pp. 1-40. See the appendix to chapter 10 for a critique of certain aspects of McClelland's views.

quently considered the earliest systematic work in political economy, was probably the first to discuss the entrepreneur. Cantillon divided the inhabitants of a country, except for princes and landlords, into two classes: entrepreneurs, including farmers and merchants, and hired people. He distinguishes between the owner and the entrepreneur, although the two categories are not clearly defined. Entrepreneurs do carry on the production and exchange of goods at some risk, facing the possibility of bankruptcy when the demand for their products is depressed.[14]

In J.B. Say's theory of distribution, the entrepreneur, though not a factor of production, has a key role. Although Say, a French economist writing in the last half of the eighteenth century, recognizes that the entrepreneur may frequently provide the capital for the enterprise, his function and remuneration is clearly differentiated from that of the capitalist. The function of the entrepreneur is to direct the application of acquired knowledge to the production of a good for human consumption. To be successful, Say maintains, the entrepreneur needs the ability to estimate future demand, to determine the appropriate quantity and timing of inputs, to judge and calculate probable production costs and selling prices, and to possess the art of superintendence and administration. Since the combination of these is not common, the quantity of successful entrepreneurs is limited, especially in industry.[15]

Although capitalism (i.e. the separation of the worker from the ownership of the means of production) developed in England prior to the seventeenth century, conspicuously few English economists have written on the theory and concept of entrepreneurship before this century. Adam Smith, writing in 1776 at the time of the putting-out system and before the advent of the factory system, distinguishes at one point between the "undertaker" (a translation of the French word, *entrepreneur*) or capitalist who manages his own capital and receives profit, and the inactive capitalist, who receives interest. However, in a subsequent reference, Smith does not even make this distinction, referring to "three different orders of people; . . . those who live by rent, . . . those who live by wages, and . . . those who live by prof-

---

14. *Essai sur la Nature du Commerce en General* (c. 1730), ed. and trans. by Henry Higgs (London: Frank Cass and Co., Ltd., 1959), pp. 47-59, 217, 388-99.

15. *A Treatise on Political Economy*, trans. by C.R. Prinsap, II (4th ed.; Boston: Wells and Lilly, 1824), 55-9.

fits" (i.e. employers, who receive profits from capital stock).[16]

Although Smith had no clear conception of the entrepreneurial function, he placed much stress on the importance of the business class. He believed that each individual would unwittingly add to wealth and welfare by furthering his own selfish ends.

In part perhaps because of the authority of Smith, the classical economists of the early nineteenth century, merged the entrepreneurial and capitalist functions, and failed to develop a theory of the differentiation between interests and profits. Not only did they have an inadequate concept of the entrepreneur - eventually the term had to be borrowed from the French - but they also lacked an adequate theory of distribution which included the entrepreneur since they had no theory of general equilibrium, unlike Frenchmen such as Richard Cantillon and Francis Quesnay. The belief of the classical school that economic relationships were determined by natural law may have forestalled the idea of a conscious agent, such as the entrepreneur, at the center of the economic process.[17]

Leon Walras, whose theory of general equilibrium in the last part of the nineteenth century has yet to be surpassed, designated the entrepreneur as the fourth factor of production who hires the others.

The entrepreneur appears as buyer on the market for productive services, and the seller on the market for goods. This definition of the entrepreneur avoids the error of the French economists who, according to Walras, consider the entrepreneur "as a worker charged with the special task of managing a firm," and the more serious error of the English economists, who identify the entrepreneur with the capitalist. Under free competition, the entrepreneur, in his role as a profit maximizer, is crucial in insuring that markets move toward an equilibrium. He enters branches of production which are profitable, thus eventually increasing output and eliminating profits (above competitive

---

16. *An Enquiry Into the Nature and Causes of the Wealth of Nations*, I (London: G. Bell and Sons, Ltd., 1912), 53-4, 262-4.

17. Say, *Treatise*, II, 54-5; and Meenakshi Tyagarajan, "The Development of the Theory of Entrepreneurship," *Indian Economic Review*, IV, No. 4 (August 1959), 135-50.

returns to the factors of production); and exits industries incurring losses, consequently decreasing the output of these goods and erasing losses.[18]

Alfred Marshall distinguished between interest and the earnings of management (or the undertaker), indicating that these are what remain of profits after capital has been deducted. The business undertakers, who bring together the capital and labor required for the work, arrange the general plan, and superintend its minor details, may range from a highly skilled industrial worker (such as a foreman) to the top management official of the firm. Undertakers at one level of the hierarchy will be substituted for those at another level, as variations take place in the ratios of the marginal product to the wage rate among the different levels of the management organization. The undertakers introduce improved methods and increase their earnings; copying by competitors results and this leads to the earnings of the initial undertakers decreasing to their initial level. This idea, not fully-developed, is a premonition of Schumpeter's theory of innovation.[19]

For Schumpeter, the entrepreneur is at the center of an integrated model of economic development incorporating a theory of profit and interest, a theory of the business cycle, and a theory of the crisis of the capitalistic system. The entrepreneur is an innovator (i.e. one who carries out new combinations). These include five cases: (1) the introduction of a new good; (2) the introduction of a new production function; (3) the opening of a new market; (4) the conquest of a new source of supply of materials; and (5) the carrying out of a new organization of an industry.[20]

The Schumpeterian pure model begins with a circular flow (similar to a stationary state), an unchanging economic process which merely reproduces itself at constant rates in a closed

---

18. *Elements of Pure Economics or the Theory of Social Wealth* (London: George Allen and Unwin, Ltd., 1954), pp. 222-3, 225.

19. *Principles of Economics* (1st ed.; London: Macmillan, 1890), pp. 142, 355, 621, 632-7.

20. *Business Cycles* (New York: McGraw-Hill Book Company, Inc., 1939), I, 102; and *The Theory of Economic Development: An Inquiry into Profits, Capital, Credit, Interest, and the Business Cycle*, trans. by Redvers Opie (New York: Oxford University Press, 1961), pp. 66, 132. Written originally in 1911.

domain, with an absence of innovators or entrepreneurs. This model, which assumes perfect competition, full employment, no capital accumulation and no technical change, helps bring out in a clearer way the impact of the entrance of entrepreneurs. No entrepreneurial function or even managerial function is required, since the ordinary routine work, the repetition of orders and operations, can be done even by workmen.

Into this flow, an entrepreneur motivated by money profits introduces an innovation, which consists of a new production function, raising the marginal productivity of the various factors of production. Major innovations generally involve the construction of new plants and are embodied in a new firm, which implies the rise to leadership of new men. The orthodox assumption that business behavior is ideally rational and prompt, and is similar for all firms, is appropriate within the precincts of tried experience and familiar motive, but breaks down when the business community encounters "new possibilities of business action which are as yet untried and about which the most complete command of routine teaches nothing."[21]

The innovator thus differs from the manager of a firm, who runs the business on established lines. The entrepreneur is the engineer of change, not its product. It is difficult to identify him in practice, since no one acts exclusively as an entrepreneur. Though frequently he will be found among heads or founders of firms and/or among the major owners or stockholders, he need not necessarily hold a high official post in the firm, nor furnish capital or bear risks. Entrepreneurs arise from all economic classes.[22]

In the stationary economy, there may be high earnings for management, monopoly gains, windfalls, or speculative gains, but there are no entrepreneurial profits. Profits are the premium for innovation, and arise from no other source. Innovation, however, sets up only a temporary monopoly gain, which is soon wiped out by imitation; for profits to continue, it is necessary to keep one step ahead of rivals with innovations. Profits result from the activities of the entrepreneur, even though they may not accrue to him in certain institutional settings.[23]

The creation of bank credit is initially associated with innovation, a breaking of the circular flow by the entrepreneur.

---

21. *Business Cycles*, I, 35-45, 130-2, 235-8.
22. Ibid. pp. 102-4.
23. Ibid. pp. 100-5.

Once a new production function has been successfully set up, imitation becomes easier for competitors. Thus, innovations are not isolated events and evenly distributed in time, place, and sector; but tend to arise in clusters as a result of varying incidences of risk. Eventually, the wave of entrepreneurial activity forces out old firms, and also exhausts the limited possibilities of gain from the innovation. As borrowing diminishes and loans are repaid, entrepreneurial activity tends to slacken and finally ceases. The differential rates of innovation and credit creation are the basis for Schumpeter's theory of the business cycle. The innovation, together with credit creation and saving, gives rise to economic growth.[24]

The concept "innovation" should be distinguished from the concept "invention." To become an innovation, an invention needs to be put into business practice. History is replete with examples of inventions, which occurred independently of any practical need, or which, more frequently, failed to obtain a sponsor or market. For example, Arthur H. Cole contends that the Stanley Steamer automobile in the United States in the early part of the twentieth century failed, not because it was inferior to the automobile with the internal combustion engine, but because of the Stanley brothers' failure to mass produce the automobiles.[25]

I want to evaluate Schumpeter's theory primarily as it relates to the question of entrepreneurship in less developed countries. The model originally purported to be valid only for western capitalism in the period of the nineteenth century prior to the rise of giant corporations.[26] The institutional assumptions

---

24. Ibid. pp. 87-159, and Richard V. Clemence and Francis S. Doody, *The Schumpeterian System* (Cambridge, Mass.: Addison-Wesley Press, Inc., 1950), pp. 9-10.

25. *Business Enterprise in its Social Setting* (Cambridge, Mass.: Harvard University Press, 1959), p. 44.

26. *Business Cycles*, I, 145. Because of this, Schumpeter's theory may be inappropriate for underdeveloped capitalist economies, since many industries in these countries, especially in manufacturing, are characterized by the dominance of a few large firms. This is to say nothing of the less developed economies which are centrally planned.

Still, despite Schumpeter's restricted focus, the scheme may have some application to other types of economies. Even in socialist economies, it seems essential that the political class, bureaucrats, managers and technicians be instrumental in the encouragement and undertaking of technical innovation and adaptation.

and theoretical interactions are so specific that, like a spark-plug made to fit one machine, it is difficult to put the Schumpeterian entrepreneur into any other model of economic development.[27] Moreover, it is not clear why there needs to be a one-to-one correspondence between new innovations and the creation of new credit. It seems unrealistic to preclude the possibility that innovations may result in the expansion of firms already existing. In fact, in the real world, characterized by imperfect competition, an organization with some time dimension might have an advantage in the development of new techniques, markets, products and organizations. It should also be noted that Schumpeter does not incorporate a premium for risk into his theory of distribution. The theory is difficult to test empirically. Though the entrepreneurial function is clear, the persons performing the function cannot be readily identified. Furthermore, the impact of an initial innovation that starts growth and fluctuations is so swamped by the secondary and tertiary effects of the model that it is virtually impossible either to demonstrate or refute the hypothesis that innovations are the source of business cycles and economic development. Finally, as evidenced in chapter four, the Schumpeterian entrepreneur has only a limited role in underdeveloped economies. However, even when the concept of the entrepreneur is broadened, it is not possible to derive a working definition which would enable other investigators to concur in the identification of entrepreneurs.

To Frank Knight, entrepreneurs bear the responsibility and the consequences of making decisions under conditions of uncertainty, i.e. where the uniqueness of the situation denies an objective, quantitatively determinate probability. In such a situation, the uncertainty cannot be eliminated by creating structures which consolidate or group a number of situations, by selecting specialized institutions (such as insurance companies) to bear the risk, by controlling the future (through overwhelming market power), by accurate power of prediction (through incurring costs of obtaining data), or by diffusion between a number of parties. However where a risk can be computed, some of these methods can be used to reduce the uncertainty.[28]

To show the impact of uncertainty upon the profits of entrepreneurs, Knight analyzes the case where every member of the competitive system is virtually omniscient. In this situation, even though change may take place, profits are absent since with

---

27. See Aitken, ed., *Explorations*, pp. 8-11.
28. *Risk, Uncertainty and Profit* (Boston: Houghton Mifflin Co., 1921), pp. 231-2, 271.

complete foreknowledge, competition adjusts things to the point where all prices would equal costs. When omniscient firms foresee potential losses, they exit the industry until losses are removed; when profits are foreseen, all-knowing firms enter the industry until the point where the increased supply erases profits.[29]

In the state where all men have perfect knowledge of the future, there are no entrepreneurs, but only laborers performing the purely routine functions of reacting in mechanical fashion to data concerning the future. However, in a world of uncertainty, the entrepreneur, a new economic functionary endowed with knowledge, judgment, foresight, confidence and organizational ability, is required. The entrepreneur, the person responsible for decisions in instances where there is unmeasurable uncertainty, can make profits, since the lack of perfect foreknowledge prevents the perfect adjustment of supply by competitors to a no-profit equilibrium.[30]

Knight's entrepreneur bears the risk, a function which Schumpeter explicitly indicates belongs to the capitalist. The ultimate decision making and control in the firm lie with the risk-bearer and not with the hired manager, even though he may be the managing director or chairman of the board of directors. Generally, it is not possible for a person to exercise only the function of entrepreneurship in a firm. The nearest approximation would be a man who borrowed all the resources for operating a firm (i.e. took the risk) and then hired a manager who was given a completely free hand.[31]

In Knight's view, it is fruitless to try to separate profit from interest, since the entrepreneur almost of necessity owns property. Profit is a residual share of income which falls to the person in *responsible* control of business, who generally also receives property income.

Unlike Schumpeter, Knight's explanation has the advantage of making profit a return to the function of entrepreneurship. However, there is no reason why the reward to the entrepreneur needs to be in the form of profits in all institutional settings. Most economists would contend that the control of the giant corporation in the United States today is generally not in the hands

---

29. Ibid. pp. 141-73, 197.
30. Ibid. pp. 232, 268-70.
31. Ibid. pp. 296-300.

of the stockholders but of management, which in many cases is self-perpetuating. Where this is true, Knight's contention that the persons who exercise the function of control in the firm also bear risk can be questioned.

The Entrepreneur in Marxist Economic Analysis

Like the majority of economists of the last two centuries, most Marxist economists have failed to recognize the function of the entrepreneur. To Karl Marx, the central figure in the economic process was the capitalist, whose role arose from his ownership of the instruments of production and not from any activity on his part. By and large, the entrepreneur was excluded, although Marx's active capitalist has some of his features. A distinction is made between the money capitalist, who receives interest, and the industrial capitalist or active capitalist, who receives that part of gross profit not paid as interest, namely "profits of enterprise." The industrial capitalist, in cases where he coordinates labor in the process of production much as a conductor directs an orchestra, is himself a laborer. In these instances, the returns of the active capitalist, unlike those of the inactive money capitalist, need not be a result of the exploitation of labor.[32]

However, the supervision of labor is much more important in modes of production based on the antithesis between the direct producer, labor, and the owner of the means of production. Labor supervision is especially important in despotic governments, and reaches its peak in the slave system. Under wage servitude in the capitalist system, the wage laborer is compelled to produce wages for himself and the supervisor, an agent of the inactive capitalist. Where wage servitude exists, the supervisor, like the capitalist, depends directly upon the exploitation of labor.[33]

In cooperative factories, where managers are paid by the workers, the labor of supervision disappears. This type of example indicates to Marx that the profits of enterprise are a fruit of exploitation by the active capitalist rather than wages for essential supervision.[34]

The lack of distinction between the entrepreneur and capi-

---

32. *Capital*, ed. by F. Engels, III (Moscow: Progress Publishers, 1966), 372-83. Originally published in 1894.
33. Ibid. III, 383-7.
34. Ibid. p. 387.

talist in the Marxian theory of distribution, as with the English classical economists, stems from a lack of clarity in differentiating interest from profits. Also, although Marx indicates a difference between the active and inactive capitalist approximating the difference between the entrepreneur and capitalist in other frameworks, he is not consistent in indicating whether the active capitalist has an essential function in the production process.

Maurice Dobb, a writer in the Marxist tradition, acknowledges that any society with modern machine techniques and extensive division of labor requires some coordinating, controlling or integrating force, which is, he indicates, the entrepreneurial function. The principal element of this function, a synthesis of the concepts of Schumpeter and Knight, is the capacity for adjustment and innovation, which includes, most importantly, the ability to make correct judgments about the future. Dobb does not question the necessity of the entrepreneurial function, but considers the most appropriate institutional framework within which the entrepreneur should operate - classless individualism, with a large number of independent producers; communism, where the entrepreneurial function is performed by agents of the community; or capitalism, under the control of a class of capitalist undertakers.[35]

The capitalist undertaker, who usually also plays the role of the capitalist, generally obtains profits as a result of some monopoly advantage. This fact does not mean that he inhibits economic progress, nor that the situation is necessarily morally undesirable. The monopoly or advantage that the undertaker exploits, except that which results from inherent ability, is the result of greater opportunities such as: (1) greater information; (2) superior access to training and education; (3) a lower discount of future earnings; (4) greater firm size; and (5) agreements to restrict entry or output. All five are facilitated by the possession of wealth or position. Capitalist undertaking in conditions of some monopoly privilege is *par excellence* a progressive force, as the economic growth of the century prior to 1926, the time of Dobb's writing, indicates. Few persons are willing to face the burden of uncertainty in an environment where they have little control. The head of a large capitalist corporation or a communist planning board is more likely to commit large resources to expanding output than is a small enter-

35. *Capitalist Enterprise and Social Progress* (London: Routledge, 1926), pp. 4, 26-41.

prise in a freely competitive economy.[36]

Despite the success of capitalism in the past century, Dobb questions whether it can, in the future, with the rise of trusts and imperialism, satisfy the demands of economic adjustment and income distribution more effectively than communism. Economic theory cannot help us very much with this problem, he continues, without new approaches, since the theory of capitalist undertaking is, as of 1926, primarily based on the assumption of a society of classless individualism.[37] Despite the analysis of imperfect competition by Joan Robinson and Edward Chamberlain in the following decade, much of Dobb's criticism of economic theory is still valid.

To Paul A. Baran, a Marxist economist, those concerned about the lack of supply of entrepreneurs have misplaced their emphasis. The entrepreneur is not the major figure responsible for capitalist development, but is, along with the capitalist, a figure that has benefited substantially from the age of modern capitalism. Furthermore, Baran charged that the study of entrepreneurship is racially and ideologically oriented. (1) Much of the literature on entrepreneurship, he claims, extols the "genius" of the entrepreneur in the capitalistic system, without trying to explain why his "genius" turned to the accumulation of capital. (2) A large part of the literature implies that less developed countries lack entrepreneurship because of a lack of character traits, such as risk-taking, imagination and frugality, presumably considered to be a strength of the Anglo-Saxon peoples. (3) Students of entrepreneurship are incorrect in maintaining that there is a lack of entrepreneurship in less developed countries. The problem is not one of inadequacy of supply but of the composition of entrepreneurship between the various sectors of the economy.[38]

Baran is correct in some of his allegations. However, although the entrepreneur has tended to become a "captive" of "bourgeois" scholars, nothing in the concept of the entrepreneurial function itself, in its broadest sense, prevents its application to socialist economies. The question of the need for certain types of entrepreneurship can be free of ideological overtones. Indigenous organizational and entrepreneurial skills are scarce in the manufacturing and mining sectors (in the sec-

---

36. Ibid. pp. 97-112, 163-4, 172.

37. Ibid. pp. 395-400.

38. *The Political Economy of Growth* (New York: Monthly Review Press, 1957), pp. 234-7.

tors with the most advanced technical requirements) in most less developed economies, whether socialist, or capitalist.[39]

Furthermore, it is scientifically indefensible to attribute differences in the supply of entrepreneurship to innate racial characteristics. No doubt, some writers on the subject have been guilty of this error. However, social scientists have consistently observed significant national, regional, ethnic and social differences in patterns of participation in a number of types of activities - in participation in music, scholarship, philosophical speculation, politics, the priesthood, and organized crime, as well as participation in major entrepreneurial positions. In eighteenth century England, a disproportionate number of scientists originated from the branch of Protestant Christianity known as Puritanism. In the United States today the representation of Jews in universities and the professions is far higher than would be expected by their population. In Nigeria, just prior to the first coup in January 1966, one-half of army officers of the rank of major or above consisted of Ibos, who comprised only one-sixth of the population. In India, the Marwari community is disproportionately represented in large industrial enterprise. Yet these high rates of activity in a sector of the socio-economic system do not necessarily imply specific character traits in the social or ethnic groups indicated. Within a country, membership of different communities, with varying histories, cultural traditions, and locations in society, may result in norms, aspirations, values and behavior which are not similar. But these dissimilar traits are the result of diverse socio-historical milieux, and not biological differences. Nevertheless, in defense of Baran, I would agree that social scientists have tended to neglect domestic class arrangements and their linkage with the stratification system which exists in the international capitalist system.

The Entrepreneur in Contemporary Economic Theory

Harvey Leibenstein points out that the entrepreneur has

---

39. L. Dupriez, *Economic Progress: Papers and Proceedings of a Round Table Held by the International Economic Association* (Louvain: Institut de Recherches Economiques et Sociales, 1955), pp. 22-4; Albert O. Hirschman, *The Strategy of Economic Development* (New Haven: Yale University Press, 1958), pp. 16-9; Gerald M. Meier and Robert E. Baldwin, *Economic Development: Theory, History, Policy* (New York: John Wiley and Sons, Inc., 1957), p. 299; and Hla Myint, *The Economics of the Developing Countries* (New York: Frederick A. Praeger, Publishers, 1966), p. 173.

only a trivial role in the type of models prevalent in present economic theory - static models which assume complete certainty.

> If all inputs are marketed and their prices are known, and if all outputs are marketed and their prices are known and if there is a definite production function that relates inputs to outputs in a determinate way, then we can always predict the profit for any activity that transforms inputs into outputs. If net profits are positive, then this should serve as a signal for entry into this market. The problems of marshaling resources and turning them into outputs appears to be a trivial activity. From this point of view it is hard to see why there should ever be a deficiency of entrepreneurship. The answer is that the standard competitive model hides the vital function of the entrepreneur.[40]

Leibenstein suggests that there is not a one-to-one correspondence between sets of inputs and outputs, nor is the complete set of inputs specified and known to all actual or potential firms in the industry, as the received theory indicates. Frequently inputs in the production function are not well-defined, and there is not a well-developed market for them. This is especially true in less developed countries. For example, if a certain type of machine has to be employed to produce a particular type of commodity, if no one in the country produces the machine, and if imports are barred, then only entrepreneurs who have access to information on how to construct the machine can enter the industry. In addition, there may not be well-organized markets for various types of management and market knowledge. To fill these gaps, the entrepreneur has to have the ability to obtain and use factors of production not well-marketed; he has to compensate for market deficiencies. In order to insure that he is not thwarted in the matrix of information, finance, markets, and inputs required, the entrepreneur may need political and family connections.[41]

The Functions of the Entrepreneur

Peter Kilby gave the most comprehensive breakdown of the

---

40. "Entrepreneurship and Development," *American Economic Review*, LVIII, No. 2 (May 1968), 72.
41. Ibid. pp. 73-4.

functions of entrepreneurship, listing thirteen roles that the entrepreneur might have to perform for the successful operation of the enterprise:

Exchange relationships

1. Perception of market opportunities (novel or imitative)
2. Gaining command over scarce resources
3. Marketing of the product and responding to competition
4. Purchasing inputs

Political administration

5. Dealing with the public bureaucracy (concessions, licenses, taxes, and so forth)
6. Management of human relations within the firm
7. Management of customer and supplier relations

Management control

8. Financial management
9. Production management (control by written records, supervision, coordinating input flows with customer orders, maintenance of equipment)

Technological

10. Acquiring and overseeing assembly of the plant
11. Industrial engineering (minimizing inputs with a given production process)
12. Upgrading processes and product quality
13. Introduction of new production techniques and products[42]

As he pointed out, the economic theorist frequently limits the entrepreneurial function to activities 1 and 2: it is assumed that the remaining skills can be purchased on the market place. The extent to which the entrepreneur can delegate these activities to competent subordinates depends upon the scale of production, the degree of development of the market for high-level manpower, the social factors which govern the amount of

---

42. Kilby, ed., *Entrepreneurship and Economic Development*, pp. 27-8.

responsibility hired personnel will show, and the efficiency of the entrepreneur in utilizing high-level managerial employees. Since many of these inputs are not well-marketed in less developed economies, the entrepreneur frequently has to perform the tasks himself. One of the important skills of the entrepreneur in less developed countries is to utilize factors of production that are not well-marketed. Empirical studies of entrepreneurs in these economies indicate that production, financial and technological management are least satisfactory.[43]

Contemporary Empirical Studies of Entrepreneurs in Less Developed Economies

Since others have reviewed the literature on entrepreneurship in less developed countries, this section can be briefer and more selective. Harris's survey of empirical studies of entrepreneurship, primarily in poor countries, is the most comprehensive available.[44] Kilby's discussion of various perspectives on entrepreneurship is not as exhaustive as the Harris survey, but emphasizes the correlation of the theoretical literature from a large number of disciplines with the existing empirical literature.[45] Here I focus on six of the leading contemporary studies of industrial entrepreneurship in less developed countries which acquire data through the use of questionnaires - Sayigh's study of Lebanon,[46] Carroll's on the Phillipines,[47] Alexander's on Greece,[48] Papanek on Pakistan,[49] and Berna[50] and

---

43. Ibid. pp. 27-35, and Leibenstein, *American Economic Review*, LVIII, No. 2, 73-4.

44. John R. Harris, "Industrial Entrepreneurship in Nigeria," pp. 40-71.

45. Kilby, ed., *Entrepreneurship*, pp. 1-40.

46. Yusif A. Sayigh, *Entrepreneurs of Lebanon: The Role of the Business Leader in a Developing Economy* (Cambridge, Mass.: Harvard University Press, 1962).

47. John J. Carroll, *The Filipino Manufacturing Entrepreneur: Agent and Product of Change* (Ithaca: Cornell University Press, 1965).

48. Alec P. Alexander, *Greek Industrialists: An Economic and Social Analysis* (Athens: Center of Planning and Economic Research, 1964).

49. Gustav F. Papanek, "The Development of Entrepreneurship," *American Economic Review*, LII, No. 2 (May 1962), 46-58, and *Pakistan's Development: Social Goals and Private Incentives* (Cambridge, Mass: Harvard University Press, 1967).

50. James J. Berna, *Industrial Entrepreneurship in Madras State* (London: Asia Publishing House, 1960).

Nafziger[51] on India.[52] Since most of these studies are included in the discussion by Harris and Kilby, my purpose is merely to emphasize aspects of the works that introduce issues relevant for an understanding of this study.

Sayigh, in his survey of 207 Lebanese entrepreneurs in 1959, carefully develops his conceptual framework and designs his questions so as to test hypotheses made by economists in the theoretical literature on entrepreneurship. In a manner similar to Schumpeter, Sayigh identifies increases in the productive capacity of an economy with the application of innovative enterprise to advances in technology. However, Schumpeter's entrepreneur is broadened to include the derivation or adaptation of innovations. Furthermore, unlike Schumpeter, the innovation need not be embodied in a new firm, but might be the basis for building or improving "an organization capable of successfully promoting the [innovative] idea and assuring the businessman a position of leadership in the field." In his search for entrepreneurs to study, Sayigh relied on files from public and semi-public bodies; chambers of commerce, industry, and agriculture; and industrial associations to aid in the selection of innovators in the manufacturing, agricultural, financial and services sectors.[53]

Sayigh, who finds that less than one-fourth of the entrepreneurs are engaged in the same sector as their father, stresses the "remarkable mobility between generations." Thirty-one percent of the fathers were in trade, 26 percent in industry, and 9 percent in the professions. The major occupation of entrepreneurs prior to their present activity was trade which together with industry comprised about two-thirds of the pre-

---

51. E. Wayne Nafziger, "Class, Caste and Community of South Indian Industrialists: An Examination of the Horatio Alger Model," *Journal of Development Studies*, XI, No. 2 (January 1975), 131-48, and "Entrepreneurship, Social Mobility and Income Redistribution: A Case Study of Industrialists in Visakhapatnam, South India," (unpublished manuscript, Honolulu, 1976).

52. The findings of Peter Kilby, *African Enterprise: The Nigerian Bread Industry* (Stanford: Hoover Institution, 1965); and Harris, "Nigerian Entrepreneurship in Industry," in Kilby, ed., *Entrepreneurship*, pp. 331-55, and "Industrial Entrepreneurship in Nigeria," which appeared soon after my own Ph.D. dissertation on Nigerian manufacturing entrepreneurs, are discussed in subsequent chapters, in the main body of this study.

53. Sayigh, *Entrepreneurs of Lebanon*, pp. 12-50.

vious occupations of respondents. In addition, apparently they perceived their own economic and social status as higher than that of their fathers.[54]

Sayigh is sanguine about the effect of concentration of entrepreneurial activity, and the limitation of access of new entrepreneurs to economic opportunities in the local market. Despite the evidence that the number of "interlocking directorates in corporations . . . must be considered high for a country with a small number of corporations," Sayigh contends that the "sustained growth" created by these corporate leaders is "widening the reach of their leavening effect to the whole economy." Ironically, "The limitation of the local market and the scarcity of natural resources, pressing on an energetic business group, make for an expansive outlook and temperament. . . . And all the while, the pressure to expand provokes a brisk competitiveness and a desire to keep the channels open and unobstructed."[55]

Carroll's 1960 survey of 92 indigenous industrial entrepreneurs, in the Philippines in establishments with more than 99 employed, has the most detailed analysis of the socio-economic background and mobility of the entrepreneurs. The differences between the actual representation of entrepreneurs by ethnic and geographical origin, and origin by size of city, on the one hand, and the expected representation based on population, on the other, are highly significant. Carroll, in explaining why entrepreneurs are disproportionately from big cities, suggests that urban culture creates the need and awareness of the possibility of entrepreneurial success, without considering the possibility that those located in the cities have greater access to business opportunities. A majority of the fathers of the entrepreneurs, and the respondents themselves immediately before their present activity, bore or shared chief responsibility for the management of at least one enterprise. Although those entrepreneurs who had fathers from the upper stratum were tremendously overrepresented, a substantial majority of the fathers were not of the upper stratum. Increasingly after 1950, with greater financial and skill barriers to business activity, entrepreneurship has become a means of enhancing or consolidating an existing upper status position. Yet, Carroll argues, in the final analysis, "mobility was quite dramatically evident," and "there has been, in fact, a very impressive amount of mobility

---

54. Ibid. pp. 69-79.
55. Ibid. pp. 67, 119-20.

in the family of the entrepreneurs."[56]

Alexander's 1961 study of 354 Greek industrialists in establishments with 50 or more workers, although based on a self-selected sample obtained by a mail questionnaire, tries to focus on "questions concerning the supply of entrepreneurs and the nature of their policies."[57] Despite a deliberate government policy to protect domestic industrial production, economic opportunities in manufacturing were relatively less attractive than in trade, because of a small domestic market, the absence of a capital market for industrialists, and the lack of availability of industrial management skills. In the Greek sample, as in Alexander's previous study of Turkish entrepreneurs,[58] big merchants are most highly overrepresented. Former craftsmen, especially well-represented in the early phases of industrialization, tended to have less drive and vision, and directed relatively small firms. Greek refugees, resulting from the exchange of minorities between Turkey and Greece in the 1920s, were especially well-represented among entrepreneurs. Alexander argues that there is considerable upward mobility in entrepreneurial activity and a lack of sharp class demarcation, partly because feudal-aristocratic survivals are weak in Greece.

Papanek studied 250 industrialists with 20 or more workers employed in Pakistan, a country with substantial industrial growth between Independence in 1947, and the time of the study, 1959. At independence, vast opportunities opened up for the Muslim business community, because of the separation from Indian industry and the exodus of the dominant Hindu businessman, resulting from Indian-Pakistani partition. The government, through protection of domestic production, subsidization by undervaluation of foreign exchange, and industrial incentive programs, such as generous depreciation allowances, increased the rate of return of manufacturing relative to trade, and stimulated the development of industrial entrepreneurship. Forty-three percent of Muslim industrialists were members of the Halai Memon, Chinioti, Dawoodi Bohra, Khoja Ismaili, and Khoja Isnashari communities, which altogether account for less than ½ percent of the Pakistani population. The previous primary occupation of 45 percent of the industrialists was trade. Papanek

---

56. Carroll, *The Filipino Entrepreneur*, pp. 97-8.

57. Alexander, *Greek Industrialists*, p. 15.

58. "Industrial Entrepreneurship in Turkey: Origins and Growth," *Economic Development and Cultural Change*, VIII, No. 4, Part I (July 1960), 349-65.

argues that the findings of his study lend support to the thesis that entrepreneurship in manufacturing arises in response to powerful economic incentives rather than significant changes in socio-psychological variables.[59] However, as Hagen maintains, Papanek provides no information concerning child-rearing practices and personality, and the evidence available concerning the small trading communities from which the entrepreneurs originated tends to suggest the possibility of substantial socio-psychological changes.[60]

Berna confined his empirical study, conducted in 1957, to manufacturing enterprises in light-engineering industry in two cities in Tamil Nadu, south India with 50 to 250 persons employed. His findings are based on interviews with entrepreneurs of 52 firms and outside sources familiar with the firms. Although the entrepreneur, "the person (or group of persons) responsible for the existence of a new industrial enterprise," is similar to aspects of the Schumpeterian concept, the discussion implies that Berna includes routine firm management as a part of the entrepreneurial function.[61]

Berna contends that traditional occupation and sub-caste (*jati*) have very little impact in determining entry into entrepreneurial endeavors. The 52 entrepreneurs are members of 10 different social communities, although 41 of the 52 are from 3 communities - the Naidu, a land-owning class from the warrior caste (*varna*); the Brahmin; and the Chettiar, a southern Indian trading community. Only four of the sample entrepreneurs are in direct line with the traditional caste-assigned family occupation. This break with the traditional occupation indicates to Berna that in explaining entrepreneurial activity "sociological factors, such as caste, attachment to traditional activities, and approval or disapproval of the social group to which a potential entrepreneur belongs are less important than economic factors such as access to capital and possession of business experience and technical knowledge."[62]

Hoselitz argues, however, that if Berna's sample is characteristic of Tamil Nadu industrial entrepreneurs in general, the

---

59. *American Economic Review*, LII, No. 2, 46-58.

60. Everett E. Hagen, "Discussion," Ibid. pp. 59-60. I mention the Hagen-Papanek controversy, as a parallel to the Hoselitz-Berna debate, below.

61. Berna, *Industrial Entrepreneurship*, pp. 1-4, 101-43.

62. Ibid. pp. 42-4, 83-6, 212-3.

social structure of the state must be undergoing a profound change. One important indication of this change is the decline in occupational choices assigned by caste. Sociological explanations are needed to explain these departures from traditional occupations, he indicates. Brahmins, for example, have been more inclined than previously to become entrepreneurs for a number of reasons: discrimination encountered in universities and government as a reaction against their favored social position in the colonial period, the decline in the number of caste-determined occupations available, an increase in status of business occupations resulting from socio-political emphasis on the need for economic growth, and the wealth and influence available for investment in training and new enterprises. In short, the socio-economic changes leading to the erosion of the Brahmins' traditional position, coupled with the present emphasis on economic development, led them to see entrepreneurship as increasingly attractive.[63] A parallel exists in Nigeria, where a large number of Yoruba and Hausa traditional political rulers thwarted the possible socio-economic decline accompanying modernization by using their wealth and influence to establish sizeable trading and manufacturing firms.[64]

Berna, in concluding that sociological factors are less important than economic factors, has raised some important questions. Hoselitz's challenge of Berna's conclusion, together with the prior Papanek-Hagen controversy, have helped clarify some of these issues. What the controversies do indicate is the limitations of a single discipline's approach to a discussion of the determinants of entrepreneurship. For example, in the case of the Brahmins, entrepreneurial activity resulted from the interaction of both social and economic factors, the impetus to the activity resulting from their declining socio-economic position, but advantages accruing from their residual wealth and influence (access to capital, good educational background).

Berna found that the largest group of entrepreneurs (12 of 52), when classified according to immediate vocational background, were graduate engineers.[65] Although he finds this difficult to explain, it is perhaps not so surprising in the light of the relatively large output of engineers and their relatively

---

63. Bert F. Hoselitz, "Entrepreneurship and Traditional Elites," *Explorations in Entrepreneurial History/Second Series*, I (Fall 1963), 36-9.

64. See below.

65. Berna, *Industrial Entrepreneurship*, pp. 60-70.

low average salary and high rate of unemployment in the post-World War II period. One notices, for example, that few industrial entrepreneurial positions are filled by ex-civil servants, who as a group have relatively high salaries, good working conditions, attractive fringe benefits and secure tenure. To explain entrepreneurial participation among groups such as graduate engineers and civil servants, it is useful to consider the alternative remuneration available, an approach used here.

My study of entrepreneurs in a newly industrializing city in coastal Andhra, India provides the data essential to consider factors related to the quantity and success of entrepreneurs.[66] Determinants of the quantity of entrepreneurs were found on the basis of differences between information on the characteristics of entrepreneurs and the population as a whole. Unlike other studies of Indian entrepreneurship, the caste composition of sample entrepreneurs was compared with that of the general population. Factors related to entrepreneurial success were found by correlating caste, paternal economic status, education, work experience, sources and amount of capital, and degree of access to government of entrepreneurs, to their income class, and the value-added (i.e. contribution to national product) of their firms.

The study examined the vertical socio-economic mobility of entrepreneurs, and the differences in economic opportunities between the privileged and underprivileged portions of the population. A disproportionately high number of the entrepreneurs (especially successful ones) are from high (twice-born) castes and from families with a high economic status. Members of the dominant castes, leading classes, and large business houses can avert the threats to their families of democratization, industrialization and modernization by using the cumulative advantages of the past - property, influence, status and so forth - to obtain the concessions, experience, education, training, and industrial capital usually essential for successful industrial undertakings. Evidence cited from other studies of capitalist and socialist industrialists supported my contention that there is limited upward socio-economic mobility to success in business.

The median education of the Andhra entrepreneur was extremely high when compared to its population, and even substantially above the medians for industrial entrepreneurs in compa-

66. Nafziger, *Journal of Development Studies*, XI, No. 2, 131-48.

rable studies in other mixed capitalist economies, such as Nigeria and the U.S. This high educational attainment was attributed primarily to the limited employment options available to graduates in government service and the private sector.

For most entrepreneurs and their families, manufacturing business entailed a step-by-step progression, and not a sharp break, from less complex economic activities with which they were familiar. More traders and merchants became entrepreneurs than any other occupational category. Former traders entered manufacturing to insure a regular source of supply, or as a result of the perception of increased opportunities for profits in industry relative to trade. The major catalyst for the shift to industry was deliberate post-Independence government policy encouraging import substitution in manufacturing, through higher tariffs and tighter import quotas.

A common pattern for major business families in the sample was to have entered in the early twentieth century a trade or light industrial sector that did not compete with British colonial or industrial interests and, given the encouragement of the Independence era, to have moved to heavier manufacturing. Private businessmen in India have not been a part of the elite, and exist at the sufferance of the political-bureaucratic leadership. Frequently, the price for obtaining political access and business security may have been concessions, favors and political loyalty.

Figure 1

Nigeria, 1963-1967

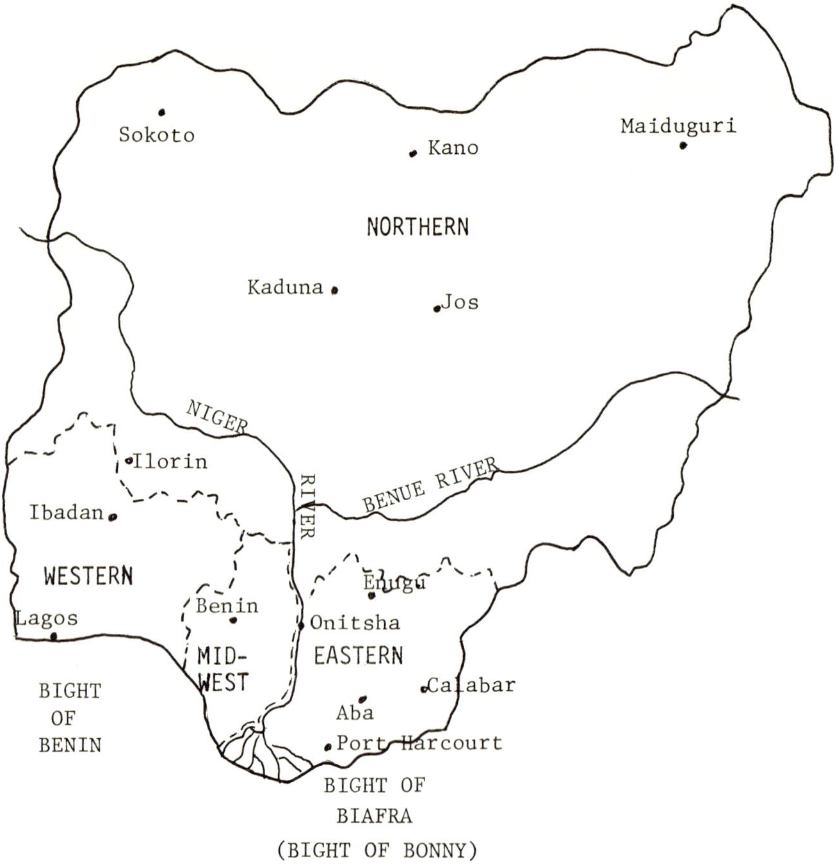

Chapter 2

A Political Economy of Nigerian Business

A study of indigenous industrialists necessitates a sketch of the economic and political background, and at the beginning of this chapter, I focus on basic data on the Nigerian economy - population, national product, growth in output, prices, employment, balance-of-payments, and the major sectors of the economy. After this, I concentrate on the interrelationship between major political events and economic trends since 1948, on the one hand, and the formation of a politico-economic elite and a domestic class structure, on the other. This sketch enables the reader to view the role of the Nigerian businessmen, especially those with substantial economic holdings, as a part of the dominant indigenous elite. International economic developments of the colonial and post-colonial periods are analyzed primarily in terms of the way in which they affected the shape of the class structure, power relations, and domestic economic policy of the Independence era. Also examined are the contradictions arising from the use of national, communal and regional sentiments by the dominant class - large businessmen, professionals, politicians, and government servants - to further their economic interests. These interests provide a basis for explaining the main weaknesses of development planning. Finally, the political and economic consequences of the growing conflict between entrepreneurs, capitalists, and government, on the one hand, and workers, on the other, are also discussed.

Nigeria, a tropical country in West Africa, lies between 4° N and 14° N latitude, and between 2° E and 15° E longitude. Her area, 356,669 square miles, is the size of the state of California, Nevada and Utah combined, or almost four times the size of the United Kingdom. The greatest distance from east to west is more than 700 miles, and from north to south about 650 miles.

Nigeria has the highest population of all African countries. The census figures (see table 2.1, p. 30) are, however, highly inflated, and Eke's population estimate of 41.3 million in 1963 and projection of 53.9 million in 1973 are probably more accurate.[1]

Table 2.1

Population of Nigeria by Region, 1952-3, 1962, 1963 and 1973 Censuses[a]
(in millions)

Region	1952-3 Census	1962 Census	1963 Census	1973 Census[c]
North	16.8	20.3	29.8	51.4
East	7.2	8.5	12.4	13.8
West and Lagos	6.4	7.7	11.0	11.4
Mid-West[b]			2.5	3.2
TOTAL	30.4	36.5	55.7	79.8

a. None of the census figures above is reliable. Even though many scholars consider the 1962 census results more accurate than those of 1963, the 1962 figures were not officially released because of political controversy (discussed below). The data from the 1963 and 1973 censuses are generally considered to be highly inflated.

b. Before 1963, the Mid-West was part of the West. When the term "the south" is used in the text this generally implies all regions other than the North (pre-1967). (See figure 1.)

c. Although the four regions and Federal Territory were divided into twelve states in May 1967, and nineteen states in February 1976, the population is distributed in this table according to the old regional boundaries.

Sources: Nigeria, Office of Statistics, *Population Census of Nigeria, 1963*, III (Lagos, 1968), 57; *West African Directory* (London: Thomas Skinner and Co., 1965), p. 270, and "Eighty Million Nigerians," *West Africa*, No. 2960 (20 May 1974), p. 590.

National Income during Civilian Rule

The sparsity of industry-wide data (especially where commodities are consumed domestically), the difficulty of assessing the representativeness of sample inquiries, and the arbitrariness of quantification based on subjective and qualitative judgments of provincial officers, limit the reliability of the estimates of Nigerian national-income statistics.[2] Despite these deficiencies, judicious use of statistics on aggregate output may be of some value. Official figures indicate that gross domestic product (GDP) at *current* prices in the fiscal year 1964/65 (beginning 1 April 1964) was £N1,1457.0 million, or about £N26 (or $73) per capita.[3] Although the inadequacies of international comparisons of statistics are well-known,[4] it is clear that in 1965 Nigeria ranked among the bottom one-fifth of the countries of the world in GDP per capita. Growth in real GDP from 1958/59 to 1965/66 was 6.0 percent per annum (computations are from table 2.2, p. 32).[5] Even though the data are unreliable, the consensus of

---

1. Ifagun I.U. Eke, "Population of Nigeria, 1952-1965," *Nigerian Journal of Economic and Social Studies*, VIII, No. 3 (November 1966), 308-9.

2. P.N.C. Okigbo, *Nigerian National Accounts, 1950-57* (Enugu: Federal Ministry of Economic Development, 1962), pp. 35-98; Nigeria, Office of Statistics, *Gross Domestic Product of Nigeria, 1958/59-1966/67* (Lagos, August 1968), pp. 3-24; and Nigeria, Ministry of Information, *Second National Development Plan, 1970-74* (Lagos, 1971), pp. 20 and 43-5. Wolfgang F. Stolper characterized plan formulation with Nigeria's aggregate economic statistics as *Planning Without Facts: Lessons in Resource Allocation from Nigeria's Development* (Cambridge, Mass: Harvard University Press, 1966), pp. 6, 41, 91-137.

3. *Gross Domestic Product of Nigeria, 1958/59-1966/67* (Lagos, 1968).

The Nigerian pound (£N) was on par with the British pound in 1964-5, and exchanged for $2.80.

4. Everett E. Hagen, *The Economics of Development* (Homewood, Ill: Richard D. Irwin, 1968), pp. 7-15; Surendra J. Patel, "The Economic Distance Between Nations: Its Origins, Measurement and Outlook," *Economic Journal*, LXXIV (March 1964), 122-9; and Simon Kuznets, "Levels and Variability of Growth Rates," *Economic Development and Cultural Change*, V, No. 1 (October 1956), 4-9.

5. Growth in real GDP from 1958/59 to 1966/67 was 5.6 percent per annum. The year, April 1965-March 1966, is probably

Table 2.2

Estimated All-Nigerian Gross Domestic Product
at Constant (1962/63) Factor Cost,
1958/59-69/70 (₤N millions)

Sector	1958/9	1959/60	1960/1	1961/2	1962/3
Agriculture, livestock, forestry, and fishing	672.2	704.5	799.9	776.9	804.8
Mining	10.2	12.1	15.8	22.3	26.8
Manufacturing and crafts	45.3	52.0	57.0	63.8	75.9
Electricity and water supply	2.8	3.5	4.2	5.2	6.0
Building and construction	35.3	47.0	55.4	57.9	57.5
Distribution	127.9	136.1	154.7	155.5	161.1
Transport	37.0	40.0	48.2	53.9	55.0
Communication	3.8	4.3	5.2	5.4	5.9
General government	39.8	47.8	49.7	49.6	51.3
Education	23.8	28.1	29.5	32.2	35.7
Health	4.0	4.6	5.3	5.2	7.2
Other services	21.8	22.7	25.3	28.1	20.2
TOTAL	1023.9	1102.7	1250.2	1256.0	1315.4

Sources: Nigeria, Office of Statistics, *Gross Domestic Product of Nigeria, 1958/59-1966/67* (Lagos, August 1968), p. 30, and O. Aboyade and A. Ayida, "The War Economy in Perspective," *Nigerian Journal of Economic and Social Studies*, XIII, No. 1 (March 1971), 29.

Table 2.2— Continued

1963/4	1964/5	1965/6	1966/7	1967/8[a]	1968/9[a]	1969/70[a]
870.8	866.7	870.9	869.5	817.3	805.8	801.8
31.3	47.5	82.4	114.4	51.5	55.6	68.4
76.8	78.8	91.7	93.1	108.9	126.3	142.7
7.3	8.1	9.2	10.7	10.0	10.5	11.2
66.0	65.0	80.0	81.3	72.3	73.4	76.3
180.9	194.9	202.7	200.9	193.9	191.0	190.0
61.4	59.3	55.6	53.3	50.1	49.8	50.4
6.7	7.9	9.2	9.4	7.8	7.8	8.1
51.3	52.1	51.6	51.6	48.1	49.1	52.0
37.8	43.0	43.7	48.2	46.3	47.3	49.2
7.5	9.4	9.8	9.3	9.0	9.1	9.7
27.9	30.7	36.2	41.4	47.2	50.5	54.0
1425.7	1463.4	1543.0	1583.1	1462.4	1475.2	1513.8

a. Includes Biafra.

economists is that population grew at a rate of 2.5-3.0 percent per annum.[6] It is likely that the growth in real GDP per capita from 1958/59 to 1965/66 was positive, and even likely that this growth was at least as high as the average rate of growth among non-communist less developed countries (i.e., countries with a GDP per capita less than $600 per annum) for the period, a rate of roughly 2.5 percent per annum.[7]

Major Sectors of the Economy

Fifty-six percent of the Nigerian labor force was engaged in agriculture in 1963, and 59 percent of GDP in 1964/65 originated in agriculture, the largest sector of the economy (see tables 2.3 and 2.4, pp. 35 and 36). Official figures indicate that the percentage of GDP contributed by the agricultural sector declined from 66 percent in 1958/59 to 41 percent in 1971/72. Despite the large margin of error in the figures, it is clear that the relative size of the agricultural sector has been declining with

---

(Footnote 5 continued from page 31.)

preferable to the year April 1966-March 1967, a year of substantial economic turmoil, as the terminal year for the computation of growth. The coups d'etat of January and July-August 1966 were accompanied and succeeded by a weakening in private investment as a result of growing anxieties about the strength of the Nigerian economy and polity, administrative difficulties in submitting viable and well-planned development projects, the disruption in the transportation and internal trade sectors stemming from the forced exodus of skilled personnel to their communal homelands, and the breakdown of economic relations between the Federation and the East. E. Wayne Nafziger, "The Economic Impact of the Nigerian Civil War," *The Journal of Modern African Studies* (*JMAS*), X, No. 2 (1972), 223-9.

6. Ifagun I.U. Eke, "Population of Nigeria, 1952-1965," *Nigerian Journal of Economic and Social Studies*, VIII, No. 3 (November 1968), 308-9; and T.M. Yesufu, "Manpower and Educational Objectives for Nigeria's Reconstruction and Development," Conference on National Reconstruction and Development in Nigeria, University of Ibadan, Ibadan, 24-9 March 1969, p. 8.

7. For figures on the growth of less developed countries, see Gerald M. Meier, *Leading Issues in Economic Development: Studies in International Poverty* (New York: Oxford University Press, 1970), pp. 21, 35, 41.

In the 1960s, the United Nations indicated the boundary line between more developed countries and less developed countries at a GDP per capita per annum of $600.

Table 2.3

Percentage of Nigerian Gross Domestic Product at Constant (1962/63) Factor Cost, 1958/59–71/72

Major sector	1958/ 59	1959/ 60	1960/ 61	1961/ 62	1962/ 63	1963/ 64	1964/ 65	1965/ 66	1966/ 67	1967/ 68	1968/ 69	1969/ 70	1970/ 71[a]	1971/ 72[a]
Agriculture, livestock, forestry and fishing	65.6	63.9	64.0	61.9	61.2	61.1	59.2	56.4	54.9	55.9	54.6	53.0	45.7	41.1
Mining	1.0	1.1	1.3	1.8	2.0	2.2	3.2	5.3	7.2	3.5	3.8	4.5	14.9	17.8
Manufacturing and crafts	4.4	4.7	4.6	5.1	5.8	5.4	5.4	6.0	5.9	7.5	8.6	9.4	8.2	8.3
Transport	3.6	3.6	3.9	4.3	4.2	4.3	4.0	5.6	3.4	3.4	3.4	3.3		
Construction, services, distribution, other sectors	25.4	26.7	26.2	26.9	26.8	27.0	28.2	26.7	28.6	29.7	29.6	29.8	31.2	32.8
TOTAL	100.0	100.0	100.0	100.0	100.0	100.0	100.0	100.0	100.0	100.0	100.0	100.0	100.0	100.0

a. Sources for the figures for 1970/71 and 1971/72 are not strictly comparable to sources in previous fiscal years.

Sources: Table 2.2, and Nigeria, Ministry of Information, *Economic and Statistical Review, 1971* (Lagos, 1972), p. 4. These fiscal years begin on 1 April.

Table 2.4

Distribution of the Labor Force by Major Occupational Group, Nigeria, 1963 Census

Occupation	Number (thousands)	Percentage of the Labor Force
Professional, technical and related	441	2.41
Administrative, executive and managerial	39	0.21
Clerical	228	1.25
Sales	2,806	15.33
Farmers, fishermen, hunters, loggers and related	10,201	55.72
Miners, quarrymen and related	14	0.08
Transport and communications	279	1.52
Crafts, production-process workers and laborers	2,190	11.96
Service, sports and recreation	871	4.76
Unspecified	891	4.87
Unemployed	345	1.88
TOTAL LABOR FORCE	18,306[a]	99.99

a. Components may not add to total because of rounding.

Source: Nigeria, Office of Statistics, *Population Census of Nigeria, 1963*, V. III, *Combined National Figures* (Lagos, 1968), 39-40.

economic growth. This drop is to be expected, since the income elasticity of demand for agricultural commodities,[8] which are mostly necessities, is low.

The dominant structural change in the Nigerian economy from 1958 to 1972 was the very rapid growth in the output of crude oil. The volume of this grew from 5,000 barrels per day in 1958 to 415,000 barrels per day in 1966, at an annual rate of 73.7 percent per annum.[9] By 1966 Nigeria, with an output of £N100 million, ranked thirteenth in the world in the value of crude-oil production.

In July 1967, after Nigeria instituted a blockade on oil tankers and Shell-B.P. halted its output in the East, Biafra's crude-oil output, produced only for refining for local requirements, dropped to 5,000 barrels per day - slightly more than 1 percent of pre-war output - before ceasing in subsequent months as a result of the fighting. In Nigeria, crude-petroleum production, confined to the off-shore wells in the Mid-West, decreased by 86.7 percent from the first half to the second half of 1967. As a result of the disruption of the civil war, the volume of crude-petroleum production declined by 42.4 percent per annum from 1966 to 1968 (computed from table 2.5). The index of this production rose sharply in 1969 as a result of the resumption of output on a limited scale in on-shore wells in the Rivers and Mid-Western States in 1969.[10] From that year to 1972, crude-oil output grew at the rate of 49.7 percent per annum. Altogether, despite the interruption of an upward trend for about two years during the civil war, the rate of growth of the volume of crude petroleum from 1963 to 1972 was 42.2 percent per annum (table 2.5).

Table 2.3 provides a different perspective on the growth of the oil sector. The steady increase in the percentage of GDP contributed by the mining sector, consisting primarily of petroleum, was interrupted by a decline from over 7 percent in 1966 to 3.5-4.5 percent in the three fiscal years affected by the war,

---

8. This is defined as the percentage change in the consumption of agricultural commodities divided by the percentage change in income.

9. Scott R. Pearson, "Nigerian Petroleum: Implications for Medium-Term Planning," in *Growth and Development of the Nigerian Economy*, ed. by Carl K. Eicher and Carl Liedholm (East Lansing: Michigan State University Press, 1970), p. 357.

10. Nafziger, *JMAS*, X, No. 2, 235-6.

1967/68-1969/70. By 1971/72, almost 18 percent of GDP originated in the mining sector.

The contribution of the manufacturing and crafts sector to GDP has grown from a little over 4 percent in 1958/59 to over 8 percent since 1968/69. Because of the slow rate of overall growth during the civil war, and the acceleration of import sub-

Table 2.5

Indices of Crude-Petroleum and Manufacturing Production (1965 = 100)

Year	Crude Petroleum	Manufacturing
1963	27.9	69.6
1964	44.0	86.1
1965	100.0	100.0
1966	152.3	111.7
1967	116.4[a]	114.2[a]
1968	50.6[a]	114.0[a]
1969	197.1[a]	150.2[a]
1970	389.1	167.4
1971	568.5	173.7
1972	662.5	198.4

a. Production figures from the secessionist areas are excluded from the third quarter of 1967 until the last quarter of 1969. However, crude-petroleum and manufacturing production was virtually at a standstill here during this period.

Sources: Nafziger, *JMAS*, X, No. 2, 235, and Central Bank of Nigeria, *Annual Report and Statement of Accounts for the Year ended 31st December 1972* (Lagos, 1973), pp. 21-2.

stitution in response to the tightening of trade restrictions, the relative contribution of manufacturing and crafts to GDP increased more rapidly during the war than the pre-war trend would have suggested (table 2.3).

The growth rate in manufacturing output from 1963 to 1972, 12.3 percent per annum, was rapid, if one compares this growth to other less developed economies. From 1963 to 1966, the year of the military take-over, growth in manufacturing output was at a rate of 17.1 percent per annum. Despite the disruption of the political crises, this rate only dropped to 14.4 percent per annum from 1966 to 1970, as the Nigerian government increased its protection of domestically-produced manufacturing goods. The relaxation of import barriers was one factor accounting for the relatively slow rate of growth of manufacturing output from 1970 to 1972, 8.9 percent per annum.

National Income during Military Rule

During the civil war, 1967/68 through 1969/70, there were sources of inaccuracies (above those in "normal" years) in Nigerian national income accounts resulting from the lack of documentation in Biafran territory.[11] Estimates from official sources (table 2.2) indicate that real GDP in all of Nigeria (including wartime Biafra) fell from the last pre-war year, 1966/67, to the final year of the civil war, 1969/70. Real GDP per capita is likely to have decreased during the war, while real net domestic product per capita is likely to have declined substantially.[12]

I shall use the term "capital exhaustion" to refer to capital consumption plus capital destruction, since there is apparently no term in the literature for the two combined. Economists widely recognize that net product - where "capital exhaustion" is

---

11. O. Aboyade, then Head of the Economic Planning Unit in the Federal Ministry of Economic Development, and A. Ayida, then Permanent Secretary of the same Ministry, indicate that "The correct story [of gross product originating in the secessionist areas during the war] may never be fully told." "The War Economy in Perspective," *Nigerian Journal of Economic and Social Studies*, XIII, No. 1 (March 1971), 28. See also Nafziger, *JMAS*, X, No. 2, 227-9.

12. Nafziger, *JMAS*, X, No. 2, 227-9, and "The Economic Impact of the Nigerian Civil War: a Reply," *JMAS*, XI, No. 3 (1973), 463-5.

subtracted - is more appropriate as a measure of economic well-being than gross product. However, because of difficulties in measuring this exhaustion, economists usually settle for gross product figures, assuming a rough parallel between growths in net and gross products. In "normal" times, this may not seriously distort the picture of growth. However, in wartime, impressions of growth are greatly distorted where capital destruction, together with depreciation, is not subtracted from gross product to obtain net product.[13]

All-Nigerian statistics indicate a real growth in GDP of 9.6 percent from 1969/70 to 1970/71,[14] 24.4 percent from 1970/71 to 1971/72, and 12.0 percent from 1971/72 to 1972/73.[15] Subsequent growth has continued at a rate substantially above the pre-war growth rate of 5.6 percent per annum. High rates of growth in the post-war period have been partly accounted for by the low level of outputs during the war, which reduced the base from which growth was calculated. Thus, a portion of the rapid growth merely compensated for output foregone as a result of the disruption and destruction of war. However, much of the more rapid rate of growth can be attributed to other factors, such as the petroleum boom of the 1970s, which especially benefitted Nigeria, the world's ninth largest producer of crude oil in 1973.

Prices, Employment, and the Balance of Payments

Nigeria, which generally pursued a conservative monetary and fiscal policy, avoided the severe inflationary pressures usually characteristic of underdeveloped countries - especially those which, like Nigeria, were plagued by political instability.

---

13. Simon S. Kuznets, *National Product in Wartime* (New York: National Bureau of Economic Research, 1945), pp. 6, 20. Even though there are no precise figures, a conservative estimate for capital destruction/gross domestic product during the war would be 5-10 percent. Nafziger, *JMAS*, X, No. 2, 242.

I have used the figures of Aboyade and Ayida, *Nigerian Journal*, XIII, No. 1, 28-9, instead of those from Nigeria, Ministry of Information, *Economic and Statistical Review, 1970* (Lagos, 1971), pp. 1, 3, which would indicate a growth rate in real GDP of 2.4 percent per annum from 1966/67 to 1969/70. The source from the Ministry of Information indicates that its figures are only "rough estimates" (p. 3).

14. *Economic and Statistical Review, 1970*, p. 3.

15. Nigeria, Ministry of Information, *Economic and Statistical Review, 1971*, p. 4.

From 1960 to 1964, the increase in the consumer price index was at a rate of only 2.2 percent per annum for lower-income groups, and only 4.6 percent per annum for middle-income groups. In the period mainly covered by this study, from 1964 to 1965, consumer prices increased by 3.5 percent and 4.1 percent for lower-income

Table 2.6

Consumer Price Indices

Year	(1) All-Cities Index or Lower-Income Groups[a]	(2) Percentage Change in (1) from Previous Year	(3) Lagos Index for Middle-Income Groups	(4) Percentage Change in (3) from Previous Year
1960	100[b]	n.a	100[b]	n.a
1962	105[b]	n.a	115[b]	n.a
1964	109.2	n.a	117.0	n.a
1965	113.0	+ 3.5	121.8	+4.1
1966	125.5	+11.1	129.6	+6.4
1967	120.8	- 3.7	127.2	-1.9
1968	120.3	- 0.4	131.3	+3.2
1969	132.3	+10.0	139.7	+6.4
1970	150.6	+13.8	152.7	+9.3
1971	174.7	+16.0	165.4	+8.3
1972	179.6	+ 2.8	172.5	+4.3

a. Weighted average price indices in Benin, Ibadan, Ilorin, Kaduna, Kano, Lagos, Sapele, Warri and Zaria in 1970-2, and fewer cities in previous years.

b. Indices stated only to the ones place.

Sources: Central Bank of Nigeria, *Annual Reports and Statements of Accounts* (Lagos).

and middle-income groups respectively. Over a longer period, from 1960 to 1972, consumer prices increased by 5.0 percent per annum for lower-income groups, and by 4.6 percent per annum for middle-income groups (table 2.6). Double-digit increases in consumer prices were confined to 1966, a year of substantial increases in food prices largely resultant from traders abandoning their customary markets during the political disturbances, and 1969-71, a period of relief, rehabilitation, and reconstruction accompanied by a rising demand for food and sustenance when distribution costs were high in war-damaged areas regained from Biafra, a food-deficit area.

Although there are no standard statistics and concepts for unemployment in Nigeria, scholarly estimates for 1963 were over 500,000 of the urban population of 9 million "unemployed" - defined here as a member of the regular labor force, fifteen years and above, who has earned insufficient during the previous twelve months to cover personal food costs. In 1964, Archibald Callaway's survey in Ibadan (the largest city, 627,370 in 1963, in sub-Saharan black Africa) indicated that 28 percent of the total labor force was unemployed, the overwhelming majority being male youths who were recent primary and secondary "graduates."[16]

The rate of unemployment increased sharply from the early 1960s to 1966-67, prior to the civil war, as a result of the drop in business activity and the decline of emigration to alien communal group areas. However, the expansion of the armed forces from about 30,000 just prior to the war, to 180,000-200,000 in both Nigeria and Biafra in 1969, reduced the rate below that of 1966. Immediately after the war the rate rose, with a disproportionate share of the unemployment in areas surrendered by Biafra. However, by early 1973, statistics from the Central Bank on the number of registered unemployed suggested that the unemployment rate was beginning to decline.[17]

---

16. Callaway, "Creating Employment for Nigeria's School Leavers," *Administration: The Quarterly Review of the Institute of Administration, University of Ife*, III, No. 1 (October, 1969), 1-11, and "Educational Expansion and the Rise of Youth Unemployment," in *The City of Ibadan*, ed. by P.C. Lloyd, A.L. Mabogunje and B. Awe (London: Cambridge University Press, 1967), pp. 198-203.

17. Central Bank of Nigeria, *Annual Report and Statement*

From the 1950s, when restrictions on the convertibility of British pounds in the overseas sterling area was lifted, to the early part of the Nigerian civil war, Nigeria's holdings of foreign exchange assets deteriorated substantially. For example, external assets at the end of the year declined from £N263.1 million in 1955 to a low of £N38.9 million in 1967. The most important long run explanations for the declining position were the significant growth in commodity imports resulting from the rapid growth in incomes in an open economy, and the rise in debt servicing and repatriated earnings from foreign lending and investment. The major immediate factor contributing to Nigeria's weak foreign exchange position in 1967/68 was military expenditures abroad, whose primary cost was equal to about one-fifth the value of merchandise exports in 1968. An external liquidity crisis was averted only by the use of stringent trade barriers and exchange controls.[18]

The favorable balance-of-payments impact of the crude-oil mining and prospecting sector was instrumental in reversing the erosion of Nigeria's external reserve position. The value of crude-oil exports increased from £N68.1 million in 1965 to £N131.0 million in 1969 to £N593.2 million in 1972, while the net positive contribution of crude oil to the balance of payments on current and capital account increased from £N35.6 million in 1965 to £N75.1 million in 1969 to £N307.5 million in 1972. Accordingly, the country's external assets grew from £N38.9 million in 1967 to £N58.0 million in 1969 to £N135.1 million in 1972, while restrictions on international trade and exchange were being relaxed. By May 1974, largely as a result of the sharp increase in the export price of petroleum, Nigeria's reserve assets had risen to £N475.2 million[19] (or 950.4 million

---

of Accounts for the Year ended 31st December 1967 (Lagos, 1968), p. 24; Central Bank, *Annual Report, 1968* (Lagos, 1969), p. 27; Yesufu, "Manpower and Educational Objectives," Reconstruction and Development Conference, 1969, pp. 8, 15-18; Central Bank, *Annual Report, 1969* (Lagos, 1970), p. 19; and Central Bank, *Monthly Reports*, passim.

18. A.E. Ekukinam, "Main Trends in Banking and Monetary Policy to 1968," in *Reconstruction and Development in Nigeria: Proceedings of a National Conference*, ed. by A.A. Ayida and H.M.A. Onititi (Ibadan: Oxford University Press, 1971), p. 353, and Nafziger, *JMAS*, X, No. 2, 230-3.

19. Nafziger, *JMAS*, X, No. 2, 230-3; *Economic and Statistical Review, 1970*, p. 12; Central Bank, *Annual Report, 1972* (Lagos, 1973), pp. 76-83; and *Standard Bank Review* (July 1974), p. 14.

nairas in the currency introduced in 1973).

The Colonial Economic Legacy

Britain's world-wide political and military suzerainty in the century or so prior to World War I enabled it to hold a commanding position in the international economy, specifically as major banker, trader, investor, and industrialist. Colonies such as Nigeria became integrated into the system as economic satellites specializing in the production of raw materials and other primary products, instrumental for the industrial development of the leading capitalist countries. Britain's own military power and resources, together with those of her capitalist allies, upheld this suzerainty.

By the middle of the nineteenth century, British traders, explorers and missionaries, protected by the navy, began to penetrate the interior of western Africa. In 1886 the Niger Company, a monopoly of the major British companies trading in the Niger River area, was granted a royal charter to exercise the political authority essential to facilitate trade in south-central Nigeria. By 1906, most of present-day Nigeria was under the control of the British government. Although the Protectorates of Northern and Southern Nigeria were amalgamated in 1914, the administration of the two territories was kept separate. The South was ruled directly by the British, in contrast to the "indirect policy" in the North, where day-to-day administrative responsibility was delegated to compliant indigenous emirs. Indirect rule was mutually advantageous; the British economized on officers and utilized a well-developed tax collection system, while the traditional rulers with British protection eliminated important sources of both internal and external opposition, and secured hegemony.[20]

World War I, however, damaged Britain's predominant position in the international economy and the United States took her place. Although World War II accelerated decolonization, Britain continued to import raw materials, and to export and invest overseas. Some degree of "political stability" (a concept which included the maintenance of an economy open to trade with, and investment from, capitalist countries) was ensured in English-

---

20. Michael Crowder, *The Story of Nigeria* (London: Faber, 1962), pp. 165-9; and G.S. Whitaker, Jr., *The Politics of Tradition: Continuity and Change in Northern Nigeria, 1946-1966* (Princeton: Princeton University Press, 1970), pp. 59-63.

speaking Africa by military bases and assistance, a junior partnership with the U.S., Commonwealth trade-and-aid arrangements, and cooperation with the indigenous elites.

After 1948 the British were more prepared to meet what they considered the reasonable demands of the Nigerian nationalist movement, thus easing the colonial burden and helping to shape a post-Independence elite favorable to British interests. In return for their cooperation, aspiring Nigerians, primarily in the south, obtained access to the power, privileges, and patronage handed over by the British in the terminal colonial period - especially in the civil service and government agencies. In the North the traditional ruling aristocracy continued to enjoy the support of the colonial regime.

Two examples illustrate the way in which the British were able to support the interests of the political elite they helped to create. First, the Harragin Salaries Commission of 1951 (consisting of British officials) established a basis for the Nigerian senior civil service to retain many of the privileges the colonial administrators had enjoyed, such as high salaries, and car and educational allowances. Secondly, the British policy of acquiescing to demands by national leaders seeking a power base in the three regions, and granting regional self-government in 1954 - six years before central self-government - reduced the eventual strength of the center. In the clamor for the politico-economic power and benefits acquired as a result of cooperation with the British, national leaders became more conservative, and radical spokesmen were excluded.[21]

Nationalism, Communalism, and Dominant Class Interests

Although the official language in Nigeria is English, there are over 200 distinct language groups, which correspond roughly to ethnic communities. The three largest communities, Hausa-Fulani, Ibo, and Yoruba, (see table 2.7, p. 46) were major rivals in the struggle for power at the center, and also dominated the politics of the three major regions prior to the civil war, the Northern, Eastern and Western respectively.

---

21. James O'Connell, "Political Integration: The Nigerian Case," in *African Integration and Disintegration: Case Studies in Economic and Political Integration*, ed. by Arthur Hazlewood (London: Oxford University Press, 1967), p. 156; and John P. Mackintosh, *Nigerian Government and Politics* (Evanston: Northwestern University Press, 1966), p. 163.

Table 2.7

Population of Major Ethnic Communities in Nigeria, 1963 Census (in thousands)

Ethnic Community	Number
Hausa	11,653
Yoruba	11,321
Ibo	9,246
Fulani	4,784
Kanuri	2,259
Ibibio	2,006
Tiv	1,394
Ijaw	1,089
Edo	955
Annang	675
Other Nigerians	10,176
Other Africans	55
Non-Africans	47
Unspecified	10
TOTAL POPULATION	55,670

Source: Nigeria, Office of Statistics, *Population Census of Nigeria, 1963*, III, *Combined National Figures* (Lagos, 1968), 10-11.

The nationalist movement, spearheaded by a socio-economic and political elite, was promoted largely by persons who identified their personal destinies with the undermining of alien rule and economic domination. Communalism or ethnic nationalism grew stronger with the struggle to obtain the benefits of modernization and self-government, especially in the last quarter of a century. The heightening of Yoruba nationalism in the West after 1948 was partly in response to the leadership of the Nigerian national movement in the 1940s by the Ibos, an overpopulated Eastern community involved in a country-wide diaspora. Hausa-Fulani nationalism was aroused later in response to rival leadership in the drive for independence, and the threat of southern economic supremacy. The dominant class accentuated the pre-colonial and colonial identification with traditional political and cultural entities, and utilized - in furtherance of their own special interests - these sentiments, which became the "political formula" used by the indigenous ruling elite to transfer potential hostility from class discrepancies (within their own ethnic groups) to the rulers and subjects of others.

Since 1949-53, when the Nigerian elite was first consulted by the British in a constitutional review, the peoples of Nigeria have engaged in a continual regional, communal, and class struggle for a share in the economic benefits resulting from decolonization and independence, and the accompanying modernization. The two coups d'etat of 1966 and the civil war of 1967-70, to be discussed below, were the most virulent of these struggles.

In the parliamentary period from 1951 to 1966 the dominant class consisted primarily of high-ranking politicians, emirs and other influential chiefs, senior civil servants and governmental administrators, and leading businessmen and professionals. This class, formed primarily during the 1950s, the last decade of the colonial period, when positions, patronage, perquisites, and economic benefits were handed over to Nigerians by the British, was most favorably placed to rule after Independence in 1960. In the south the older leaders of the nationalist movement were joined by a rising educated new group of influential politicians, civil servants, lawyers, doctors, teachers, businessmen, and a few far-sighted chiefs.[22] In the North, power was retained by the traditional Hausa-Fulani ruling oligarchy in the upper North, supported by civil servants, Native Authority employees, district

---

22. Richard L. Sklar, *Nigerian Political Parties: Power in an Emergent African Nation* (Princeton: Princeton University Press, 1963).

and village heads, and judges, together with a smattering of new men, such as former headmaster Alhaji Sir Abubakar Tafawa Balewa, Federal Prime Minister from 1957 to 1966.

During 1951-60 each of the three major political parties, which played leading roles in unifying and locally mobilizing the socio-economic elite, achieved security and hegemony in one region only. A majority in the regional parliament and cooperation with the ruling coalition at the center enabled this elite to dispense a wide range of political favors and economic sanctions, thus retaining its own position and power, and maintaining the subordination of the underprivileged classes. Positions and employment in government service and public corporations, licenses for market stalls, permits for agricultural export production, and land rights for the establishment of enterprises, were allocated by the governing elite. Each major party was supported by a bank, which received substantial public funds and contributed to the viability of the party's newspaper.

At all levels - the local and regional in 1951, and the center after 1957 - the dominant class was in a position to employ a range of controls, extending over local councils, district administration, police and courts, to subdue any dissident minority. Thus the political elite attracted clients and socially inferior groups not only in the upper North, where the Muslim religion legitimized the traditional hierarchy, but even in Iboland, where there had been a wide dispersion of power prior to the twentieth century.[23] Although the elite of each region preferred to close ranks, in order to share the fruits of office and to prevent any challenge to their position, contradictions developed in which policies to enhance the regional security of one privileged group threatened the security of others.

Partly because of the dominance of a political and religious ideology which legitimized authority and inequality, class consciousness and mobilization was minimal. Although the National Council of Nigeria and the Cameroons (N.C.N.C.), the prime vehicle for the nationalist movement at its establishment in 1944, started as a pan-regional organization with some radical and trade union support, when the first elections were held in 1951, its strength remained only in the East, and Lagos. As noted

---

23. Stanley Diamond, *Nigeria: Model of a Colonial Failure* (New York: American Committee on Africa, 1966), p. 34; and Margery Perham, *Native Administration in Nigeria* (London: Oxford University Press, 1962), p. 234.

below, the Action Group (A.G.), which around the time of Independence in 1960 became the first major party to try to mobilize its support on a pan-regional and class basis, was undercut by the ruling, regionally oriented, parties. From time to time labor parties were formed, but they won virtually no seats because of the small size of the wage-earning class and the cross-pressures between communal and class-oriented parties.[24]

Regional Economic Interests and Political Enmities, 1949-67

One of the first threats to regional security occurred during 1949-53 when the Northern ruling class opposed any plan for Nigerian self-government where southerners - not sympathetic to the maintenance of the authority of the traditional aristocracy - were dominant. The British support of this Northern resistance, together with southern impatience for early self-government, led in an agreement in 1953-4 to leave the Northern Region intact with a majority of representatives in the Federal legislature. However, one of the contradictions which emerged, as subsequent events demonstrated, was that the quest for security by the Northern aristocracy - which required supremacy at the center - became a danger to the parties based in the other regions.

After Independence, the first major party to be challenged in its region of primary strength was the Action Group, the Western ruling party and Federal opposition party until 1962. Some members of the A.G. under its leader, Chief Obafemi Awolowo, planned to reorient its support to a broader constituency, comprising individuals and classes from all regions (including the upper North) who felt excluded from the distribution of patronage and positions, and who might be attracted by a program of egalitarian socialism. The shift in strategy by the A.G. came after its campaign for seats, and agitation for the creation of new states, in minority areas in the North and East during the 1950s. These actions bitterly antagonized the ruling coalition - especially the Northern People's Congress (N.P.C.), the instrument of the powerful aristocracy whose survival depended upon dominance in an undivided North hegemonic at the center.

A minority, primarily supported by conservative business elements who wished to protect their regional economic interests,

---

24. Robert Melson, "Marxists in the Nigerian Labor Movement" (unpublished Ph.D. dissertation, Massachusetts Institute of Technology, Cambridge, 1967), pp. 35-84.

broke from the A.G.; and many of those who remained were dissatisfied with its pan-regional, anti-capitalist strategy. The dissident faction instigated a disturbance in the Western parliament, which provided an excuse for the Federal coalition to declare a state of emergency in 1962, and to suspend the A.G. government of the region for six months.

During the next two years the ruling alliance used several politico-legal measures to crush the A.G., to depose its leader, and to facilitate the rise of a more compliant party in the West. The report of an inquiry into the misappropriation of public funds by A.G. officers, and a ten-year prison sentence for Awolowo for treason in an alleged attempt at a coup d'etat, effectively emasculated the radical wing of the A.G. Constitutional moves were initiated which eventually severed the Mid-West from the Western Region in 1963. After the suspension of the regional parliament was lifted, the dissidents of the A.G. formed the nucleus of a new coalition, which in 1964 became the Nigerian National Democratic Party (N.N.D.P.), the majority party in the West and a member of the ruling coalition at the center.[25]

A crisis resulted when partial returns from the 1962 Nigerian census for parliamentary representation indicated that the majority of the population was in the south rather than the North. Accusations from the North concerning the inflation of figures, especially in the East, led to the suppression of the results. A Northern-inspired re-count in 1963, not surprisingly, gave the North a majority which closely approximated the proportion in the previous official (1952-53) census. Despite protests from the East, the West supported its Northern ally in the Federal parliament, the 1963 figures were accepted and a challenge to Northern supremacy was averted.

The 1964-65 election threatened to undermine the security of the Ibo dominant class - i.e. civil servants, businessmen, and professionals - behind the Eastern-based N.C.N.C. This party joined with the A.G. to form the United Progressive Grand Alliance (U.P.G.A.) in opposition to the N.P.C.-N.N.D.P. coalition, the Nigerian National Alliance (N.N.A.). Although the U.P.G.A.

---

25. For a more complete treatment of the political struggle in the West, see Richard L. Sklar, "Nigerian Politics: The Ordeal of Chief Awolowo, 1960-65," in *Politics in Africa: Seven Cases*, ed. by Gwendolen M. Carter (New York: Harcourt, Brace & World, Inc., 1966), pp. 119-65.

started the campaign with confidence, its candidates and spokesmen encountered harassment and violence, and some were arrested while making their nominations in the North. The N.C.N.C., well aware of the fragility of Federal opposition parties such as the A.G. in 1962 - feared that, with a loss of membership in the coalition Federal government, they might lose their regional base as a result of appeals by the ruling parties to minorities and dissident or opportunistic politicians. Eventually the U.P.G.A. staged an election boycott, anticipating that President Nnamdi Azikiwe, an Ibo sympathetic to the N.C.N.C., would use this as a pretense for postponing the elections and installing a caretaker prime minister - presumably favorable to the U.P.G.A. - supported by the army, which was led by a disproportionate number of Ibo officers.

However, the army and the police supported Prime Minister Balewa and the winning N.N.A. coalition. Major-General Welby-Everard, soon to be retired as General Officer Commanding the Nigerian Army (G.O.C.), had no inclination to act contrary to the legal advice from the Chief Justice which supported the Prime Minister.[26] Major-General J.T. Aguiyi-Ironsi, the highest Nigerian officer, was an Ibo, but his promotion to G.O.C. was possible with the departure of British personnel the following month and he had no wish to jeopardize it. Balewa's consultation with top officers in the armed forces helped ensure their loyalty, as they were still largely free of communalism and the civilian government retained a certain legitimacy. Although the East contemplated secession, the Federation was kept together temporarily because of an agreement between Balewa and Azikiwe: elections in boycotted areas were to be scheduled later, but everywhere else the results were to be recognized, and the N.C.N.C. was to become a member of a grand coalition with the N.N.A. Nevertheless, the N.C.N.C. lost a few ministerial portfolios, and experienced insecurity from the knowledge that their presence in the coalition government was no longer essential, and that they could be disposed of when convenient.

The military intervention in politics on 15 January 1966, in which Prime Minister Balewa, Federal Finance Minister Festus

---

26. O'Connell, "Political Integration," in *African Integration*, ed. by Hazlewood, p. 170; Mackintosh, *Nigerian Government*, pp. 586-7; and Robin Luckham, *The Nigerian Military - A Sociological Analysis of Authority and Revolt, 1960-67* (Cambridge: Cambridge University Press, 1971), pp. 237-8.

Okotie-Eboh, Northern Premier Ahmadu Bello, Western Premier S.L. Akintola, and nine army officers were killed, was spearheaded by young Ibo majors. There is some evidence that the rebellion was instigated to forestall drastic measures to quash opposition elements in the West (and other parts of the south), expected as a result of a meeting of several leading politicians from the ruling alliance and a few army officers. On 17 January the principal architect of the coup, Major Chukwuma Nzeogwu, surrendered to another Ibo, Ironsi, who as G.O.C. became Supreme Commander of the new Federal military government. Despite the fact that the ethnic composition of the mutineers and victims led some to suspect that the coup was an attempt to establish Ibo suzerainty, initial reactions were not unfavorable, in part because of the disillusionment with the corruption, favoritism and disorder accompanying civilian rule.

Subsequent statements from the 15 January conspirators indicated that their objectives were to eliminate a corrupt political order, establish a radical socialist regime, and destroy Northern political dominance. The efforts of the army mutineers and the Ironsi government can be interpreted, in part, as an attempt to insure the security of the southern regions and, more specifically, the Ibo community, by the removal of the firm hold of Northern emirs and administrators on the Federal government. The stresses resulting from the regional and communal competition for a share of the economic pie had been transmitted to the army, and had politicized its officer corps. Perhaps the conspirators perceived that their positions and promotions were endangered by policies of regional quotas for lower ranks, and regional balance for officer recruits, which enhanced the share of the educationally-backward North. In addition, some radical and southern soldiers resented the way in which the army was used by the ruling coalition for political purposes in the Western party struggle in 1962, the riots of the Tivs (a dissident lower Northern community) in 1964, the election crisis during 1964-65, and finally in the repression of opponents during the rigged Western election of October 1965.

Within a few months, potential opposition elements, especially in the North, became convinced that Ironsi was using the center's powerful political and economic levers primarily on behalf of the Ibo and other southern communities. On 23 May a government decree imposed a unitary state and a unified civil service, banned parties and communal organizations of a political character, and implied the possibility of a continuance of the regime for three years. This decree was introduced at a time when the fear of Ibo hegemony, present since the coup, had been exacerbated by Ironsi's dependence on advice from fellow Ibos, and his failure to punish the mutineers. The unification of the civil service together with the earlier repudiation by the Northern Military Governor of the policy of "Northernization" of the private and government sectors, aroused anxieties in the North concerning the loss of jobs to better-educated Nigerians. The decree was followed by a weekend of riots there against Ibos and other southerners.

The dominant economic interests behind Ironsi, the Ibos in the Federal administration, the joint-stock companies in Lagos and the East, did not unite with other elites in the south, and even some of the Ibos in the East were disenchanted. In fact, the new regime managed to antagonize radical Nigerians in the armed forces, and in the West and lower North, who were opposed to the previous civilian government. It even alienated the influential aristocracy of the upper North, although doing little to undercut its power. Prior to 1966, this ruling group had been able to control some of the lower Northern communities, not only through negative measures such as economic sanctions and political reprisals, but through positive inducements such as a policy of regional preferences in employment in the modern sector, which especially benefited their educated classes. Ironsi, by undermining the long-standing practice of Northernization of employment, failed to drive a wedge between the elites of the upper and lower North, and united them.[27]

On 28 July 1966 General Ironsi and a number of other Ibo officers were killed by a counter-coup, launched in a charged atmosphere in which rumors circulated rampantly of an Ibo plan to annihilate key Northerners. The disorders within the army continued until a few days later, when Lieutenant-Colonel Yakabu Gowon, from the Angas, a minority community in the lower North, emerged as the Head of State. After some early doubts concerning the viability of a unified Nigeria, one of the first acts of the new leader was to return the country to the Federal structure existing before the May decree. Gowon was more representative of the soldiers, civil servants, and educated classes of the lower North than upper Northern politicians.

The rift between the Eastern and Federal military governments, which eventually widened into a civil war, began immediately after the second coup. The East recognized the Gowon government as only an interim regime, on the grounds that Gowon was not the highest-ranking army officer, and on the basis of an

---

27. The lower North (or "Middle Belt") consists of present-day Kwara, Niger, Benue, Plateau, and Gongola states.

understanding by the Eastern government that he was to retain power only until the military had the opportunity to decide on the country's future. In addition, the violence directed against persons of Eastern origin in the North, and the subsequent flight to their communal homelands in 1966, diminished the economic advantages to the East of continuing in the Federation, and strengthened the forces giving an impetus to disintegration. Finally, the failure of the coup in the East and the departure of Northern soldiers from that region in August 1966 meant that its Military Governor, Lieutenant-Colonel Odumegwu Ojukwu, had effective control of all troops there.

In addition to the transfer of power from civilian politicians to military officers between 1965 and late 1966, there was a shift away from the major ethnic communities, especially the Hausa-Fulanis and Ibos, to the minorities in the lower North, Mid-West, and non-Ibo areas of the East. Indicative of this was the formation on 27 May 1966 of twelve states from the previous four regions and Federal Territory. The creation of six states in the old Northern Region formalized the decline of the traditional aristocracy in the upper North, whose previous hegemony was based on political control of the whole region, comprising a majority of the population in the Federation. The new structure cut off two minority states from the previous ruling community in the East, the Ibos. It severed a major industrial center, Port Harcourt, and a large part of the oil-producing areas, from the Ibo majority in the landlocked East-Central state (now Anambra and Imo states). On 30 May 1967, the Eastern leaders, with little support from local non-Ibos, moved to protect their regional hegemony by declaring the East to be the independent Republic of Biafra.

Secession threatened the new ruling elite in Nigeria, the high-ranking military leaders and government servants, and the minority communities, whose interests coincided with a strong central government. The West, contrary to indications early in May, remained in the Federation, where their economic interests lay. Although Ibos held a smaller number of posts in the Federal civil service than Yorubas, they provided strong competition for certain positions, and here was a chance for the Westerners to make gains at the center by supporting the Federation against Eastern secession. In addition, the appointment of Chief Awolowo (freed from prison in 1966) to be Vice-Chairman of the Federal Executive Council and Federal Commissioner for Finance, together with the Biafran attack on a Western city, may also have been important factors in the West's decision to opt for the Federation.

From the previous discussion it is now possible to see the

main causes behind the tendency towards disintegration since World War II: the struggles between the dominant elites of the East, the West, and the North; the contentions between majority and minority groups within each region; and the conflicts between classes. Contradictions arose when the security of one regional elite interfered with that of another. The Northern traditional rulers and administrators, through coercion, the sanction of religion, and the control of major economic benefits, prevented opposition elements in the lower North and Kano Province from making inroads into their parliamentary representation. Control of the giant Northern Region was sufficient for dominance at the Federal level. However, this threatened the security of the bourgeoisie and government officials in the south, who faced the dilemma of whether to align with the conservative North, or to join with radical socialist groups in the south and the opposition parties in the North in a "progressive" coalition. Radicals and Northern rulers were recognized as incompatible in a Federal alliance, because many politicians felt that significant social progress was not possible unless the Northern "feudalists" were removed.

Nevertheless, membership of a ruling coalition aligned with the North was a powerful attraction for the major southern parties, and the insecurity of opposition was a strong repellent. This type of coalition was inclined towards conservatism or reaction, opposing the populist programs of trade unions, and radical intellectuals and civil servants. However, during 1960-62, Chief Awolowo, the leader of the opposition party in the Federal parliament, who had long been personally inclined towards socialism, reacted to his somewhat vulnerable position by trying to become the spokesman for the dispossessed and underprivileged, and for anti-imperialism. The subsequent attempts by the conservative Federal coalition to crush the A.G. during 1962-63, and the A.G.-N.C.N.C. alliance during 1964-65, set the stage for the army mutinies and the civil war.

Trans-national Linkages after Independence

The colonial pattern of division of labor under international capitalism continued in the post-Independence civilian era. As late as 1965, despite a substantial growth in the relative importance of secondary exports, 7.8 percent of exports and 80.9 percent of imports were secondary products (chemicals, machinery, transport equipment, and manufactured goods), while 91.8 percent of exports and 17.8 of imports were primary products (food, raw materials, minerals, and organic oils and fats). Despite the steady decline in the relative importance of trade with Britain in the previous decade, 38.5 percent of exports and 30.9 percent of imports were with that nation in 1965.[28] Almost all Nigeria's trade was with the developed capitalist economies, and only a trace (less than 5 percent) was with the socialist and less developed countries. The colonial nexus in international trade has remained fairly strong, even in the Independence period, as a result of the legacy from economic policies which discouraged industrial growth, the high degree of integration of poor capitalist countries in the world economy, and the inducements to the indigenous elite to cooperate with the metropolitan nations.

Prior to the 1970s, virtually all of Nigeria's foreign exchange assets were in the form of sterling. Under the post-war modified gold-exchange standard of the International Monetary Fund, British sterling was a key currency in international trade. In essence, a country that accumulates sterling, as Nigeria did in the twenty years prior to 1955, extends credit to Britain, facilitating her long-term investments in underdeveloped economies. In the period of restrictions on sterling convertibility, from World War II to 1958, Nigeria contributed dollar earnings to the common sterling pool in such a way as to increase the importance of imports from the U.K.[29] This strengthened the balance-of-payments position of the sterling area, and the international financial position of the U.K.

Hakam's estimates indicated that in 1964 nearly 75 percent of the book value of industrial assets, from firms in Nigeria with a value of £N25,000 (about $70,000) or more, was foreign; the British accounted for slightly more than 50 percent of the total value.[30] According to the 1965 *Industrial Survey* of manufacturing establishments with ten or more employed, foreign private ownership comprised 62 percent of total ownership, and 85

---

28. The pattern of international trade with Britain in 1965 was close to that of the world as a whole, with secondary products accounting for 14.1 percent of exports and 91.8 percent of imports, and with primary products making up 85.9 percent of exports and 8.2 percent of imports. Nigeria, Office of Statistics, *Annual Abstract of Statistics: Nigeria, 1967* (Lagos, 1968), pp. 87-90.

29. H.M.A. Onitiri, "Nigeria's International Economic Relations: A Survey," *Nigerian Journal of Economic and Social Studies*, III, No. 3 (November 1961), 15-18.

30. "Industrial" refers to manufacturing, assembling, and processing. A.N. Hakam, "The Motivation to Invest and the Locational Pattern of Foreign Private Industrial Investments in Nigeria," ibid., VIII, No. 1 (March 1966), 49-65.

percent of total private ownership, in the manufacturing sector in Nigeria (if ownership shares are measured by paid-up capital) (table 2.8, p. 58). Foreign interests continued to dominate new registrations of manufacturing companies on the eve of the 1966 army mutiny. Seventy-eight percent of the thirty-three largest manufacturing companies registered during 1964-65 represented some foreign ownership or management. Arthur Lewis estimated that Nigerian income comprised less than 30 percent of the 1963 value-added in foreign large-scale manufacturing firms. Debt servicing became a major problem for the military government, as the net international outflow of private direct investment income was greater than the net inflow of private direct investment, by £N73.4 million to £N55.0 million in 1966, a reversal from 1965 when it was less than the net inflow by £N6.14 million to £N53.4 million, and 1960-4 when its annual average was less than the net inflow by £N33.0 million to £N12.3 million.[31]

The fact that in Nigerian manufacturing in 1965 foreigners accounted for as much as 24.7 percent of the total wages and salaries but only 2.4 percent of the total employment (table 2.8) suggests that they were highly represented among high-level personnel in the industrial sector. According to estimates from table 3.1, p. 84, 55.3 percent of the 2,355 professional and managerial personnel in manufacturing firms in Nigeria in 1965 with 100 or more employed were foreign.

Another colonial legacy, partially responsible for the primacy of the foreign industrial sector, was the dominance of overseas banks, which were dubious concerning the potential viability of indigenous firms. As late as 1965, 90 percent of total demand deposits were held in banks where foreign capital was at least a majority. The foreign sector was also favored by policies of industrial discrimination. Where the expansion of new enterprises was considered to be of high priority they were given income-tax holidays of from two to five years; but this was mostly extended to large-scale and relatively heavy industry, which was primarily foreign. Of the 145 "pioneer" companies so

31. "Foreign large-scale manufacturing" refers to firms with ten or more persons employed where all paid-up capital has been supplied by non-Nigerians. Permanent and quasi-permanent residents of non-African origin are considered foreign. Samuel A. Aluko, *Fiscal Incentives for Industrial Development in Nigeria* (New York: United Nations Department of Economic and Social Affairs, 1967), p. 14; W. Arthur Lewis, *Reflections on Nigeria's Economic Growth* (Paris: Organisation for Economic Cooperation and Development, 1967), p. 26; and Nigeria, *Annual Abstract*, 1967, p. 4.

Table 2.8

The Relative Size of Foreign Ownership and Employment in Nigerian Manufacturing Industries, 1965

ISIC No.[a]	(see facing page for letter code explanation) c	d	e	f	g	h	i	j
201	393	0.569	0.508	0.298	0.394	1,056	0.020	0.275
202	153	0.940	0.833	0.046	0.725	256	0.030	0.352
203	--	--	--	--	--	524	0.004	0.130
205	1,104	0.935	0.833	0.022	0.869	584	0.059	0.470
206	572	0.537	0.144	0.404	0.468	2,559	0.007	0.120
208	490	0.639	0.000	0.361	0.640	950	0.027	0.232
207,211	1,887	0.899	0.952	0.018	0.161	2,857	0.012	0.241
209,220	6,354	0.903	0.128	0.095	0.890	2,563	0.018	0.189
213	5,228	0.803	0.306	0.134	0.545	2,984	0.030	0.278
214	797	0.970	0.969	0.015	0.503	868	0.029	0.311
231,232	5,962	0.952	0.894	0.033	0.662	11,554	0.027	0.293
241	732	0.696	0.485	0.234	0.535	1,761	0.029	0.292
243	110	0.600	0.000	0.400	0.600	652	0.013	0.136
244	476	0.589	0.562	0.269	0.386	1,379	0.024	0.348
251	2,910	0.557	0.244	0.387	0.487	8,176	0.009	0.194
259	5	0.000	0.000	1.000	0.000	104	0.000	0.000
260	801	0.688	0.200	0.289	0.639	4,251	0.019	0.176
272	970	0.669	0.000	0.330	0.669	686	0.035	0.384
280	2,824	0.646	0.858	0.095	0.193	5,708	0.035	0.086
291,293	336	0.892	0.359	0.080	0.666	726	0.023	0.218
300	6,218	0.842	0.589	0.120	0.643	6,843	0.017	0.268
311	300	0.912	0.816	0.063	0.660	295	0.057	0.428
312	3,612	0.908	0.616	0.065	0.650	7,057	0.007	0.163
313	816	0.934	0.600	0.025	0.938	407	0.078	0.488
331	245	0.910	0.000	0.090	0.910	352	0.034	0.338
332,333	380	0.871	0.935	0.021	0.144	882	0.011	0.172
334	5,261	0.335	0.312	0.253	0.127	2,393	0.022	0.201
339	2,792	0.959	0.857	0.038	0.737	1,480	0.025	0.387
341,342	1,250	0.971	0.826	0.025	0.857	694	0.057	0.455
350	4,006	0.954	0.589	0.043	0.896	6,620	0.045	0.351
370	369	0.902	0.330	0.092	0.853	759	0.023	0.253
381	60	0.000	1.000	0.000	0.000	352	0.011	0.125
383,385	1,105	1.000	0.000	0.000	1.000	1,880	0.024	0.263
Other [b]	9,037	0.950	0.853	0.046	0.726	15,530	0.213	0.278
TOTAL	67,467	0.848	0.676	0.111	0.619	97,051	0.024	0.247

a. Following are the industries which correspond to the International Standard Industrial Classification (ISIC) code in the table:

ISIC No.	Industries	ISIC No.	Industries
201	Meat products	272	Paper products
202	Dairy products	280	Printing
203	Fruit canning	291,293	Tanning and travel goods
205	Grain mill products	300	Rubber products
206	Bakery products	311	Basic industrial chemicals
208	Sugar confectionary	312	Vegetable oil milling
207,211	Sugar and spirit distillery	313	Paints
209,220	Miscellaneous food products	331	Bricks and tiles
213	Beer brewing	332,333	Pottery and glass products
214	Soft drinks	334	Cement
231,232	Manufacture of textiles	339	Concrete products
241	Footwear	341,342	Basic metals
243	Wearing apparel	350	Metal products
244	Made-up textile goods (excluding wearing apparel)	370	Electrical equipment
251	Saw milling	381	Boat building and repairs
259	Other wood products	383,385	Motor vehicle and bicycle assembly
260	Furniture and fixtures		

b. ISIC numbers for other industries are 319, 321, 329, 360, 384, 391, 394 and 399.

c. Paid up capital. (£N'000)

d. Foreign private ownership/total private ownership.

e. Nigerian public ownership/total Nigerian ownership.

f. Nigerian private ownership/total ownership.

g. Foreign private ownership/total ownership.

h. Total employed, refering to the total number of workers engaged, i.e. working proprietors, paid employees, unpaid apprentices and unpaid family workers.

i. Number of non-Nigerians employed/total employed.

j. Wages and salaries of non-Nigerians/total wages and salaries.

Source: Nigeria, Office of Statistics, *Industrial Survey of Nigeria, 1964 and 1965* (Lagos, 1968), pp. 32, 34, 37.

designated between 1952 and 1966, only six were exclusively Nigerian holdings. Foreign firms benefited disproportionately from many other governmental concessions, such as accelerated depreciation allowances, import duty relief, equity and loan finance, and land acquisition provisions, not to mention improved public services.[32]

Unlike most developed countries in their early stages of industrialization, foreign merchants and manufacturers, rather than domestic entrepreneurs, took the lead in the development of import-substitution industries in Nigeria. A primary motive for the establishment of foreign enterprise, according to empirical studies, was to transform a highly competitive market in international trade to one where competition was virtually eliminated. Ironically, the greatest pressure for increased protection for manufacturing was not from the government, or even from domestic producers, but from foreign capitalists and their local collaborators.[33]

Foreign dominance of the manufacturing sector was accompanied by high rates of industrial concentration. Table 2.9, p. 62, indicates that the total value-added of the largest four establishments in thirty-one manufacturing industries as a percentage of the total value-added in the thirty-one industries was 69.0 percent in Nigeria in 1965 in comparison to 3.7 percent in the same thirty-one industries in the U.S. in 1947. In addition, the total employment of the largest four firms in these industries as a percentage of total employment was 72.2 percent in Nigeria compared to 3.3 percent in the U.S. (The appendix to this chapter indicates that Nigerian and U.S. data are very comparable. Also see this appendix for the basis for the selection of industries, and the method of computation of concentration rates.) The overwhelming majority of the foreign firms have been multinational corporations, companies with their headquarters located in some country other than Nigeria. Although foreign subsidiary firms dominated production in Nigeria's nascent industrial sector, the output of these subsidiary enterprises was usually only a fraction of the output of the parent companies.

---

32. Ola Oni, "Development and Features of the Nigerian Financial System - A Marxist Approach," *Nigerian Journal of Economic and Social Studies*, VIII, No. 3, (November 1966), 386-91; and Aluko, *Fiscal Incentives*, pp. 49-65.

33. Peter Kilby, *Industrialization in an Open Economy: Nigeria, 1945-1966* (Cambridge: Cambridge University Press, 1969), pp. 48-59; and Hakam, *Nigerian Journal*, VIII, No. 1, 49-65.

The control of this technology has been concentrated in the advanced economies of North America, Western Europe, and Japan. Ronald Müller's data on patents granted by a group of mixed and capitalist less developed countries indicate that over 90 percent of the patents were granted to foreigners. If the number of patents is weighted by their economic or technological worth (i.e. volume of sales or value-added), most less developed countries would find that the weighted patents granted to foreigners would be over 99 percent.[34]

A major argument for overseas investment has been the necessity to transfer techniques of modern production to Nigeria. However, the advantages to Nigeria from the substantial contribution of foreign firms to national output should be weighed against some possible disadvantages, which need to be examined in future research. Incentives in large foreign firms may be structured so as to discourage them from transmitting to domestic counterparts the knowledge or skills upon which commercial success is based. The interests of many indigenous capitalists tend to become associated with those of their foreign partners or benefactors. In addition, as long as small-scale African enterprises are overwhelmed by the larger firms, domestic entrepreneurs may not be successful in climbing step by step to larger industrial units.

Manufacturing concerns controlled by Lebanese, Greeks, Syrians, Cypriots, and Palestinians (referred to as "Levantines") need to be distinguished from western (and Japanese) industrial enterprises. Although most of the families of Levantine businessmen came to Nigeria between 1910 and 1940, they are considered foreign by the Nigerian government, despite their quasi-permanent residence in Nigeria (at least through the 1960s). Initially involved in transport and small-scale trade, they have proceeded from small beginnings to develop a number of important industrial units. Their operations are on a smaller scale than those of westerners,[35] and few have headquarters outside Nigeria.[36] The Lebanese seem to be especially resented by their Nigerian competitors, even though the 1964 book value of their

34. "The Multinational Corporation and the Underdevelopment of the Third World," in *The Political Economy of Development and Underdevelopment*, ed. by Charles K. Wilber (New York: Random House, 1973), pp. 126-7.

35. Kilby, *Industrialization*, p. 61.

36. At least the latter is generally believed, although there has been little research on the possibility of business holdings by Levantine entrepreneurs and families both in Nigeria and abroad.

Table 2.9

A Comparison between the Concentration Rates[a] of Value-added and Employment in Selected Manufacturing Industries in Nigeria, 1965, and the U.S., 1947

(see facing page for letter code explanation)

ISIC No.[b]	c	d	e	f	g Nigeria	g U.S.	h Nigeria	h U.S.
201	10	3,974	1,056	275,441	0.747	0.097	0.869	0.055
202	4	7,816	256	207,669	1.000	0.018	1.000	0.021
205	6	4,206	584	113,217	0.963	0.066	0.999	0.069
206	70	7,123	2,559	297,368	0.297	0.028	0.408	0.044
208	6	1,754	250	91,710	0.908	0.085	0.782	0.113
207, 211	3	825	2,857	73,542	1.000	0.090	1.000	0.124
209, 220	9	6,691	2,563	150,794	0.884	0.049	1.000	0.072
213	6	493	2,984	85,058	0.767	0.138	0.590	0.164
214	13	5,618	868	79,397	0.647	0.031	0.788	0.036
231, 232	34	3,715	11,554	864,309	0.553	0.025	0.715	0.024
241	21	1,314	1,761	257,428	0.566	0.084	0.587	0.102
243	15	24,706	652	940,939	0.440	0.011	0.357	0.010
244	6	6,254	1,379	127,631	0.950	0.077	0.894	0.055
251	46	19,039	8,176	380,456	0.729	0.203	0.750	0.290
259	4	2,349	104	65,514	1.000	0.059	1.000	0.037
260	55	7,687	4,251	322,384	0.312	0.031	0.582	0.037
272	8	8,315	686	701,296	0.855	0.015	0.864	0.010
280	77	28,986	5,708	715,450	0.374	0.025	0.452	0.047
300	35	849	6,843	230,967	0.441	0.116	0.255	0.094
311	6	975	295	271,624	0.902	0.085	0.941	0.079
312	62	1,194	7,057	43,431	0.481	0.066	0.490	0.077
313	8	1,456	407	67,807	0.730	0.096	0.840	0.089
331	7	711	352	36,945	0.871	0.084	0.791	0.088
332, 333	7	1,792	882	148,633	0.939	0.085	0.979	0.096
334	5	155	2,073	35,662	0.969	0.083	0.959	0.084
339	12	6,158	1,480	46,821	0.680	0.027	0.371	0.031
341, 342	3	4,552	694	1,030,042	1.000	0.026	1.000	0.019
350	40	17,545	6,620	1,020,490	0.360	0.020	0.340	0.015
370	10	3,973	759	801,359	0.674	0.044	0.853	0.037
381	3	809	352	19,455	1.000	0.232	1.000	0.211
383, 385	11	1,980	1,880	716,736	0.854	0.197	0.932	0.032
TOTAL	613	183,014	80,221	10,118,075	0.722	0.033	0.690	0.037

a. Concentration rate refers to the size of the four largest establishments in the industry/the size of the total industry.

b. For the industries which correspond to the ISIC code in the table, see note a, table 2.8.

c. Total number of establishments, Nigeria.

d. Total number of establishments, U.S.

e. Total employment, Nigeria.

f. Total employment, U.S.

g. Total number employed from the largest four establishments in each industry in terms of employment size/total number employed in the industry.

h. Total value-added of the largest four establishments in each industry in terms of employment size/total value-added in the industry.

Source: Nigeria, *Industrial Survey, 1964 and 1965*, pp. 40-1; and U.S., Department of Commerce, Bureau of the Census, *Census of Manufacturers: 1947*, Vol. II, *Statistics by Industry* (Washington, D.C.: U.S. Government Printing Office, 1949).

---

industrial assets, from firms in Nigeria with a value of £N25,000 of more, was only 8 percent of assets held by Europeans or North Americans.[37] Levantine firms in the footwear industry have resisted the Nigerianization of management and capital as much as European footwear firms, although the lack of further evidence precludes wider generalization.

The political class profited from foreign investment during the civilian regime, 1960-66. In some cases, external interests formed partnerships with members of the governing elite or their business constituents, or with the parastatal corporations, which widened the patronage and income base of the class. Frequently, leading politicians benefited from foreign firms through "rake-offs" on their contracts, intermediary roles in land deals, sales of inputs and services, and positions on the boards of directors.

Business interests by foreigners in Nigeria were generally

37. Greeks, Syrians, Cypriots, and Palestinians are not mentioned in the statistics, although some may be included in the category, "other," whose holdings of industrial assets are 11 percent of citizens from Europe or the United States. Hakam, *Nigerian Journal*, VIII, No. 1, 65.

supplemented by overseas political, military, and economic assistance, designed to help support those who wished to keep the country open to foreign investment and trade. British capital cemented the pro-British sympathy of the Northern-dominated civilian government. The Northern ruling aristocracy, highly sympathetic to British economic and military interests in Nigeria, and opposed to the influence of communist countries, could reasonably expect the British to resist any threat to Northern hegemony and regional security, including threats from radical socialists or from potential southern-dominated ruling coalitions. By attracting British capital, the North minimized the threat of a high concentration of southern entrepreneurship, technical expertness, and labor in its economy; the British were more sensitive to Northernization in employment, and had respect for the old authoritarian social system.

British foreign policy during the Nigerian Independence period, as manifested especially during the 1966-70 crises, was consistent with support for an economically integrated area that would leave the Federation open to international trade and investment. The mutineers of 15 January 1966, whose objective in part was to establish a radical socialist regime, surrendered the following week to General Ironsi, who announced that policies favorable to foreign capital would be continued. The extent to which the British, represented at the rump cabinet meeting the day after the coup, influenced these policies is not certain. After the July 1966 coup, British and (in some cases) American diplomats were influential in dissuading Gowon from announcing the disintegration of the Federation, and in discouraging those who attended the September Constitutional conference and the January 1967 Aburi conference from agreeing on confederation. However, Federation was clearly unacceptable to the East, which was close to *de facto* secession long before the end of 1966.

Northern Nigeria has been frequently characterized as "feudal." But while the authoritarian patron-client system was reminiscent of interpersonal relations under feudalism, the region's overseas economic links demonstrated a high degree of integration within the international capitalist network.[38] There is

---

38. The counterpart to a high degree of integration within the world capitalist system is a low degree of interregional economic integration (e.g., trade flows and migration), a partial determinant of the extent of political cohesion. I have examined aspects of this question in "Economic Aspects of the Nigerian Civil War," in *Civil Wars in the Twentieth Century*, ed. by Robin

evidence that the North was as dependent upon the capitalist world for trade and investment as Nigeria as a whole.[39] Also, gains accrued to the Northern rulers from their close political ties with Britain and her capitalist allies. Once the power of this oligarchy had been broken through the two military coups and the creation of twelve states, the foundation was laid for the decline of the influence of the capitalist world, and a greater emphasis upon economic ties with communist countries, and policies to counter foreign industrial concentration in Nigeria.

Development Planning

The earliest national plans, during 1946-55 and 1955-60 (later extended to 1962), were framed by colonial administrators. Even the First National Development Plan, 1962-68, after Independence, was drawn up primarily by foreign economists. They were in favor of "automatic" decision-making by private units, a dismissal of major discrepancies between financial and social profitability, a stress on marginal adjustment rather than fundamental structural change, an accent on a high economic pay-off from directly productive investment (as opposed to an indirect return from social overheads), the eschewal of increased tax rates at high-income levels (for fear of dampening private incentive), a conservative monetary and fiscal policy with an emphasis upon a relatively small plan size, an economy open to foreign trade and investment, and a substantial reliance on overseas assistance. Although political leaders and, to a lesser extent, government officials were involved in the selection of certain projects, they provided little overall direction or specification of

---

Higham (Lexington: University of Kentucky Press, 1972), pp. 187-8; and "Inter-Regional Economic Relations in the Nigerian Footwear Industry," *JMAS*, VI, No. 4 (1968), 535-41.

39. Adebayo Adedeji, *Nigerian Federal Finance: Its Development, Problems, and Prospects* (London: Hutchinson, 1969), pp. 122-4; P.N.C. Okigbo, *Nigerian National Accounts, 1950-57* (Enugu: Federal Ministry of Economic Development, 1961), pp. 52-9; and Hakam, *Nigerian Journal*, VIII, No. 1, 59-60. Cf. André Gunder Frank, *Capitalism and Underdevelopment in Latin America: Historical Studies of Chile and Brazil* (New York: Monthly Review Press, 1969), pp. 3-6, who argues that Latin America's underdevelopment stems from a satellite position in the international capitalist system, and not from a legacy of domestic feudalism.

goals.[40] However, despite their lack of involvement in formulating the plan, Nigerians were charged with its administration.

Arthur Lewis suggests that the main weaknesses of the 1962-68 plan were as follows: incomplete feasibility studies and inadequate evaluation of projects, meager public participation followed by excessive political intervention in the making of economic decisions, insufficient attention to the small indigenous sector, and unsatisfactory machinery for implementing developments in the public sector.[41] The author claims that if a strong central program had been designed to foster economic development among the masses, the power and privileges of the ruling elite would have been threatened--especially in the North. A dispersion of economic power to the multiplicity of petty traders, craftsmen, and small industrialists, without a *quid quo pro*, would have threatened the economic interests of the political leaders - the viability and monopoly return of the public corporations which serve as a basis for the disposal of patronage, and the large private business interests. Only 83.1 percent of the £N676.8 million capital expenditure planned for the public sector was spent; ironically its percentage shortfall was even greater during 1962-64 than in the later years of political crisis.[42] One reason for the shortfall was that when the plan was formulated there was no clear identification of feasible industrial projects, and virtually no details of supporting government policies. The lack of preparatory work by professional accountants, economists, engineers, managers, and planners resulted from ineffective coordination, a shortage of high-level manpower, and the introduction of political criteria for determining projects.

The dominant class, virtually devoid of goals and priorities that could be articulated to the masses, and preoccupied with the preservation of their system of patronage, did not encourage decision-making by local authorities, or consultation with the public. Members of parliament energetically pushed projects that

---

40. Wolfgang F. Stolper, Head of the Economic Planning Unit at that time, discusses "The Main Features of the 1962-1968 National Plan," in *Nigerian Journal of Economic and Social Studies*, IV, No. 2 (July 1962), 85-91. Sayre P. Schatz, "Nigeria's First National Development Plan (1962-68): An Appraisal," ibid. V, No. 2 (July 1963), 221-35, and Reginald H. Green, "Four African Development Plans: Ghana, Kenya, Nigeria, and Tanzania," *JMAS*, III, No. 2 (1965), 253-74, provide cogent criticisms of the plan.

41. *Reflections*, pp. 37-9.

42. Nigeria, Ministry of Information, *Second National Development Plan, 1970-74* (Lagos, n.d.), pp. 11-14.

would enhance their clientage base, regardless of any relationship to the plan's objectives. Decisions on expenditures involving millions of pounds were made on the basis of conversations between politicians without documents or expert advice, and with little knowledge of easily ascertainable facts. Parliament was not equipped, and did not have the will, to make important decisions concerning the plan, because of a preoccupation with the distribution of bounty to the faithful.[43]

It is not surprising that the dominant class had no desire to establish adequate machinery to implement and evaluate the plan independently. If such an apparatus had been controlled by professionals or civil servants not oriented towards the interests of the political leaders, the system from which the leaders profited would have been undermined. The lack of departmental annual reports, the secrecy of official information, and the paucity of program evaluation, together with political intervention, allowed personal advancement to remain the political elite's main objective. An emphasis upon socio-economic development for the low-income classes was obviously no priority to a ruling regime preoccupied with this struggle.

Class Conflict and Formation

A major restive element in Nigeria has been the relatively deprived and politically discontented members of the educated classes. During the decolonization period of the 1950s and the 1960s, rapid indigenization led to a large number of elite positions in the civil service, armed forces, police, government corporations, and universities opening to them. However, by the mid-1960s foreigners had been almost completely replaced by relatively youthful Nigerians and only a few vacancies remained. For example, the number of Nigerians holding the 4,000 plus senior posts in the Federal public service increased from 19.3 percent in 1953 to 74.9 percent in 1961 to virtually all in 1965. In addition, Nigerians filled the majority of new positions created after the regional public services came into being in 1954.[44]

Younger men, who had developed high aspirations for good

---

43. A. Akene Ayida, "Development Objectives," Reconstruction and Development Conference, 1969, p. 10.

44. Mackintosh, *Nigerian Government*, pp. 188-9; and K.W.J. Post, *The Nigerian Federal Election of 1959: Politics and Admistration in a Developing Political System* (London: Oxford University Press, 1963), p. 23.

positions and rapid promotion on the basis of observing the careers of slightly older men, became frustrated with the abrupt decline in openings. This discontent was exacerbated among southerners who found that jobs were more abundant in the North where foreigners had retired at a slower rate during 1955-65. The substantial student unrest, especially in southern universities, may have stemmed, in part, from frustration over the sharp decline in high-level employment. A similar drop in the rate of openings and promotions was a major factor explaining the low morale in the army prior to the revolt by the officers in January 1966. There was a limit to the expansion of senior positions that the ruling class could provide to placate the disgruntled younger educated group.

By the middle of the 1960s the scramble for the few remaining posts was very intense, and communal competition for these contributed to the enmity and bitterness which sparked off the crises of 1966 and 1967.

The most visible aspect of class conflict has been that between the workers and the government, in the dual role of ruler and major employer. By and large, labor has been relatively weak and unorganized in Nigeria, with the overwhelming majority "self-employed" in agriculture, petty trade, or crafts. Thus wage-paid employment comprised only about 5 percent, and trade union members only 2 percent (300,000), of the economically active population of 17.6 million in 1962. In addition, the reluctance of the British Colonial Office to strengthen trade union rights, the dependence upon foreign financial support, and the thwarting of labor political organizations by nationalist leaders, hampered the development of a strong united movement. Following the general strike of 1945, the trade unions were divided between the "moderates," supported by western confederations, and oriented towards immediate goals of higher wages and better working conditions under the existing capitalist system, and the "leftists," devoted to the creation of a socialist economy and a more centralized government, and affiliated with communist and/or revolutionary pan-African confederations. Furthermore, after independence the "moderates" and Marxists were each split into two factions by leadership struggles, personal feuds and ideological differences.

Nevertheless, these four superordinate central labor organizations amalgamated during 1963-64 as the Joint Action Committee (J.A.C.) to pressure the government to raise wages and salaries. After a delay in publishing the report of the Morgan Commission, and after a wage offer by the government below the recommended level, the J.A.C. mobilized 800,000 supporters to stop work for thirteen days in June 1964. Even though this general strike represented less than 5 percent of the economically-active population, it disrupted the vital economic and administrative services of the country, and especially affected the upper-income classes. Partly because the U.P.G.A. coalition supported the workers' demands, they secured an improvement on the government's original offer, no dismissals during the strike period and payment of wages, plus a consideration of the Commission's recommendations on industrial relations and the machinery for a continuing wage review. Although the strike caught the government unawares and demonstrated its fragility, the J.A.C. could not translate this victory into further political strength, because labor unity did not survive for long. The government recognized the moderate United Labour Congress, which lost interest in the J.A.C. when it judged it could not hold its position against the "leftists." The election alignment between radical labor leaders and U.P.G.A. miscarried after the latter refused to endorse the candidates of the labor parties.[45]

Labor discontent resulted from a growing sense of injustice at the wide gap between the wages of white-collar and blue-collar workers. To be sure, the 1963-64 GDP per capita of members of the households of daily-paid and semi-skilled workers was probably as high as that of the total labor force, which consisted of 56 percent in agriculture.[46] However, in the fiscal year 1963/64 (beginning 1 April), supervisors in the public service were paid 33 times as much as these workers, compared to a multiple of 5 to 10 in the U.S. and about 5 in the U.S.S.R.

---

45. William H. Friedland, "Paradoxes of African Trade Unionism: Organizational Chaos and Political Potential," *Africa Report*, X, No. 6 (June 1965), 6-10; Melson, "Marxists in the Nigerian Labor Movement," pp. 30-87; and Kilby, *Industrialization*, pp. 202, 267.

46. If the average wages of the daily-paid workers in government service are assumed to be equal to the average of all such workers, their annual wages were 3.7 times the GDP per capita in 1963-4. (Aluko estimates that comparable ratios between wages and income per capita were 2:1 in the U.S. and 1.5:1 in Western Europe.) However, the ratio of these workers to total members in their households is 1:3, if it is assumed that this ratio is equal to that of the total number in the labor force to the total population. Aluko, "Wages, Costs and Prices," Reconstruction and Development Conference, p. 18; and *Population Census of Nigeria, 1963*, III (Lagos, 1968). Agricultural workers include "farmers, fishermen, hunters, loggers and related workers." Ibid. p. 39.

Furthermore, personal income tax rates were low (i.e. a 3.2-6.0 percent average rate for single persons in the 99th percentile income class - an annual income of £N700), and regressive (or, at best, approximately proportional) in all regions except the East.[47] To exacerbate the frustration, the government had not increased wages since 1959, despite an increase in overall prices by 3.1 percent per annum, and an estimated annual real growth in GDP per capita of about 2 percent from the fiscal years 1960/61 to 1963/64.[48]

After Independence, with the British no longer the whipping-boy, many workers gradually began to feel that the political elite was making no effort to erase the inequities of the colonial wage structure; and this together with frequent exposés of corruption among African leaders, diminished the acceptance of the wide income gap, especially among the younger and more articulate urban workers.[49] In addition, the high rate of unemployment and the communal competition for jobs contributed to the unrest.

The general strike in 1964, a response to the deep-seated worker dissatisfaction, posed a challenge to the legitimacy and authority of the civilian government, demonstrated its ineptness and powerlessness, raised questions about the future use of the army and police for the repression of popular demands, and in-

---

47. Aluko, "Wages, Costs and Prices," Reconstruction and Development Conference, 1969, p. 16; and Adedeji, *Nigerian Federal Finance*, p. 188. O. Teriba and O.A. Philips, "Income Distribution and National Integration," *Nigerian Journal of Economic and Social Studies*, XIII, No. 1 (March 1971), 91-4, present evidence indicating that the personal income distribution is less equitable in Nigeria than in the U.S., the U.K., and the "average" less developed country.

48. The real growth rate in GDP was 4.5 percent per annum, while an educated guess for population growth was 2.5 percent per year. Office of Statistics, *Gross Domestic Product of Nigeria, 1958/59-1966/67* (Lagos, 1968), pp. 25, 30; *Second National Development Plan, 1970-74*, p. 77; and Ifagun Eke, *Nigerian Journal*, VIII, No. 3, 308-9.

49. Contrary to the myth, there was a substantial amount of inequality in wealth and income per head among those engaged in agriculture. See Polly Hill, "The Myth of the Amorphous Peasantry: A Northern Nigerian Case Study," *Nigerian Journal*, X, No. 2 (July 1968), 239-60. However, in part because of a lack of education and urbanity, peasants were not as restive about inequality as workers.

creased the likelihood of further attempts by dissident forces to use political violence to effect political change.[50] Much of organized labor supported the progressive opposition to the Northern-dominated coalition in the 1964-65 election boycott and constitutional crisis, and at the end of 1965 workers helped to foment the mass violence directed against a Northern-supported Western regional government with little popular support.

Communal Competition for Employment

As alluded to above, communal identity received its staying power because it was the major framework used by the political elite for the distribution of jobs to clients. The Ibos were at the center of the communal competition for employment and business activity - if we leave aside the clash between the dominant and minority ethnic groups in the regions, discussed previously. Ibos, other southerners (especially Yorubas), and Northerners competed for positions in trade, transportation, civil service, public corporations, and foreign firms in the North. The major contenders for key positions in the Federal civil service, and for other jobs in the modern sectors of Lagos, the capital, and the Western Region, were the Ibos and Yorubas.

In 1963 the East had a population density of 420 persons per square mile compared to 156 in Nigeria as a whole. Although there was little farming land in the East, 70 percent of its labor force was engaged in agriculture during 1963-4. The Ibo-speaking area was especially hindered by a high density (712 persons per square mile in the Onitsha-Owerri Provinces), and poor agricultural land, and had long been a food-deficit area.[51] This over-population, together with certain other socio-historical factors which tended to make the Ibos enterprising and aggressive, induced them to migrate.[52]

As far as the North was concerned, immigration was possible only because of the protection of the colonial regime. The growth in the number of southerners in the North paralleled that in the Kano *Sabon Gari* (non-Northern residential ghetto), which changed from about 2,000 in 1921 (mostly Yorubas) to 21,000 in 1954 and 40,000 in 1964 (mostly Ibos). Southerners were dominant in much of the trade and transport, and in employment in

---

50. Robin Cohen, *Labour and Politics in Nigeria, 1945-71* (New York: Africana Publishing Co., 1974), pp. 166-8.

51. *Population Census of Nigeria, 1963*, III, 54, 57.

52. I have discussed these factors in *JMAS*, VI, No. 4, 532-3, 537 and 540.

the public corporations (e.g. postal services and railways) and foreign firms. The Kano riots in May 1953, in which thirty-six died, were directed against southerners partly because so many Northerners were worried about prospects for employment and business in their own region, with an independent government under the control of non-Northerners. Indeed, even by 1955, there was scarcely a single Northerner in the administrative class of the Northern civil service.[53]

The large numbers of southerners in the Northern economy stemmed primarily from their substantially greater attainment of formal education. In the colonial period, the need for an educated class of civil servants and clerks in the North was obviated by "indirect" rule through indigenous chiefs and admistrators. In addition, the British cooperated with local rulers to restrict Christian missions, and their primary and secondary schools, since these were threats to the Northern socio-political oligarchy. Thus, as late as 1960, the male primary enrollment rate (i.e. males enrolled in primary school as a percentage of males aged 6-14), and the corresponding secondary rate (with males aged 13-18 as the denominator) were 11 and 1 percent respectively in the North, compared to 81 and 11 percent in the south.[54]

The reaction to competition resulting from uneven economic and educational development in the regions was the policy of Northernization instituted in late 1955, which gave priority in many positions to the local ethnic communities. As a result of this policy, Northerners in the superscale, administrative and professional, and executive and higher technical classes of the Northern civil service increased from virtually none in 1955 to 14 percent of about 2,000 in 1958, surpassing 50 percent by the middle of 1961. Regionalization was directed more against southerners, who represented a long run danger to Northern political power in the country, than foreigners. From June 1958 to October 1959, the number of southerners in the Northern public

---

53. John N. Paden, "Communal Competition, Conflict, and Violence in Kano," in *Nigeria: Modernization and the Politics of Communalism*, ed. by Robert Melson and Howard Wolpe (East Lansing: Michigan State University Press, 1971), pp. 121-2; and B.J. Dudley, *Parties and Politics in Northern Nigeria* (London: Frank Cass and Co., Ltd., 1968), p. 219.

54. Peter Kilby, "Technical Education in Nigeria," *Bulletin of the Oxford University Institute of Economics and Statistics*, XXVI, No. 2 (May 1964), 183-4.

service declined from 294 to 1.[55] Regional employment preference helped solidify the bureaucracy as the instrument of the traditional aristocracy and administration, to whom civil servants owed their positions. Furthermore, Northernization, by expanding the employment of educated Northerners, especially benefited the more advanced lower North, and expedited an alliance of convenience (at times shaky) between the upper Northern rulers and the educated classes of the lower areas.

However, in 1965, the modern sector of the Northern private economy was still dominated by southerners, Levantines, and Europeans, who were, in general, sending their earnings out of the North. The alien values especially of southern Nigerians posed a threat to the Hausa-Muslim way of life and social structure. Yet the growing enmity in the urban areas was less a conflict of values than a competition for the benefits of modernization which both groups prized highly, but in which the majority of Northerners were at a disadvantage as a result of their later arrival on the scene, and their lesser education. Already there were the beginnings of a restive group of unemployed in the major Northern centers.

The resentment against southern migrants reached a peak in the weeks following 23 May 1966, when the Ibo-led Ironsi regime announced a unitary civil service. The uneasiness concerning the impact of this on economic opportunities for Northerners in their own region helped to inflame the disorders in May and July. Afterwards, at the September *ad hoc* Constitutional conference, those supporting the Northern traditional rulers were jolted by the North's *volte face* (influenced by lower Northern elements, especially in the army) from a position favoring retention of the regions to one backing the creation of new states. In an environment of distrust and animosity, this provided the immediate spark for popular violence and disorders directed against Ibos and other southerners in the North during September and October 1966. These operations appeared too far-reaching and well ordered to have been entirely spontaneous, and can be interpreted as a desperate last-ditch strike by the insecure upper Northern elite at the most vulnerable group available. In all, several thousand southerners were killed in the North during 1966.

In the year prior to 1 April 1967, interregional migration in Nigeria was estimated at about 1.7 million. Most were persons returning to their regions of communal origin, and could be clas-

55. Dudley, *Parties and Politics*, pp. 220-1.

sified, according to Aluko, as refugees since they moved because of fear, force, or edict. In April 1967, 3 percent of the Nigerian population was characterized as refugees, i.e. persons who had fled from one region to another in the previous year. Aluko's figures indicated that about 98 percent of the migrants were Ibos and others returning to their ethnic homelands in the East.[56]

The major competitors for high-level positions within the Federation were the two ethnic groups most advanced in education, the Yorubas and the Ibos. After 1948 as positions at the center were rapidly opened to Nigerians, the Yorubas, who had previously held almost exclusive control in indigenous jobs in the Federal service, were challenged substantially by the Ibos. Competitive modernization became political rivalry, culminating in the formation of the A.G. as adversary to the N.C.N.C. in 1951. In 1964, as vacancies dwindled, the contest intensified. Enmity grew when in 1965 a board with a Yoruba majority arbitrarily replaced the Ibo Vice-Chancellor with a Yoruba at Lagos University.[57]

Communal competition was intensified by policies instigated in response to the large body of unemployed, discussed above in this chapter. In an atmosphere of apprehension and suspicion, the response to such problems was to intensify policies of regional discrimination in employment. This geographical segmentation of the labor market contributed to numerous cases of specific shortages in one region alongside surpluses elsewhere, as a result of the lack of migration as an equilibrating device.

The Post-war Military Regime

Positions in the post-war military government have been more broadly based in terms of ethnic communities than in the pre-war civilian regime. The pre-war elites of the three major ethnic communities have been, by and large, deposed, and their ability to use their regional base to control the center has declined as the number of administrative units has increased. Most of the underpinnings of the power of the Northern ruling aristocracy, such as the local councils, the courts of the emirs, and Native Authority Police, are now incorporated as part

---

56. Samuel A. Aluko, "Displaced Nigerians," *West Africa* (15 April 1967), pp. 495, 497-8.

57. James O'Connell, "Authority and Community in Nigeria," in *Nigeria*, ed. by Melson and Wolpe, p. 633.

of a national system. Members of pre-war opposition parties and politicians from minority communities replaced leaders from the pre-war ruling alliance.

Since 1966-67, with a military government and the creation of twelve states, power has become more centralized in Nigeria. Economic strength has shifted away from interest-groups in the regions, including merchants and medium-sized industrialists, to those at the center, such as government servants, and high-level personnel in the large public corporations.

In the post-war period, prior to the deposing of General Gowon from the position of Head of State on 29 July 1975, the Supreme Military Council - consisting of Gowon, the Military State Governors, and senior military and police officers - was the highest governing body. But this rarely met in practice, and it was the Federal Executive Council, consisting of appointed civilian heads of administrative departments, and military leaders, which exercised day-to-day authority. In practice, decisions were made informally by a group of Gowon's closest associates and advisors, primarily a few senior civil servants and key permanent secretaries from the ministries. This heavy reliance on advice from the public service stood in contrast to the infrequent consultation under the pre-war government.[58]

From 1965 to 1971 the armed forces expanded from about 10,500 to around 250,000. The ratio of armed personnel to the total population, which at about 1:5,500 was lower than Sierra Leone (1:2,500), Tanzania (1:1,700), Ghana (1:800) and Zaïre (1:480) in 1965, was one of the highest in Africa (1:220) by 1971.[59] The relative size of the force had not decreased by 1974, when the Federal military government rescinded the return to civilian rule scheduled for 1976.

Although the Second Plan, 1970-74, was written by indigenous economists, planners and bureaucrats, there was little consultation with local governing units, and hardly any indication as to how targets were to be achieved and specific projects executed. Nigeria's position with regard to changes in foreign reserve assets improved rapidly, from -£N8.8 million in 1966 to

---

58. Pauline H. Baker, "The Politics of Nigerian Military Rule," *Africa Report*, XVI, No. 2 (February 1971), 20.

59. B.J. Dudley, "The Military and Development," *Nigerian Journal of Economic and Social Studies*, XIII, No. 2 (July 1971), 163-74.

+£N7.6 million in 1969, to +£N29.3 million in 1970, and to +£N59.7 million in 1971. This was largely the result of an increase in the net positive contribution of the oil sector to the balance on current and capital account, from £N43.4 million in 1966 to £N53.3 million in 1969, to £N131.9 million in 1970, and to £N290.4 million in 1971.[60]

Labor discontent has not diminished in the post-war period. In December 1969 the military government issued a decree which froze wages and banned strikes for one year. Despite the institution of price controls on several commodities in July 1970, the average consumer price-index for low-income groups increased by 9 percent in 1970, due largely to the lack of controls on food, clothing and accommodation. In response to labor unrest, the government appointed the Wages and Salaries Review Commission to consider the workers' grievances. Although the Commission awarded wage increases in December 1970 and in October 1971 to all public servants, and recommended increases to private employees, the measures led to a further widening of the absolute gap between high-level and unskilled labor.

In the post-war era the government instituted policies to reduce the relative size of the foreign sector. Among the reasons for its action were: the lukewarm support of a number of countries for the Federal government during the war; the decline of the civilian politicians and indigenous high-level personnel who gained from the presence of foreign capitalists; and the enhanced power of the civil servants, intelligentsia, and local industrialists, especially from the south, who favor a de-emphasis on foreign investment. In 1974, a Nigerian public oil company acquired 55 percent of the equity shares in foreign oil producing companies. A decree in mid-1971 increased the number of industries reserved for Nigerians, raised the requirements for indigenous equity participation in a number of enterprises, and tightened quotas for foreign business personnel.

Conclusion

Although the average level of material well-being in Nigeria is low, its post-Independence growth in GDP per capita, even prior to the 1974-75 oil boom, appears to have been rapid. This

---

60. Nafziger, *JMAS*, X, No. 2, 231; and Nigeria, Ministry of Economic Development, *Economic and Statistical Review, 1971* (Lagos, 1972), p. 11, and *Second National Development Plan, 1970-74: First Progress Report* (Lagos, 1972), pp. 53-6.

economic growth was accompanied by a steady relative increase in the manufacturing and mining sector at the expense of the declining relative position of agriculture. Consumer prices, prior to 1975, were relatively stable, especially when compared to other less developed economies. As a result of the rapid growth in crude-petroleum output, Nigeria's foreign exchange crisis of the last half of the 1960s was replaced by a rapidly accelerating international reserve position in the early 1970s.

In the terminal colonial period, the British government became more oriented toward meeting what they considered the reasonable demands of the Nigerian nationalist movement, which was spearheaded in large part by an economic elite. Through this policy towards the movement, the British helped shape a post-Independence elite favorable to its interests. In return for their cooperation, aspiring Nigerians obtained access to power, privileges, and patronage available as a result of the replacement of British with Nigerians in political and civil service positions in the terminal colonial period. This political elite controlled the access to large business ventures and public service jobs, and were instrumental in determining the policies which affected their business interests and those of their domestic and foreign allies. The colonial nexus in international trade, finance, and investment remained fairly strong in the Independence period (after 1960). Some of the reasons for the retention of this nexus were the legacy from colonial economic policies which discouraged indigenous industrial development, the import restrictions on industrial goods by developed capitalist economies, and the inducement (including military and economic support) to the Nigerian elite to cooperate with the metropolitan economy.

Appendix: The Measurement of Concentration in Nigerian and U.S. Manufacturing

This appendix explains how the inter-industry concentration rates in manufacturing in Nigeria in 1965, and in the U.S. in 1947 were obtained. These rates are based upon data obtained by making assumptions essential to find a correspondence between individual firms and quantitative data on value-added and employment in the *Industrial Survey of Nigeria, 1964 and 1965* and the U.S. Department of Commerce, Bureau of the Census, *Census of Manufacturers: 1947*. There are several reason for choosing the *Industrial Survey* for 1965 for Nigeria. First, my study of entrepreneurs in Nigerian manufacturing especially focuses on the years, 1964-65. Secondly, data from the *Industrial Survey* after 1965 are distorted by the disruption of the economy surrounding the two coups d'etat of 1966, and the severance of the Eastern Region during the civil war of 1967-70. Thirdly, several types of information collected in 1964, particularly on paid-up capital, were not valid because of ambiguities in the questionnaire, which were clarified in 1965.[61] The 1947 *Census of Manufacturers* was chosen, since I was unaware of any other U.S. census volume that had data by industry that was comparable to the Nigerian data in 1965.

Of the thirty-three Nigerian industries of 1965 (listed above in table 2.8), each producing goods that are more or less satisfactory substitutes for each other, thirty-one U.S. industries (listed in table 2.9) could be delineated in a similar fashion. Since establishments with less than ten employed are not included in the figures on Nigerian industry, establishments with 1-9 employed were deleted from computations of concentration in the U.S. Otherwise the categories of average employment size are fairly comparable. In Nigeria these categories are 10-19, 20-49, 50-99, 100-299, 300-499, 500-999, and 1,000 and over. The only variations from this in the case of the U.S. are a division of categories between 249 and 250 (rather than between 299 and 300), and an extra category of 2,500 employees and over. This addition has little impact on relative concentration rates, since only ten of 613 establishments in Nigeria in table 2.9 had an employment of 1,000 or more.[62] Finally, the definition of employment in Nigeria and the U.S. is the same.

To measure the degree of industrial concentration in Nigeria

---

61. *Industrial Survey of Nigeria, 1964 and 1965*, p. 21.
62. Ibid. p. 38.

and U.S. manufacturing, the concept of a concentration rate was used, which indicates the proportion of value-added and employment contributed by the largest four establishments of an industry. The delineation of an industry in the Nigerian *Industrial Survey* conforms to one or two three-digit numbers, classified according to the International Standard Industrial Classification (ISIC) code.

Philip C. Packard, in his study of concentration in manufacturing in 1963 and 1965, indicated that it is not possible to identify intra-industry concentration in Nigeria.[63] However, the key to utilizing the data in the Nigerian *Industrial Survey* and the U.S. *Census of Manufacturers* for purposes of measuring intra-industry concentration in value-added (i.e. total value-added of the largest four establishments in each industry in terms of employment size as a percentage of the total value-added) is to make the following two simplifying assumptions. (1) All establishments within a given employment size category (i.e. 10-19, 20-49, 50-99, 100-299, 300-499, 500-999, 1,000 and over) have the same value-added - namely the total value-added for that employment size category divided by the number of establishments. (This assumption tends to understate slightly the concentration in value-added, since there is some variation in the value-added of establishments in the same employment size category, but there is no reason to believe that this understatement introduces any systematic bias into the comparative figures for the U.S. and Nigeria.) (2) Each establishment in a higher employment size category also has a greater value-added than any of the establishments in a lower employment size category.

For 1965, the *Industrial Survey* indicates the distribution of establishments within each industry group by employment size, and furthermore the distribution of value-added within each industry by the employment size of establishments. In the computation of total value-added of the largest four firms in the vegetable oil milling industry (ISIC No. 312) in 1965, e.g., assumption (1) allows the addition of £N1.296 million (for the one establishment with an employment of 1,000 and over) to £N0.737 million (the aggregate for the two establishments with an employment of 500-999) to £N0.372 million (for one of the four establishments tied for fourth place with an employment of 300-499, whose value-added is calculated by dividing the aggregate value-

---

63. "A Note on Concentration and Profit Rates within the Manufacturing Sector 1963 and 1965," *Nigerian Journal of Economic and Social Studies*, XI, No. 3 (November 1969), 386.

added for the four establishments, £N1.487 by 4 in order to get value-added equal to £N2.405 million, which is 0.490 (the concentration rate) of total value-added in the industry, £N4.912.[64] Assumption (2) enables a person to eliminate from consideration the 55 firms with less than 300 employed when computing the value-added of the largest four establishments.

The way to measure intra-industry concentration in employment (i.e. total number employed from the largest four firms in each industry in terms of employment size as a percentage of the total number employed) is to use Joe S. Bain's technique[65] for averaging the statistically possible maximum and statistically possible minimum values for employment. For example, in the vegetable oil milling industry, I added 1,889 (the employment for one establishment with an employment of 1,000 and over) to 1,059 (the aggregate employment for the two establishments with an employment of 500-999) to 499 (the statistical maximum for the largest establishments, in terms of employment, of the four establishments in the employment size category of 300-499 whose total employment is 1,556) in order to obtain 3,447, the statistical maximum. The statistical minimum for the fourth largest establishment in employment, 389 (calculated by assuming that all four establishments in the employment size category, 300-499, are assumed to have the same employment) is added to 1,889 plus 1,059 to obtain 3,337, the statistical minimum for the aggregate employment of the four largest establishments.

The average of the statistically possible minimum and statistically possible maximum for the aggregate employment of the four largest establishments is 3,392. When this figure is divided by 7,057, the total employment in the industry, the concentration rate for employment is 0.481 (table 2.9).[66]

---

64. *Industrial Survey*, pp. 38, 41.

65. *International Differences in Industrial Structure: Eight Nations in the 1950's* (New Haven: Yale University Press, 1966), pp. 27-8.

66. The figures for the calculation are in *Industrial Survey*, pp. 38, 41.

Chapter 3

The Supply of and Demand for Nigerian Entrepreneurs and Managers[1]

This chapter, like the previous one, is intended to provide a broad context in which to study Nigerian entrepreneurship, but the emphasis here is upon formal economic analysis. The entrepreneur, from the perspective of the economic analyst, is a factor of production - a factor that combines the resources used in the production of a good or service. Although economists have analyzed the factor markets for labor and capital, they have, because of conceptual problems, been reluctant to discuss the market for entrepreneurs. This chapter analyzes the market for entrepreneurs of indigenous firms[2] in Nigeria. Starting with the data available on the quantity and remuneration of entrepreneurs, and with additional information and a few assumptions, it offers some generalizations about the nature of the supply of and demand for entrepreneurs of Nigerian firms.

Even though it is not possible to measure annual returns to entrepreneurship empirically, it is possible to obtain information on 1965 annual returns for persons in entrepreneurial positions in industry. Hired managers with entrepreneurial re-

---

1. The material in this chapter borrows from E. Wayne Nafziger, "Nigerian Entrepreneurship: A Study of Indigenous Businessmen in the Footwear Industry," (unpublished Ph.D. dissertation, University of Illinois, 1967), pp. 148-61, and "The Market for Nigerian Entrepreneurs," in *South of the Sahara: Development in African Economies*, ed. by Sayre P. Schatz (Philadelphia: Temple University Press, 1972), pp. 61-87.

2. Indigenous firms are those in which at least one-half of the capital is Nigerian, i.e. owned by Nigerian citizens of African origin and/or government statutory corporations. Other firms are designated as "foreign" firms.

sponsibility and self-employed entrepreneurs operate on the same factor market, since both can move from one type of position to another. In equilibrium, where profits above competitive returns to factors were eliminated, the annual returns for persons in self-employed entrepreneurial positions would approximate annual salaries for persons hired to exercise comparable entrepreneurial and managerial responsibilities in other firms, since both concepts of remuneration exclude risk premiums and returns to capital. Thus the 1965 modal salary for a person exercising the top entrepreneurial responsibility in an indigenous manufacturing firm represents approximately the modal entrepreneurial remuneration for a self-employed person with the same responsibility.

Entrepreneurial Remuneration

In 1965 the modal salary for the foreign major entrepreneur in an indigenous manufacturing firm with a net worth of £N75,000-125,000 and 100-200 employed was about £N2,500 yearly. International travel and fringe benefits cost the firm an additional £N1,500 per annum. The modal salary for an indigenous top entrepreneur of a firm of the same size was about £N800 per year plus training costs and fringe benefits, which frequently were substantial.

The 1965 annual wages for top entrepreneurs in firms with about £N3,000 net worth and twenty employed ranged from about £N180 in the East to about £N300 in the North. On the other hand, most of the entrepreneurs of firms with less than five workers earned very little above a subsistence wage. The following 1965 Nigerian wage rates are given for purposes of comparison: typist: £N240, automobile driver: £N200, school nurse: £N200, unskilled industrial worker: £N84, and journeyman: £N48.[3]

The Quantity of Entrepreneurs

Table 3.1, p. 89, based primarily on official data, gives some indication of the scarcity of indigenous industrial entrepreneurs in firms with an employment of twenty-five or more. Virtually all the entrepreneurs of these firms are listed as managerial or professional personnel. In 1965, there were about

---

3. Wage rates for the first three categories of labor are found in Nigeria, Ministry of Information, *Estimates of the Government of the Federal Republic of Nigeria, 1965-66 (Approved)* (Lagos, 1965), pp. 67, 122, 143.

6,800 indigenous and 2,300 foreign managerial and professional personnel in the approximately 2,400 indigenous firms with ten or more workers. Probably no more than 4,000 indigenes and 1,500 foreigners held decision-making responsibility concerning the employment and organization of factors of production in these firms. In the same year, there were about 1,900 indigenous and about 1,800 foreign managerial and professional personnel in the manufacturing firms with fifty or more workers, and of these it is unlikely that more than 1,300 indigenous and 1,100 foreign personnel held entrepreneurial or managerial responsibility.

The Demand for Entrepreneurs

How can the scarcity and remuneration of industrial entrepreneurs be explained in terms of demand and supply? The demand schedule for entrepreneurship is a function of its marginal net revenue productivity (i.e. the increment in revenue product corresponding to an additional unit of the entrepreneurial input, other things remaining equal). The marginal product of entrepreneurship is dependent upon the level of technique and the quantity of other factors of production, such as capital (including social overhead capital), labor of various levels of skill, and natural resources.

Schatz contends that lack of entrepreneurship stems primarily from impediments in the economic environment, such as a lack of available technique and complementary resources (i.e. lack of demand) rather than a lack of entrepreneurial capacity (i.e. lack of supply). He argues that even with entrepreneurial ability comparable to the advanced economies, profit opportunities would have been lacking due to an unfavorable economic environment.[4]

The author concurs with Schatz's contention that numerous impediments in the economic environment restrain the demand for entrepreneurship. Demand is dampened by the scarcity of capital.[5] (Among African countries, Nigeria, with a rate of 13 per-

---

4. Sayre P. Schatz, "Economic Environment and Private Enterprise in West Africa," *Economic Bulletin*, VII, No. 4 (December 1963), 42-56.

5. See S.A. Aluko, "The Educated in Business: The Calabar Home Farm - A Case Study," *Nigerian Journal of Economic and Social Studies*, VIII, No. 2 (July 1966), 200.

Schatz does not support this statement. *Development Bank*

Table 3.1

Estimates of Professional and Managerial Employees in Manufacturing Firms with Ten or More Employed, 1965[a]

Size of Firm (by employment)	Number of Indigenous Firms	Number of Foreign Firms	Total Number of Firms
10-24	1,888	42	1,930
25-49	318	94	412
50-99	112	75	187
100-199	52	47	99
200-499	27	38	65
500-999	8	16	24
1000-1999	3	4	7
2000 & over	2	3	5
TOTAL	2,410	319	2,729

a. Table 3.1 was computed primarily on the basis of Nigeria, Office of Statistics, *Industrial Survey of Nigeria, 1964 and 1965* (Lagos, 1968), pp. 32, 37-8. The distribution of managerial and professional personnel by firm size and the extent of coverage by the Federal industrial surveys were estimated on the basis of the preceding source and Nigeria, Ministry of Commerce and Industry, *Industrial Directory, 1964* (Lagos, n.d.) and an unpublished supplement in 1965; Eastern Nigeria, Ministry of Economic Planning, *Eastern Nigeria Industrial Directory* (Enugu, 1963); Midwestern Nigeria, *Midwestern Nigeria Industrial Survey, 1964*

Table 3.1— Continued

Number of Indigenous Professional and Managerial Personnel in Indigenous Firms	Number of Indigenous Professional and Managerial Personnel in Foreign Firms	Number of Foreign Professional and Managerial Personnel in All Manufacturing Firms	Number of Professional and Managerial Personnel in All Manufacturing Firms
3,766	82	174	4,022
957	216	286	1,459
468	227	511	1,206
223	155	362	740
170	190	423	783
71	106	252	429
36	41	141	218
27	34	124	185
5,718	1,051	2,273	9,042

(Footnote a continued)

(Benin, n.d.); Northern Nigeria, Ministry of Economic Planning, *Northern Nigeria Industrial Directory* (Kaduna, 1965); Personal Interview, Assistant Trade Officer, Western Nigeria, 6 May. 1965; Nigeria, Ministry of Commerce and Industry, Registration of Business Names, Lagos, August 1965; Nigeria, Ministry of Labour, Lagos, August 1965; Peter Kilby, *Development of Small Industry in Eastern Nigeria* (Enugu: Eastern Ministry of Information, 1963); and information in chapter 5 and the appendix.

cent, ranked eighth among ten in gross fixed investment as a percentage of gross national product in 1962/63.[6] The inadequacy of social overhead capital, such as schools, transport facilities, and public utilities is another factor reducing demand. Slow and irregular deliveries and unsatisfactory servicing of much of the equipment, materials and supplies, often purchased abroad, must also be considered.[7] In addition, demand is discouraged by wage rates above equilibrium in the large industrial sector, resulting from political pressure to pay the government minimum wage,[8] and, to a lesser extent, from trade union pressure.[9] The scarcity of high and intermediate-level manpower (consultants, technicians, supervisors and foremen, etc.) is another impediment to demand.[10] In Nigeria also, access to technical knowledge is limited, partly because of the lack of programs and personnel to assist in the transfer of technology from abroad.[11] The small size of the Nigerian market resulting from low per capita income is another obstacle. Finally, the percep-

---

(Footnote 5 continued from page 83.)

Lending in Nigeria: The Federal Loans Board (Ibadan: Oxford University Press, 1965), and "The Capital Shortage Illusion: Government Lending in Nigeria," *Oxford Economic Papers*, XVII, No. 2 (July 1965), 309-16. See, however, the author's discussion of the difference between the concepts of capital "shortage" and "scarcity." "A Reconsideration of 'Capital Surplus' in Nigeria," *Nigerian Journal of Economic and Social Studies*, X, No. 1 (March 1968), 111-6.

6. United Nations, Statistical Office, Department of Economic and Social Affairs, *Statistical Yearbook, 1964* (New York, 1965), pp. 529-35. See also W. Arthur Lewis, *Reflections on Nigeria's Economic Growth* (Paris: Development Centre of the Organisation for Economic Cooperation and Development, 1967), p. 27.

7. Schatz, *Economic Bulletin*, VII, No. 4, 43-8.

8. See Gerald K. Helleiner, *Peasant Agriculture, Government and Economic Growth in Nigeria* (Homewood, Ill.: Richard D. Irwin, Inc., 1966), pp. 323-5; and John P. Henderson, "Wage Policy in Africa," (paper presented to the Conference on African Economic Development, Temple University, Philadelphia, 18-19 April, 1968).

9. W.M. Warren, "Urban Real Wages and the Nigerian Trade Union Movement, 1939-1960," *Economic Development and Cultural Change*, XV, No. 1 (October 1966), 35-6.

10. Schatz, *Economic Bulletin*, VII, No. 4, 45-7; Helleiner, *Peasant Agriculture, Government and Economic Growth*, pp. 330-1; and Nigeria, Ministry of Economic Development, *National Development Plan, 1962-68* (Lagos, n.d.), p. 15.

11. See Aluko, *Nigerian Journal*, VIII, No. 2, 200-1.

tion by prospective industrialists, whether valid or not, that government officials were frequently indifferent, obstructionist, inefficient, discriminatory and corrupt in their dealings with business decreases the demand for entrepreneurs.[12]

On the other hand, Helleiner argues that the fact that foreign owned and managed firms (which encounter the same economic environment as indigenous enterprises) have been generally much more successful than have Nigerian enterprises suggests that the explanation may lie in lack of entrepreneurial capacity and experience.[13] Thus, Helleiner's view is that the scarcity of entrepreneurship is largely a result of lack of supply rather than of a deficiency in demand.

Since both indigenous and foreign entrepreneurs are placed in the same economic context, one might expect the marginal productivity of (and demand for) both types of entrepreneurial inputs to be the same, where the inputs are assumed to be of identical quality. However, as a result of the heteorogeneity of input quality arising from the fact that education, training, experience and socio-cultural milieu are more conducive to the development of entrepreneurship in western countries, the schedule of expected returns to (or demand for) foreign entrepreneurs is greater than for Nigerian entrepreneurs. In addition, the fact that the foreign entrepreneur may have had access to more capital, advanced techniques, and highly-skilled manpower frequently results in a higher marginal productivity of entrepreneurial units. While exchange restrictions, immigrant quotas and pressures for Nigerianization restrain the demand for foreign entrepreneurs, one would expect, on balance, the demand for foreign entrepreneurs to exceed that for indigenous entrepreneurs.

In light of the relatively low remuneration and quantity of large indigenous entrepreneurs, it is most consistent to conclude that the lack of supply discussed below is combined with a weak demand for Nigerian entrepreneurs.[14] (See figure 2, p.88.)

---

12. Schatz, *Economic Bulletin*, VII, No. 4, 48-9; and Schatz and S.I. Edokpayi, "Economic Attitudes of Nigerian Businessmen," *Nigerian Journal of Economic and Social Studies*, IV, No. 3 (November 1962), 257-68.

13. Helleiner, *Peasant Agriculture, Government and Economic Growth*, p. 265; and John R. Harris, "Industrial Entrepreneurship in Nigeria" (Ph.D. dissertation, Northwestern University, 1967), pp. 17-39.

14. Cf. Harris, "Industrial Entrepreneurship," pp. 23-39.

This weak demand, together with an abundant supply of small-scale entrepreneurs, can explain the relatively low remuneration and relatively high quantity of small-scale entrepreneurs. On the other hand, the relatively high remuneration of foreign

Figure 2

The Market for Indigenous Industrial Entrepreneurs in Large Firms

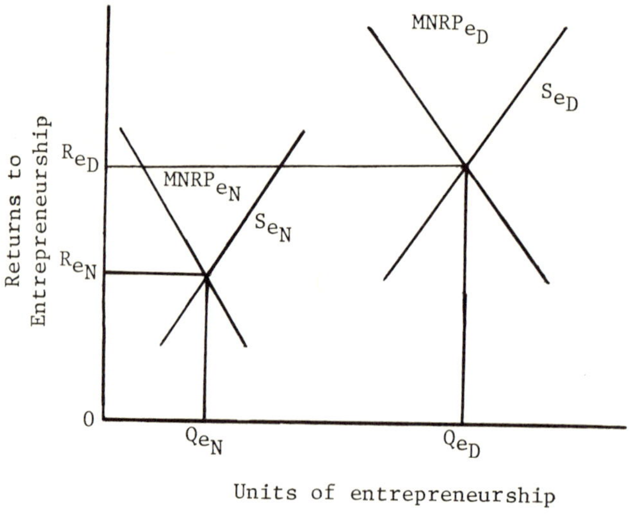

<u>Legend to figure 2:</u>

$MNRP_e$ -- Marginal net revenue productivity of (or demand for) entrepreneurship
S_e -- Supply of entrepreneurship
Q_e -- Equilibrium quantity of entrepreneurship
R_e -- Equilibrium returns to entrepreneurship
N -- Variable pertaining to Nigeria
D -- Variable pertaining to a developed economy (with the same population)

entrepreneurs indicates that the limited supply is combined with a demand that is somewhat greater than that for indigenous entrepreneurs.

The Supply of Foreign Entrepreneurs in Indigenous Firms

Despite the fact that salaries in Nigeria were competitive with their European counterparts, it has still been difficult to induce foreign personnel into indigenous firms. A man from abroad wants decidedly increased income if he is to give up his home environment and its securities, assume added costs of travel and dislocation, and subject himself and his family to a less satisfactory environment in terms of health facilities and education, not to mention possible political insecurities.

Frequently, positions with Nigerian firms have proved temporary, since after one to three years, the firm may have expected to have trained indigenes to assume management. The former manager may then find difficulty in locating a satisfactory position on his return and will probably have lost opportunities for promotion, retirement benefits and professional contacts.

Where skilled managers have helped the firm achieve a large market share within the industry, it is easier to attract potentially good management material.[15] But the less established firm may be trapped in a "vicious circle," unable to attract competent foreign managers because of a poor competitive position.

It is also difficult for an indigenous entrepreneur to attract a foreign partner with capital and expertness. Expected returns must be lucrative indeed to induce foreigners to invest in an underdeveloped country like Nigeria, without majority control. A study by Schatz and Edokpayi indicates that Nigerians believe lack of knowledge and experience on their part to be one of the foreigner's major objection to forming a partnership with a Nigerian.[16]

---

15. A. Soyade and A. Oyejide, "Market Share and Profitability in Commercial Banking: The Case of Nigeria," discussion paper 75-02, Department of Economics, University of Ibadan, 1975.

16. *Nigerian Journal*, IV, No. 3, 266.

Cases where foreign capitalists have over 50 percent of equity are not discussed, since by definition the firm is not indigenous.

The Supply of Indigenous Entrepreneurs of Large Firms

The lack of Nigerian industrial entrepreneurship is a result partly of a lack of supply. Even though foreign managers were far more expensive than Nigerians of comparable skills[17], a large percentage of the managerial personnel in the firms are foreigners. In outline some of the major factors impeding supply are: high remuneration in competing occupations; low level of educational attainment; lack of appropriate training and deficiency of experience in high-level positions; lack of governmental encouragement; and socio-political barriers to migration.

The high salaries in occupations requiring a comparable level of skill, such as employment in foreign firms and government, are a major factor impeding the supply of indigenous entrepreneurs. Political pressures have increased the demand for (and salary of) indigenous managers in foreign firms. Similarly, government officials and high-ranking civil servants receive attractive salaries, additional allowances, fringe benefits and working conditions (see table 3.2, p. 91).[18] The civil servant also enjoys much more job security than the entrepreneur. In light of the relatively low average earnings and the high degree of risk in entrepreneurial activity, it is not surprising that high-level manpower is more likely to be attracted by the civil service and foreign firms.[19]

---

17. Wolfgang Stolper, *Planning Without Facts: Lessons in Resource Allocation from Nigeria's Development* (Cambridge, Mass.: Harvard University Press, 1966), p. 301; Schatz, *Economic Bulletin*, VII, No. 4, 46-7; and F.A. Wells and W.A. Warmington, *Studies in Industrialization: Nigeria and the Cameroons* (London: Oxford University Press, 1962), p. 88.

18. See "The Civil Service," *Nigerian Opinion*, I, No. 8 (August 1965), 3-4; and Richard Burghart, "Ministerial Emoluments in Nigeria," *Nigerian Opinion*, I, No. 8 (August 1965), 10-12.

19. A probable major reason for the high salaries of top-ranking government bureaucrats is the institutional rigidity that maintained intact the high salaries required to induce qualified Britons to take civil service positions in the colonial period, and the concentration of oligopolistic power in the hands of government officials and civil servants. Hugh H. Smythe and Mable M. Smythe, *The New Nigerian Elite* (Stanford: Stanford University Press, 1960), pp. 132-3, see high government salaries as a psychological necessity for the Nigerian government elite in order to retain the status attached to civil ser-

Table 3.2

Annual Salary for Selected Government Officials and Civil Servants in the Federal and Regional Governments, 1965 (£N)

	Federal	North	West	Mid-West	East
Minister with Cabinet Rank	2700	2700	2700	2700	2700
Minister with Portfolio	2250	2250	1620	1620	2160
Permanent Secretary	2940	2820	2940	2940	2940
Deputy Permanent Secretary	--	2495	--	--	--
Principal Assistant Secretary	--	--	--	--	2500
Senior Assistant Secretary	2300	--	2300	2300	2290
Parliamentary Secretary	1800	1800	1350	1350	1350

Sources: Nigeria, Ministry of Information, *Estimates of the Government of the Federal Republic of Nigeria, 1965-66 (Approved)* (Lagos, 1965); Northern Nigeria, *Estimates of the Government of Northern Nigeria, 1965-66 (Approved)* (Kaduna: Government Printer, 1965); Western Nigeria, *Western Nigeria Estimates, 1965-66 (Approved)* (Ibadan, 1965); Mid-Western Nigeria, Ministry of Internal Affairs, *Mid-Western Nigeria Estimates, 1965-66 (Approved)* (Benin City, 1965); and Eastern Nigeria, *Approved Estimates of Eastern Nigeria, 1965-66* (Enugu, 1965).

(Footnote 19 continued from page 90.)

vice positions under the British.

The remuneration of foreign civil servants has been the same as that of Nigerian civil servants of identical rank. Although the supply of foreigners available from the colonial period is large, the demand for foreigners has not been keen, because of their assumed lesser orientation toward Nigerian goals, and the greater pressure in the public sector for control of policy levers in the hands of Nigerians. As a result, Nigerians have an advantage over foreigners in the civil service relative to entrepreneurial positions.

The government sector in Nigeria is large enough[20] to have a significant impact upon the supply of manpower in the rest of the economy. Relatively lower government salaries would result in an increase in the supply of Nigerian top entrepreneurs. Though the effect in the short run might be small, the effect in the long run would be to induce more Nigerians to acquire entrepreneurial skills.

Another restrictive factor is the low level of educational attainment in Nigeria. The average educational level of sample entrepreneurs of large firms is some attendance at secondary school (see chapter 7).[21] Statistics on age structure and education[22] and figures on enrollment rates[23] indicate that around 1965 no more than 25 percent of the population (seven years of age or older) had four or more years of schooling and no more than 3 percent of the population had a minimum of a secondary-school certificate.

Entrepreneurs in large, complex firms need the ability to communicate in writing within and outside the firm, the possibilities of obtaining access to new ideas and developments through reading and other forms of communication, and the ability to make computations for management control and firm analysis - skills which are dependent upon educational attainment. However, Nigerian manpower with some secondary education is in short supply. Added to the low average educational attainment is the low quality of primary and secondary education and its lack of relevance to the Nigerian socio-historical tradition, socio-cultural setting, and economic and occupational structure.[24]

---

20. Nigeria, Office of Statistics, *Digest of Statistics*, XVI, No. 1 (January 1967), 8, and *Annual Abstract of Statistics, 1964* (Lagos, April 1965), p. 28.

21. Peter Kilby, *African Enterprise: The Nigerian Bread Industry* (Stanford: The Hoover Institution on War, Revolution, and Peace, 1965), p. 94; and John R. Harris, "Industrial Entrepreneurship in Nigeria," pp. 269-70, also find that entrepreneurs in large firms are much better-educated than the population as a whole.

22. Nigeria, *Annual Abstract, 1964*, pp. 13-14.

23. Kilby, "Technical Education in Nigeria," *Bulletin of the Oxford University Institute of Economics and Statistics*, XXVI (May 1964), 182; and Nigeria, Office of Statistics, *Annual Abstract of Statistics, 1963* (Lagos, August 1963), p. 25.

24. Kilby, *Oxford Bulletin*, XXVI, 183, and Helleiner, *Peasant Agriculture, Government and Economic Growth*, pp. 305-10.

The lack of training adapted to the development of entrepreneurial skills needed in large industry also reduces supply. Until recently "the need for high-level managerial institutional training was completely neglected in the higher institutions."[25] The technical and vocational schools, which might be an alternative source of supply of trained entrepreneurs, accounted for only 3 percent of the 1959-63 enrollment in post-primary schools below the university level.[26] Moreover, the technical and trade schools and centers also suffer from low-quality instruction, irrelevant training programs and an orientation toward production specialists rather than management generalists.

Other educational factors impeding the supply of indigenous entrepreneurs for large firms are the shortage of secondary graduates with mathematics and science training, the unduly lengthy training period required in most technical and trade institutes, and the low prestige associated with technical training compared with the high prestige of university training.[27]

Public agencies, because of their brisk demand for technicians, hire over 90 percent of the technical institute graduates.[28] The prevailing remuneration of top entrepreneurs of manufacturing firms employing 60 to 70 persons has been competitive with the starting salaries received by these graduates as mechanics or technicians. But it is unlikely that new graduates could provide the entrepreneurial leadership for firms of this complexity. In designing the length and types of courses, public training institutes need to be more responsive to price signals reflecting skill requirements in the private industrial sector.

The inexperience of Nigerians in business, especially in manufacturing, has also inhibited the supply of entrepreneurs. The low priority given to industrialization before Independence

---

25. Aluko, *Nigerian Journal*, VIII, No. 2 (July 1966), 198.
26. Ibid. and Nigeria, Ministry of Education, *Statistics of Education in Nigeria, 1963*, III, No. 1 (Lagos, 1965), 11-3.
27. Kilby, *Industrialization in an Open Economy: Nigeria 1945-1966* (London: Cambridge University Press, 1969), pp. 234-266, and *Oxford Bulletin*, XXVI, 190-2; and Nigeria, Ministry of Education, *Investment in Education: The Report of the Commission on Post-School Certificate and Higher Education in Nigeria* (Lagos, 1960), p. 5.
28. Kilby, *Oxford Bulletin*, XXVI, 182-91.

in 1960, the relatively small size of the industrial sector in the 1960s and the dominance of foreign firms in large manufacturing must in part account for this.[29]

Governmental obstructionism, ineffectiveness and antipathy toward business not only lessens the demand for entrepreneurship but also impedes its supply. Problems with government such as delays in obtaining pioneer industry status, tax rebates, immigrant quotas, and acquiring land; complaints of discrimination, favoritism and the requirement of bribery; levying and enforcement of taxes in a seemingly inconsistent manner; and the lack of extension services and basic economic and business data contributed to the lack of entrepreneurial supply.[30]

Another contributory factor, discussed further in chapter 9, is the socio-political barriers to migration. Most entrepreneurs have not felt sufficiently confident of long run stability and safety to establish a manufacturing firm with a substantial amount of fixed capital in another ethnic group area.

Unlike many less developed economies, socio-cultural impediments to entrepreneurial participation are few, especially in the south. The favorable attitudes toward business endeavors and pecuniary achievements facilitate entrepreneurship. As Harris and Rowe state:

> Theories of entrepreneurship as a manifestation of social deviance, or theories of underdevelopment related to a lack of entrepreneurial spirit are inapplicable to Nigeria. Nigerians appear to be actively seeking material rewards and entrepreneurship as such is socially honored. . . . Nigerians are alert to profit opportunities and can find the necessary capital for industrial projects which

---

29. It is almost certain that the total value-added by the estimated 183 large foreign manufacturing firms was more than that of the estimated 204 large indigenous firms in 1965 (see Table 3.1). Foreign firms, because of greater access to advanced techniques and capital equipment, had a higher average productivity of labor. See A.M. Hakam, "The Motivation to Invest and the Locational Pattern of Foreign Private Industrial Investments in Nigeria," *Nigerian Journal of Economic and Social Studies*, VIII, No. 1 (March 1966), 49.

30. See chapter 7, and Schatz, *Nigerian Journal*, IV, No. 3, 257-68, and *Economic Bulletin*, VII, No. 4, 48-9.

seem to be within their capability to exploit.[31]

The Relationship between the Foreign and Nigerian Markets

In 1965, the typical salary of a European in a top managerial position with an indigenous Nigerian firm, having a net worth of £N75,000-125,000 and 100-200 employed, would be £N2,500 per annum. This salary, plus cheap housing, family allowances, low taxes, and reimbursement for direct moving costs and home leaves, would, at best, have attracted a works (or production) manager or sales manager from the same size of firm in England who had been earning £2,200-2,500 yearly;[32] but, in many cases, the firm may have had to accept an assistant works manager or an export sales manager, who might be earning £1,800-2,100 per year in the same size of firm in England.[33] As indicated, the modal salary for an indigenous top entrepreneur of a firm of the same size was about £N800 yearly.

The differences in modal salaries between Nigerians and Europeans of the same skill arise, not only because of the greater availability of technical skills and complementary factors in the latter, but because the Nigerian and European markets for entrepreneurs were separate. This lack of international standardization results in very localized and imperfect markets.[34]

Europeans can operate both on the Nigerian and European markets, since many of the production and organizational techniques in Nigeria are borrowed from Europe. Thus the lower limit for the salary of Europeans in Nigeria is set by the remuneration paid on the European market plus a transfer inducement. Nigerians, however, are available only on the Nigerian market, since they are not familiar with European business mores and values, labor practices and conventions, marketing practices,

---

31. John R. Harris and Mary P. Rowe, "Entrepreneurial Patterns in the Nigerian Sawmilling Industry," *Nigerian Journal of Economic and Social Studies*, VIII, No. 1 (March 1966), 94. See also Peter Kilby, "African Labour Productivity Reconsidered," *Economic Journal*, LXXI (June 1961), 283.

32. In 1965, the Nigerian pound was on par with the British pound.

33. Cf. A.J. Merett and D.A.G. Monk, *Inflation, Taxation and Executive Remuneration* (London: Hallam Press Limited, 1967), pp. 44-7.

34. Ibid. p. 82.

economic institutions, and cultural traits. Major differentials in remuneration between Nigerians and Europeans of the same quality on the Nigerian market continue to persist because of the Nigerian manager's lack of options on the European market and his lower supply price.

As the number of Nigerians with training and experience increases, Nigerians will hold an increasing proportion of entrepreneurial positions in indigenous firms. Whenever Nigerian and European entrepreneurs of the same quality are available to the firm, the Nigerian will be hired since he can be obtained more cheaply.

Knowledge about the Market for Entrepreneurs

A number of initial entrepreneurs of large industrial firms have very little knowledge about the market for entrepreneurs and managers. As indicated by several sample firms with poor records, some minimal technical and entrepreneurial competence is necessary to assess needed skills and evaluate candidates for management responsibility (see chapter 6). This is especially significant when only foreign entrepreneurs, with little local knowledge, are available.

The Supply of Indigenous Entrepreneurs of Petty Firms

Official sources indicate that the number of petty manufacturing firms (those with less than ten employed) number in the hundreds of thousands.[35] Barriers to entry are minimal, as a small firm can be started with meager skill and perhaps as little as £N25. Frequently the extended family provides the funds needed for apprentice training and the establishment of the enterprise, if the entrepreneur lacks sufficient capital. Although entrepreneurs encountered more problems in raising capital for the expansion of the firm, most successful firms had access to retained earnings.[36]

The high rate of unemployment and underemployment serves as

---

35. Nigeria, Office of Statistics, *Survey of Rural Household Enterprises* (Lagos, 1965). See also the sources cited in the footnote to table 3.1 - especially those of the Federal Ministries of Labour and of Commerce and Industry, and the Kilby report.

36. See chapter 7 below; Harris and Rowe, *Nigerian Journal*, VIII, No. 1, 67-95; and Schatz, *Development Bank Lending in Nigeria*, pp. 89-101.

a further inducement to the establishment of petty enterprises,[37] and the supply of petty businessmen is not hindered appreciably by the low level of education in Nigeria. Callaway's study of 5,135 small entrepreneurs in Ibadan indicates that only 36 percent had some primary education[38] compared to about 30-35 percent of the population of the city with the same age distribution.[39] Because of the low skill requirements of small industry and the fact that apprentice training may be more closely related to business occupations, the lack of formal education does not seem to be a significant barrier to entrepreneurial activity in petty firms.

The nature of government policies reduces the supply of petty entrepreneurs just as it does that of large entrepreneurs. In fact, petty entrepreneurs, lacking political power, suffer even more from government apathy and red tape than do large entrepreneurs.

The training of the entrepreneur is discussed in chapters 7 and 10. Training can change the aggregate supply of entrepreneurs and their composition by firm size. Many training programs have been designed with little consideration for the market for entrepreneurs.

Why are the wages of small entrepreneurs high in the North and low in the East? The major determinant of the supply of petty entrepreneurs is the supply of apprentice course graduates. Whereas the number of these graduates in the North is relatively small, the number in the East is relatively large (chapter 7). Thus the supply of petty entrepreneurs in the East is relatively large and their wages relatively low. As in-

---

37. Peter T. Bauer, *West African Trade: A Study of Competition, Oligopoly and Monopoly in a Changing Economy* (Cambridge: Cambridge University Press, 1954), pp. 18-21. See also Archibald Callaway, "School Leavers and the Developing Economy of Nigeria," in *The Nigerian Political Scene*, ed. by Robert O. Tilman and Taylor Cole (Durham, N.C.: Duke University Commonwealth-Studies Center, 1962), pp. 220-38.

38. Archibald Callaway, "From Traditional Crafts to Modern Industries," *Odu: University of Ife Journal of African Studies*, II, No. 1 (July 1965), 36. See also chapter 7 below.

39. Kilby, *Oxford Bulletin*, XXVI, p. 182; Nigeria, *Annual Abstract, 1964*, pp. 12, 14; Helleiner, *Peasant Agriculture, Government and Economic Growth*, pp. 305-6; and Callaway, *Odu*, II, No. 1, 28-51.

dicated in chapter 9, these interregional differences in wages to petty entrepreneurs have persisted because of socio-political barriers to migration. Of course, these barriers not only widen the regional differentials in the supply of entrepreneurs, but also decrease their aggregate supply.

Summary

In 1965, the modal salary for a foreign top entrepreneur in an indigenous manufacturing firm with a net worth of £N75,000-125,000 and 100-200 employed was about £N2,500 yearly plus international travel and fringe benefits, compared to £N800 per year plus fringe benefits for an indigenous top entrepreneur. The difference in modal salaries arose from the segmentation of foreign and Nigerian markets, and the lesser demand for indigenous entrepreneurs as a result of the lack of complementary factors and available techniques, and the heterogeneity of resource quality.

Annual wages for top entrepreneurs in firms with about £N3,000 net worth and twenty employed ranged from £N180 per annum in the East to £N300 per annum in the North. These interregional differences persisted because of socio-political barriers to migration.

Industrial entrepreneurship in Nigeria is very scarce. It is estimated that in 1965 there were 1,300 indigenous and 1,100 foreign entrepreneurs in manufacturing in Nigeria with fifty or more workers.

Although the demand for foreign entrepreneurs exceeds that for indigenous entrepreneurs, the quantity of foreign entrepreneurs is relatively small because of the limited supply. Factors depressing the supply of foreign entrepreneurs are the uncertainty, the costs of moving, and the possible loss of professional position in the home country.

The lack of indigenous industrial entrepreneurship stems from deficiencies in both supply and demand. Demand is dampened by the lack of complementary factors and the low level of available techniques. Major factors impeding supply are the high remuneration in competing occupations, the low level of educational attainment, the lack of appropriate training, the deficiency of experience in high-level positions, the lack of encouragement by government, and the socio-political barriers to migration.

Chapter 4

Procedures, Methods, Definitions and Questions

This chapter indicates the major emphases of this study, which was conceived during a Research Assistantship (December 1964-December 1965) at the Economic Development Institute at the University of Nigeria - Enugu Campus, in Enugu, the capital of what was then Eastern Nigeria. Enugu served as a base from which I travelled throughout Nigeria to conduct interviews with entrepreneurs, other respondents in the firms, and outside sources. I conducted all the interviews myself.[1] In June-August 1969, June 1970, and May 1976, I returned to Nigeria to obtain more information on the broader context in which entrepreneurial activity was conducted.

Sample Entrepreneurs and Firms

An industry approach to the study was taken in order to facilitate the making of comparisons among entrepreneurs and their firms. The footwear industry was chosen for two reasons. First, this industry afforded the opportunity of studying a great diversity of firm size.[2] Secondly, there were more outside sources of information available in the footwear industry

---

1. The appendix discusses sources of information on the firms. For details on the interview and the questionnaire, see E. Wayne Nafziger, "Nigerian Entrepreneurship: A Study of Indigenous Businessmen in the Footwear Industry" (unpublished Ph.D. dissertation, University of Illinois, 1967), pp. 207-20.

2. On the basis of empirical data, Kenneth A. Bohr classifies the "boots and shoes" industry as an industry with no prevalent employment size. "Investment Criteria for Manufacturing Industries in Underdeveloped Countries," *Review of Economics and Statistics*, XXXVI, No. 2 (May 1954), 157-66. Tables 5.1-5.4, and 5.7, pp. 113-116, and p. 122, indicate a wide range

than in most industries in Nigeria. In most cases, there is no reason to believe that determinants of entrepreneurship in footwear manufacturing differ significantly from that in manufacturing as a whole in Nigeria.

The statistical universe consists of the forty-one indigenous[3] footwear manufacturing firms, with an average 1964 employment of eight or more, which were listed in the ten 1964-65 federal and regional directories.[4] "Manufacturing" involves the making of goods and articles, either by hand or with machinery.

Most of the analysis of the study is based upon the sample of twenty-five indigenous firms from the universe from which the author could obtain reasonably reliable data on value of output. Eighteen sample firms comprise a sub-sample on which reliable data on profit rates for the fiscal years, 1964 and/or 1965, were available.[5]

---

in the three measures of firm size in the Nigerian footwear industry - net worth, employment and the value of output. With a greater diversity in firm size, there is a greater potential for growth in output, a subject of interest to the student of entrepreneurship.

3. See above p. 81, n. 2, for the definition of "indigenous" firms.

4. The ten directories are the following: Nigeria, Ministry of Commerce and Industry, Quantitative Information on the Footwear Industry (Lagos, May 1965); Nigeria, Ministry of Commerce and Industry, *Industrial Directory, 1964* (Lagos, 1964); Eastern Nigeria, Ministry of Economic Planning, *Eastern Nigeria Industrial Directory* (Enugu, 1963); Mid-Western Nigeria, Mid-Western Nigeria Industrial Survey, 1964 (unpublished document, Benin City, 1964); Northern Nigeria, Ministry of Economic Planning, *Northern Nigeria Industrial Directory* (Kaduna, 1965); Personal Interview with the Assistant Trade Officer in the Western Region, May 1965; Nigeria, Parliament, *Parliamentary Debates* (House of Representatives), Vol. XVIII, No. 10 (5 April 1965), for the list of footwear firms registered for excise tax purposes; Nigeria, Ministry of Commerce and Industry, Registration of Business Names, Lagos, 1965; Nigeria, Ministry of Labour, Registration of Businesses, Lagos, 1965; and Nigeria, Office of Statistics, Supplement to the Industrial Directory, 1965, Lagos, 1965.

5. The appendix elaborates on sources of information, sources for quantitative data, major adjustments to the data, and sample bias. I conducted interviews with representatives

In some cases, to facilitate analysis, the firms are divided into two size categories. The boundary between the categories is meant to correspond, by and large, to a separation between the firm characterized by a modern shoe factory, advanced more capital-intensive techniques, a routinized production line, a specialized division of labor and machine tasks, a hired labor force, and a complex entrepreneurial and management structure, on the one hand, and an enterprise with a less modern, shoemaker's workshop, a simple more labor-intensive technology, not more than a few simple machines, and a labor force predominantly consisting of apprentices, journeymen, and family workers who learn most of the operation in making a shoe from face-to-face supervision by a proprietor. Thus, the firms are divided into large firms - those with a 1964 average net worth of £N5,000 or more, and small firms - those with a 1964 average net worth of less than £N5,000.[6] Entrepreneurs in small and large firms are known as small and large entrepreneurs respectively.

The Concept of the Entrepreneur

From among the various concepts of the entrepreneur suggested, it is necessary to find one that is not only satisfactory theoretically, but can also be used empirically in a field study in less developed countries. There are at least three important conceptualizations of the entrepreneur in orthodox economics literature: as the fourth factor of production who coordinates and hires the others (Walras); as the innovator, i.e. one who carries out new combinations (Schumpeter); and as the ultimate decision-maker in the enterprise, the one who commits the capital and bears the risk (Knight).

The Walrasian definition has advantages for the theory of general equilibrium, which discusses the role of the entrepreneur as a profit maximizer entering and leaving the industry; but it is not sufficiently rigorous for the interviewer in the field to identify with certainty the person or persons in a firm who coordinate and hire land, labor, and capital. Similarly, Schumpeter's concept of the entrepreneur is somewhat limited in less developed countries, since the majority of indigenous

---

of sixty-six non-sample footwear manufacturing firms (including ten foreign firms), and ninety footwear trading firms.

6. See table 6.1 for an indication of the size of the firms. All five large indigenous footwear firms are included in the sample.

Schumpeterian entrepreneurs are trading entrepreneurs whose innovations are the opening of new markets. In light of the possibilities of technical transfer from advanced economies, no undue emphasis should, in my view, be put on the development of entirely new combinations. Furthermore, the opportunity cost of technical, executive and organizational skills in underdeveloped economies may be too high to allow their use in developing new combinations in the Schumpeterian sense. Usually, fewer high-level skills are expended if combinations are adapted from economically advanced countries.[7]

Schumpeter's concept of the entrepreneur could be broadened to include those who adapt and modify already-existing innovations.[8] Most business activity in a non-stationary state involves the necessity of some innovation, since each firm faces unique factors (most obviously location and date of establishment). A firm's economic setting, in addition, changes over time. Absolute imitation is therefore impossible, and techniques developed outside the firm must be adapted to its own circumstances. This is especially true in the case of a firm in a less developed country borrowing technology from an advanced economy with different relative factor prices - for example, a higher price of labor relative to capital. Such adaptations require innovation, if "innovation" is used in a less restric-

---

7. Cf. however Douglas Rimmer, "Schumpeter and Underdeveloped Countries," *Quarterly Journal of Economics*, LXXV (August 1961), 433-50.

8. Schumpeter did not consider the imitator to be an entrepreneur. Nevertheless, see Henry G. Aubrey, "Industrial Investment Decisions," *Journal of Economic History*, XV (December 1955), 338; Margaret Katzin, "The Role of the Small Entrepreneur," in *Economic Transition in Africa*, ed. by Melville J. Herskovits and Mitchell Harwitz (Evanston, Ill.: Northwestern University Press, 1964), p. 183; and James J. Berna, *Industrial Entrepreneurship in Madras State* (New York: Asia Publishing House, 1960), p. 4. Joseph A. Schumpeter, *The Theory of Economic Development*, trans. by Redvers Opie (New York: Oxford University Press, 1961), pp. 132, 229-30, and *Business Cycles* (New York: McGraw-Hill Book Company, 1939), I, 102, 131, 137, has contrasted the "imitating" entrepreneur with the "innovating" entrepreneur. Entrepreneurs who adopt innovations already in existence could be said to be involved in both imitation and innovation.

tive sense than Schumpeter used it.[9] However this modification of the Schumpeterian framework has not proved workable in practice. Two independent field researchers would not be able to agree upon innovations and innovators within a given universe of firms.[10] Moreover, the entrepreneur is, in the modified Schumpeterian framework, no longer very distinctive among businessmen.

This study uses a concept similar to Knight's, where the entrepreneur is the ultimate decision-maker in the enterprise. It is he who commits the (ownership) capital and bears the risk (not the hired manager).[11] However, in some instances, more than one person owned capital within the firm. To cope with the problem of identifying quantities of entrepreneurship, it is assumed that there is one unit - the entrepreneur - in each firm. The entrepreneur is identified as the person with the largest capital share in the enterprise (or where these shares are equal, the person with the principal responsibility for making the decision to commit the capital to the firm). In the case of one sample firm, Southeastern Shoe, the entrepreneur, the board chairman, Mr. S.E. Dindu, represents a regional statutory corporation, the Eastern Nigeria Development Corporation, which contributed 80 percent of the share capital of the firm. (Throughout the study, pseudonyms are used to disguise the identity of the firms and entrepreneurs.) For two sample firms, Lagos Supreme and Aba Shoe Works, the existing entrepreneur, although not the same as the initial entrepreneur, has been top decision-maker long enough to carry paramount responsibility for the performance of the firm.[12]

---

9. On the other hand, even Schumpeter's "new combinations" involve a degree of imitation. The history of technological change provides few abrupt breaks from the past. T.S. Ashton, *The Industrial Revolution* (New York: Oxford University Press, 1948), p. 2.

10. Sayigh (see p. 21 above) is probably more successful than any other researcher in translating the modified Schumpeterian concept into a working definition. Nevertheless, it is unlikely that another investigator working independently would agree with Sayigh in his selection of 207 innovators.

11. The crucial decision in the firm is the selection of men to make decisions; "any other sort of decision-making or exercise of judgment is automatically reduced to a routine function." Frank Knight, *Risk, Uncertainty and Profit* (Boston: Houghton Mifflin Co., 1921), pp. 296-8.

12. Much of the responsibility of the substantial losses of Lagos Supreme in 1964 can be attributed to Mr. L.G. Ade-

The terms "entrepreneur" and "initial entrepreneur" are fairly concrete, referring to individuals. However, the terms "entrepreneurial input" and "entrepreneurship" are more abstract, and lack an exact empirical correspondence. Conceptually, the entrepreneurial inputs in a larger, more complex firm (where most resources of production are organized and coordinated) are considered to embody more "units of entrepreneurship" than that in a smaller firm.

Indices of Entrepreneurial Success

Few of the existing studies on entrepreneurship in less developed economies utilize measures of entrepreneurial or firm success,[13] because of the difficulty of obtaining access to firm records. In this study, however, access was gained to the records of a number of firms,[14] and thus data were available for measuring entrepreneurial success. The major critiera used to gauge entrepreneurial success are 1965 value of output, and 1964 rate of profit.[15]

Williams, the entrepreneur from 1961 to the time of the study. The poor performance of the firm was partially due to the entrepreneur's inability to acquire technical and management personnel with expertness in the plastics footwear industry.

The rapid expansion of output and significant increase in profits of Aba Shoe Works in 1965 were associated with the transfer of the major entrepreneurial responsibility from the aged Mr. I.R. Okenyi to his son, Mr. A.B. Okenyi, a graduate of a secondary commercial school, and an intensive and highly-individualized three-month course for managers of shoe firms at the Industrial Development Centre in Owerri, Eastern Nigeria.

13. James J. Berna, *Industrial Entrepreneurship in Madras State* (London: Asia Publishing House, 1960), pp. 144-76, does discuss firm growth. But the growth referred to is the growth of inputs, capital and labor. This growth is no measure of firm performance unless one assumes fixed input-output coefficients, in which case entrepreneurship has no effect upon output.

14. The appendix indicates how data from the firms were obtained.

15. Since ownership and control are generally not separated in the firms in this study, entrepreneurs generally receive some profits. The person designated as entrepreneur received income from both interest and profit in 24 of the 25 sample firms. The income of the entrepreneur in the other firm, Southeastern Shoe, is partly a function of the profits of the enterprise.

Measurements of entrepreneurial success would not be sig-

Neo-classical economists, in the theory of resource remuneration, maintain that "Profits perform . . . effectively the task of allocating resources among alternative lines of production," and that a person's income reflects what he is worth to the firm, and to society as a whole.[16] According to some of these economists, profitability has no ideological content,[17] but is a measure of efficiency[18] and the growth of available resources.[19] However, I make no claims that profit or its rate bear a close relationship to social contribution. An underlying assumption of pure competition is not warranted, as evidence on market imperfections, monopolistic restraints, barriers to the entry of new firms, and government support to inefficient enterprises indicates. Resource earnings are distorted by substantial variations between actual and equilibrium factor and commodity prices. A major distortion is created by differential controls, taxes, and subsidies imposed by government. Furthermore, there are substantial divergences between the private and social cost and benefit of industrial production, which arise from such things as the development of human skills, and forward and backward linkages with other producers. Nevertheless, the rate of profit, together with the value of output,[20] can be considered

---

nificantly affected by the age of the firm, since there is no relationship between its age and either value of output or rate of profit.

If X equals the age of the firm on 1 July 1964 (rounded off to the nearest year) and Y percentage rate of profit: $Y = -41.7 + 3.0X$. If the *t*-test is used, the regression coefficient is not significant at the 5 percent level ($t = 1.30$).

When Y is value of output, $Y = 119.6 + 1988.8X$. The regression coefficient is not significant at the 5 percent level ($t = 1.71$).

16. Campbell R. McConnell, *Economics: Principles, Problems, and Policies* (5th ed., New York: McGraw-Hill Book Company, Inc., 1972), pp. 576, 530-1.

17. Wolfgang F. Stolper, *Planning Without Facts: Lessons in Resource Allocation from Nigeria's Development* (Cambridge, Mass.: Harvard University Press, 1966), pp. 84, 139.

18. Murray D. Bryce, *Industrial Development: A Guide for Accelerating Economic Growth* (New York: McGraw-Hill Book Company, Inc., 1960), 121, and Bela A. Balassa, "An Abstract Model of Capitalism," in *Capitalism, Market Socialism and Central Planning*, ed. by Wayne A. Leeman (Boston: Houghton Mifflin Company, 1963), pp. 13-6.

19. Stolper, *Planning Without Facts*, pp. 70, 139.

20. Conceptually, the value-added of an establishment might

measures of success *from the standpoint of the individual firm and enterprise.*

Definitions of Profit, Output, Investment, Employment and Net Worth

Profit is defined as revenue plus changes in inventories[21] minus costs. Revenue equals the total proceeds[22] from footwear sales and apprentice fees. Costs include, *inter alia*, implicit returns to the businessman's own factor resources. For example, the businessman's capital is assumed to receive a competitive rate of return; the figure of 7 percent, the 1964 median return to bonds on the Lagos Stock Exchange, is employed. In addition, wages of management in unincorporated enterprises[23] are imputed when this has not been done in the firm's profit and loss statement. Conceptually, the wage for a proprietor or partner would equal the wage required for a hired manager to do the same job.[24]

Rate of profit is equal to profit divided by the net worth of the firm.[25] The value of output equals total proceeds from the sale of footwear plus changes in inventories of work-in-progress and finished goods. The number employed, a measure of workers engaged, includes working proprietors, paid employees, unpaid apprentices and unpaid family workers. In large firms,

---

be preferable to value of output as an indicator of business success. Value-added, which equals the value of output minus purchases from other firms, measures the resource earnings of the firm, and thus its contribution to gross national product. However, in a single industry, rankings of value of output tend to correspond to rankings of value-added. In the footwear industry, there is even reason to believe that the value of output of an enterprise is not far from being directly proportional to its value-added.

21. These include changes in the inventories of work-in-progress and finished goods.

22. Total proceeds include accounts receivable at the end of the period, but do not include proceeds from accounts receivable of the previous period.

23. The term for "incorporated enterprises" in Nigeria is "limited companies."

24. Chapters 8 and 9 consider wages to management by region and firm size.

25. The net worth of the firm equals its assets minus its liabilities.

the number of paid workers is usually equal to the number of workers engaged. However, the measure of employment usually exceeds the number of paid workers in small firms, which rely heavily on apprentices and family workers.[26] Investment refers to an increase in assets over a period of time.

The Primary Foci of this Study

The major empirical studies of entrepreneurship in less developed countries have information on the education, training, occupational and socio-economic background, communal origin, sources of initial capital, and relationship to government of the entrepreneurs. However, most of the works lack the data essential to consider factors related to entrepreneurial quantity and success. Here determinants of this quantity are found on the basis of differences between data on the characteristics of entrepreneurs and the population as a whole. One crucial differentiation, discussed in few other studies, is that between the socio-economic status of the entrepreneur and the general population. Factors related to entrepreneurial success are found by correlating socio-economic class, education, training, work experience, and sources and amounts of capital to the rate of profit and the value of output of their firms. Few other studies have access to these measures, which can be considered indicators of business success.

Several factors limit the scope of the topics discussed in an empirical study on entrepreneurship. Clearly, where data are collected by interview, only a limited number of questions can be asked since respondents have pressing duties and only a limited attention span. The cost of asking one question is the foregone opportunity of asking another question.

Some of the factors considered in the selection of questions should be indicated. First, questions pertaining to propositions well-established in the literature of entrepreneurship, and unlikely to generate new information and new challenges, were usually omitted. However, questions were framed to test the consensus of the existing literature on important questions, where I had doubts and disagreements.

Secondly, certain interesting questions of a theoretical nature could not be asked without substantial cost in time and rapport with the entrepreneur, e.g. What kind of relationship do

---

26. See chapter 8 for a discussion of apprentice contracts.

entrepreneurs and/or capitalists have with workers? From the pre-test of the first draft of the interview schedule in nine firms, it was clear that respondents, where they were willing to answer at all, tended to be biased. Independent sources of information, available on other questions, are fewer. Competitors, suppliers, and customers in business, as representatives of the capitalist class, are less likely to supply independent information on labor relations. On the other hand, interviews with workers would lessen the investigator's rapport with the entrepreneur and the amount of other information elicited, and change the whole nature of the field study.

Finally, my own professional background and research capabilities predisposed me towards certain questions, and precluded others. This is true, even though the study is multi-disciplinary. Thus, although I have evaluated the literature on achievement motivation and entrepreneurship from the standpoint of the social scientist,[27] I do not have the competence to test and score for need for achievement.

As a result of these factors certain topics were not stressed in questions. Little emphasis was placed upon motivation or "inner driving forces" for becoming entrepreneurs.[28] Entrepreneurs were either puzzled that anyone would ask "Why did you go into business?", or indicated a pecuniary motivation. One entrepreneur, in response to this inquiry, replied, "I thought I could make more money in business," and the expression on his face seemed to ask the question, "Why else?" In addition, the faulty and selective memory of the entrepreneur is less likely to distort impressions and misrepresent past occurrences when recalling, e.g., employment, previous work experience, and sources of capital than when recounting motives, either in answer to an open-ended question or a choice of responses, which are usually neither comprehensive nor mutually exclusive. It seems unlikely that an analyst, on the basis of a multiple-choice question concerning motives,[29] can surmise that "more of the respondents were led to their [entrepreneurial] career by natural inclination to it than by anything else - that is, they felt an attraction to that career *in itself* apart from the attraction of profit prospects, the desire to follow father's busi-

---

27. See chapter 10 and its appendix.

28. Cf. Yusif A. Sayigh, *Entrepreneurs of Lebanon: The Role of the Business Leader in a Developing Economy* (Cambridge: Harvard University Press, 1962), p. 106.

29. Ibid. pp. 150-1.

ness career, the pressure of urging by elders, the urge to contradict father, or the prestige expected in the career chosen."[30]

Rather than querying personal motivation, therefore, questions were directed towards acquiring data for the analysis of the role of education, training, work experience, access to capital, and paternal occupation and economic status in preparing the person for entry into industrial entrepreneurship (chapters 7 and 8). In general, questions requiring the entrepreneur to analyze his situation were not selected, in preference to those asking for his impression of facts. The respondent's own conception of the entrepreneurial role was not requested as has been the case in some studies of entrepreneurship.[31] The cost in further information foregone of obtaining this is high and entrepreneurs have few insights to add to the existing information.

---

30. Ibid. p. 76. Italics in original.
31. Ibid. pp. 51-120.

Chapter 5

The Nigerian Footwear Industry

The empirical data gathered for this study are based on the footwear industry. As indicated in chapter 4, the footwear industry was selected because of the substantial accessibility of reliable data on firms, and the great diversity of firm size in the industry.

According to Everett E. Hagen, one of the industries prevalent in the early stages of industrialization is footwear, because of its wide use and the familiarity of its production in simpler and rougher forms.[1] Despite the low level of industrialization in Nigeria, a large percentage of the footwear manufacturing firms were indigenous, because of the backlog of experience and the availability of simple techniques.

This chapter presents information on the Nigerian footwear industry including a description of processes of production; a regional distribution of firms by firm size; statistics on employment, investment and value of output in 1964; time series on output, imports and consumption; and the size and importance of the foreign sector.

Processes of Production[2]

In the largest and most capital-intensive Nigerian footwear

---

1. *The Economics of Development* (Homewood: Richard D. Irwin, 1968), p. 102.

2. This description of the process of producing men's leather shoes in large firms draws from the following sources: United Shoe Machinery Corporation, *How American Shoes Are Made* (Boston: By the Author, 1961); Fred Hammond Nichols, compiler, *The Building of a Shoe* (Lynn, Mass.: The Nichols Press, 1912);

firms, the first step in making men's leather shoes is to cut shoe upper parts from sheets of leather by means of cutting machines which press metal dies through leather skins. The patterns of the dies are shaped to correspond to the type of shoe desired. Upper skiving machines are then used to reduce the edges of the upper parts, so that they can be folded or joined to another part. Sewing machines are used to sew the lining and upper parts together. Meanwhile insoles have been temporarily tacked to the lasts by insole tacking machines. Lasts are reproductions of the approximate shape of the foot. Tack lasting machines are then used to tack the assembled upper to the bottom of the last. After this, pulling over machines draw the upper firmly and smoothly forward over the last, and fasten it into place. Outsole and heels are then attached to the insole by cementing and vulcanizing. The last is then taken from the shoe. Finally, the shoe is cleaned, finished, polished and sprayed, with the aid of machines and power equipment.

On the other hand, the leather shoe firm with less than four persons employed uses much simpler processes in making a shoe. Paper patterns are used to trace the insoles and upper parts in a sheet of leather, and the outsoles in a sheet of rubber. The various parts are cut with a cutting knife. Upper parts and lining are sewed together by hand stitching. The insoles and upper are formed around the last, and smoothed by hand. A rasp is used instead of a finishing machine to smooth the outsole after cementing. Rags are used for the final step of cleaning and polishing.

To manufacture plastic footwear, injector molding machines are used.[3] A plastic footwear firm established in 1965 in the

---

and Jerome N. Afuba, "A Feasibility Study of an Eastern Shoe Firm," (Economic Development Institute Working Paper No. 1, University of Nigeria, Enugu, March 1965), pp. 5-7.

3. Sources used to describe the process of plastic footwear manufacturing are: "Vinyl Polymers and Copolymers," *Modern Plastics Encyclopedia, 1965*, XLII, No. 1a (1964), ed. by Joel Frados (New York: B.F. Goodrich Chemical Co., 1964), 271. S.E. Rusinoff, *Manufacturing Processes* (Chicago: American Technological Society, 1949), pp. 338-9, 356-61; John Sasso, ed., *Plastics Handbook for Product Engineers* (New York: Pitman Publishing Co., 1941), pp. 94-8, 200-2, 211-13. A Technical Advisor to the Federal Ministry of Commerce and Industry, Lagos, Nigeria, 12-13 May 1965, and plastic footwear representatives, interviewed by the author, are sources for both technical and economic data on plastic footwear manufacturing.

Lagos metropolitan area in the Western Region (now Lagos state)[4] employs seven operators and one supervisor for each molding machine. Each of its four machines cost £N12,500 in February 1965, with a set of seven molds costing £N4,000.

The first step in the process is to feed polyvinyl chloride (PVC)[5] granules through a hopper into a pressure cylinder. The PVC is heated until it reaches a fluid state. The fluid is forced by hydraulic pressure through a vent into a closed mold cavity. The temperature of the mold is kept sufficiently cold so that the plastic material is no longer fluid. Pressure of around 17,000 to 20,000 pounds per square inch needs to be applied long enough so that the shoe or sandal cools and becomes hard. After a defined length of time, the mold opens automatically. The shoe is then removed by one of the operators. For most machines with a set of six or seven molds, a shoe or sandal can be removed at least every fifteen seconds. Except for servicing and repairing, this rate can be sustained.

The timing and the sequence of operations in most of the injector molding machines in use in Nigerian plastic footwear factories are highly automatic. Although machinery and supervisory costs are higher with the more automatic processes, labor costs are lower, as very little skill is required by the operators. Relatively unskilled operators can regulate the flow of PVC granules into the feed hopper, check the pressure and temperature of the machine, remove the shoe or sandal, and clean out excess material from the mold. Extraordinary problems are referred to the supervisor.

The Industry

Despite deficiencies in the data, some generalizations on the urban footwear industry can be made for 1964[6] The industry

---

4. Cities with major footwear firms in Lagos state are Ikeja, Ebute Metta and Mushin.

5. The advantages of using PVC in manufacturing plastic footwear are its strength, flexibility, chemical and water resistance, resistance to abrasion, and adaptability to unlimited color possibilities. *Modern Plastics Encyclopedia, 1965*, XLII, No. 1a, 27.

6. In addition to tables 5.1-5.3, this information is based on tables analagous to table 5.2, part A, for each region. See E. Wayne Nafziger, "Nigerian Entrepreneurship: A Study of Indigenous Businessmen in the Footwear Industry" (unpublished Ph.D. dissertation, University of Illinois, 1967), pp. 267-8.

comprised about 3,000 firms with 8,000 to 10,000 persons employed. Net worth and value of output were about £N2 million and £N3 million respectively. Foreign firms accounted for roughly two-thirds of this net worth and value of output (see tables 5.1-5.3, pp. 113-116). A majority of the firms with twenty-five or more workers were located in the Lagos metropolitan area. Probably more than half of the firms with less than twenty-five workers were in the Eastern Region. The Lago metropolitan area probably accounted for more than one-half of both

Table 5.1

Estimates of Numbers of Indigenous Footwear Firms in Urban Areas, March 1965[a]

Region	Size of Firms by Employment					
	1-5	6-9	10-24	25-99	100 or more	Total
East	1,450	40	32	3	1	1,526
Mid-West	300	8	2	0	1	311
North	730	8	1	1	0	740
West	330	9	10	1	0	350
Federal Territory	40	10	6	2	0	58
TOTAL	2,850	75	51	7	2	2,985

a. "Urban areas" are defined as "all compact centers of over 10,000 inhabitants." K.M. Buchanan and J.C. Pugh, *Land and People in Nigeria* (London: University of London Press, 1965), p. 63. "Footwear firms" include economic units in which at least one person derives 50 percent or more of his annual income from the making or repair of footwear. The estimates in this table are based mainly on the ten directories listed on p.100, n. 4 above. All this information was checked against the author's field research and, among other useful sources, Peter Kilby, *The Development of Small Industry in Eastern Nigeria* (Enugu: Eastern Region Ministry of Information, 1963). For the procedures used to obtain the estimates in tables 5.1-5.3, see E. Wayne Nafziger, "Nigerian Entrepreneurship: A Study of Indigenous Businessmen in the Footwear Industry," pp. 255-63.

Table 5.2

Estimates of Number of Firms, Employment, Net Worth and Value of Output in the Indigenous Footwear Manufacturing Industry in Urban Areas, 1964[a]

	Number of Firms	Employment	Net Worth (£N)	Value of Output (£N)
(A) The Employment size of the firms				
100 or more	2	365	360,000	224,800
25-99	6	320	115,200	123,000
10-24	47	642	58,230	119,640
6-9	74	530	14,325	33,800
1-5	2,765	6,258	101,900	488,500
TOTAL	2,885	8,115	649,655	989,740
(B) Regions				
East	1,472	3,825	201,700	388,520
Mid-West	311	967	262,080	259,640
North	710	1,399	47,775	107,150
West	340	945	108,700	208,720
Federal Territory	52	979	29,400	25,600
TOTAL	2,885	8,115	649,655	989,740

a. In addition to the sources cited for table 5.1, the estimates of employment, net worth, and value of output are based on information supplied by persons working in the Northern Ministry of Trade and Industry, the Northern Nigeria Development Corporation, the Ministry of Trade and Industry in Kano, the Industrial Development Centres in Owerri and Zaria, the National Manpower Board, the Federal Ministry of Commerce and Industry, the Federal Office of Statistics, and the Eastern Region Fund for Agricultural and Industrial Development.

Table 5.3

Estimates of Number of Firms, Employment, Net Worth and Value of Output among Foreign Footwear Manufacturing Firms, 1964[a]

Size of Firms by Employment	Number of Firms	Employment	Net Worth (£N)	Value of Output (£N)
100 or more	2	870	1,050,000	1,237,550
25-99	7	233	420,000	495,000
TOTAL	9	1,103	1,470,000	1,732,550

a. This table refers only to firms with twenty-five or more workers employed.

the net worth of footwear enterprises and the value of footwear output of the Federation. Probably more than one-half of the employment in the industry was with Eastern firms. The Eastern Region led in the value of output of indigenous firms.

The Federal Office of Statistics, on the basis of an enumeration of several survey villages in each region, estimated that the number of rural household enterprises in 1965 was 12,020, a majority of which were in the Northern Region (table 5.4, p. 116). Most of these establishments were one-man operations on a part-time basis, using techniques even more labor-intensive than those of the small leather shoe firm described above, and oriented toward the modest consumption needs of the local village. Frequently the basic materials for the shoes or sandals were used rubber tires. It is not likely that the total value of output of these firms exceeded £N800,000 in 1964.

Trends in Output, Consumption, and Imports

The domestic output of footwear in urban firms with ten or more employed increased from 50,000 pairs per annum in 1956 to 20,100,000 in 1971, a rate of growth of 49.1 percent per annum (table 5.5, p. 118). If the output of urban and rural firms with less than ten employed were included, the growth rate was much slower. For example, inclusion of these smaller firms decreased the growth rate of the volume of domestic output of footwear

Table 5.4

Estimates of Number of Rural Household Footwear Enterprises by Region, 1965

East	2,930
Mid-West	860
North	6,510
West	1,720
TOTAL	12,020

Source: Nigeria, Office of Statistics, *Survey of Rural Household Enterprises* (Lagos, 1965).

firms from 1960 to 1964 from 266.7 percent per annum to only 18.8 percent per annum.

The number of pairs of imported footwear increased during the last thirteen years of colonial rule from 753,000 in 1947 to a peak of 8,787,000 in 1960, a rate of growth of 20.8 percent per annum. As a result of a program of tariff protection (see table 5.6, p. 119) and industrial investment incentives, imports dropped at a rate of 19.4 percent per annum between 1960 and 1971, when only 816,000 were imported. The number of pairs produced domestically as a percentage of the total number of pairs consumed increased from less than 6 percent of 400,000 in 1946, to 6 percent of 9,387,000 in 1960, to 66 percent of 11,910,000 in 1964, to 96 percent of 15,104,000 in 1969 (table 5.5).

The Significance of the Foreign Sector

The footwear manufacturing industry, like most of the Nigerian industrial sector, has been characterized by a high rate of concentration in output, value-added and capital expenditures, and domination by foreign firms. Although Nigerians headed establishments which produced footwear throughout the late colonial period, they lacked the techniques and skills essential for output on a large scale.

Nigeria's post-Independence strategy of emulating the process of large-scale, capital-intensive industrialization in the West, necessitated the acquisition of advanced technology abroad. It might have been possible for Nigeria to have emphasized the expansion of the production of indigenous-type consumer goods, such as handicraft footwear. At the same time, the country might have severely limited the entry of foreign firms which generally produce western-type consumer goods on a mass scale. Indigenous production would have required less capital imports, foreign exchange, and technology transfers than "modern" western-type consumer goods. Over time, Nigeria might have developed new technology through "learning by doing" on the part of its entrepreneurs, managers, technicians and workers. Since, for example, the footwear industry is not characterized by a prevalent size of firm or plant,[7] shoemakers could have obtained essential management skills and technical knowledge for more complex economic activities on a step-by-step basis, as the enterprise gradually expanded. Whatever expertness could not be acquired by learning on the job, conferring with other footwear industrialists, and reading technical journals, might have been got from technical and management assistance from industrial extension centers or technical training institutes, through technology purchase contracts, technical collaboration agreements with or patent licensing from foreign firms, or by hiring a foreign or domestic technician with appropriate skills. The existing domestic and foreign technology could then have been imitated and adapted when needed. One could conceive of the technical and management skills of a craftsman expanding little by little so that in a number of years he might become a modern manufacturer. This could be achieved with production under the control of Nigerians, rather than foreigners.

There are, however, several problems associated with a strategy which emphasizes technological learning on the part of small, indigenous businessmen. First, a country which formulates an industrial policy at independence does not start from "scratch." In Nigeria, in 1960, there were a number of companies already manufacturing or with permits to manufacture, which had to be considered. In addition, legal commitments and regulations that permit foreign capital and entrepreneurship to enter a country relatively freely (such as existed in Nigeria) cannot easily be rescinded. Such foreign enterprises may provide overwhelming competition for indigenous businesses. The major obstacles to their development may be, not their lack of diligence, determination, resourcefulness, innovation, or thrift, but the concentration of large enterprises in the industrial sector,[8] and few ef-

---

7. Kenneth A. Bohr, "Investment Criteria for Manufacturing Industries in Underdeveloped Countries," *Review of Economics and Statistics*, XXXVI, No. 2 (May 1954), 157-66.

8. See, e.g., James McCrory, *Case Studies in Latent Industrial Potential: Small Industry in a North Indian Town*

Table 5.5

Domestic Consumption[a] of Imported Footwear and Domestically Produced Manufactured Footwear in Firms with Ten or More Employed, 1960-71

(1)	(2)	(3)	(4)	(5)
Year	Imported Footwear (thousands of pairs)	Domestically Produced Footwear (thousands of pairs)	Total (thousands of pairs)	Column 3/ Column 4[b]
1946	400	< 25	400	0.06
1947	753	< 25	750	0.03
1948	1,393	< 25	1,400	0.02
1949	1,431	< 25	1,450	0.02
1950	1,431	< 50	1,500	0.03
1951	2,509	< 50	2,550	0.02
1952	2,270	< 50	2,300	0.02
1953	3,508	< 50	3,550	0.01
1954	4,723	< 50	4,750	0.01
1955	4,706	< 50	4,750[c]	0.01
1956	6,201	50	6,251	0.01
1957	4,786	100	4,886	0.02
1958	5,833	250	6,083	0.04
1959	6,116	300	6,416	0.05
1960	8,787	600	9,387	0.06
1961	7,219	2,200	9,419	0.23
1962	5,869	3,600	9,469	0.38
1963	5,574	5,000	10,574	0.47
1964	4,010	7,900	11,910	0.66
1965	2,141	8,800	10,941	0.80
1966	1,466	9,300	10,766	0.86
1967	1,272[d]	10,400[d]	11,672[d]	0.89
1968	624[d]	10,700[d]	11,324[d]	0.94
1969	504[d]	14,600[d]	15,104[d]	0.96
1970	594[d]	21,200[d]	21,794[d]	0.97
1971	816	20,100	20,916	0.96

a. Recorded exports, whose volume never exceeded one-tenth of a percent of import volume, are not subtracted.

b. For this calculation, the < sign is ignored for the figure in column 3.

c. Approximation.

d. Excludes the three Eastern states from June 1967 through February 1970.

Sources: Nigeria, Office of Statistics, *Nigeria Trade Summary*, Lagos, various years; Nigeria, Office of Statistics, *Economic Indicators*, Lagos, various issues; and Nigeria, Ministry of Commerce and Industry.

Table 5.6

Nigerian Footwear Import Duties (as a percentage of value and/or per pair)

	Date of Commencement					
Type of footwear	Aug. 1948	Aug. 1954	Apr. 1958	Mar. 1962	Aug. 1964	Aug. 1965
(a) Children's	16 2/3%	20%	25%	33 1/3%	33 1/3%	33 1/3%
(b) Other						
(1) canvas and rubber	16 2/3%	20%	25%	33 1/3%	6d or 40%[a]	6s or 50%[a]
(2) other material	16 2/3%	20%	25%	33 1/3%	10s6d or 40%[a]	£N1 5s0d or 50%[a]

a. The higher of the two is levied.

12d (pence) = 1 s (shilling); 20 shillings = £N1.

Sources: Joseph C. Miller, "Nigerian Tax Legislation: An Outline," (report to the Economic Development Institute, University of Nigeria, Enugu, 1965); and Nigeria, *Supplement to Official Gazette Extraordinary, L. N. 92*, Vol. LII, No. 65 (18 April 1965), B509.

fective measures to reduce monopoly power.

As the previous exposition points out, a poor country needs to acquire some technology from abroad, even when it pursues a strategy which emphasizes indigenous enterprise. The analysis of the foreign sector in chapter 2 above indicates that the control of industrial techniques has been concentrated in a few advanced economies; for firms under the control of nationals to obtain this technology is expensive.

Given this expense, it can be argued that foreign technology should be acquired by attracting foreign enterprise. Furthermore, the priority placed upon large-scale capital-intensive industrialization in Nigeria provides even more reason to encourage foreign assistance and investment. Nevertheless, the following discussion of the role of the foreign company in the footwear industry in Nigeria, together with the more general discussion in chapter 2, raises some questions about the costs of overseas enterprise.

Seven of the nine foreign firms in the footwear industry in 1965 were multinational corporations, a company with its headquarters located in some country other than Nigeria.[9] Although two of the headquarters are in Greece and India, and rank low in total output among multinational footwear companies, five of the companies have headquarters in Western Europe or North America, and are among the top fifty companies in the world in footwear output. Nigerian output accounted for less than 1 percent of the total output of the five major multinational companies, and less than 20 percent for the other two international companies. Nevertheless, foreign firms and individuals (primarily multinational corporations) accounted for 70.4 percent of the net worth, and 63.2 percent of the value of output in 1964 in the Nigerian urban footwear industry. These percentages closely approximate the percentages one would get from computations on the basis of figures on indigenous and foreign firms in tables 5.2 and 5.3 except for a few differences where indigenous firms have some foreign ownership, and foreign firms some indigenous ownership.

(Footnote 8 continued from page 117.)

(Delhi: Government of India, Ministry of Commerce and Industry, 1956), pp. 3-4.

9. The Lebanese owners of two foreign firms were quasi-permanent residents in Nigeria.

Other sources confirm the importance of foreign ownership in the footwear industry. For example, computations based on the *Industrial Survey, 1965* of the Federal Office of Statistics indicate that foreign private ownership comprised 53.5 percent of total ownership[10] and 69.6 percent of total private ownership in the industry in 1965 (table 2.8).

The dominance of foreigners in the ownership structure of the industry was associated with the importance of foreigners among entrepreneurial, management and technical personnel of the industry. Although the 1965 *Industrial Survey* does not classify non-Nigerian employees according to skill level, one can assume that, with rigorous government regulations concerning expatriate quotas and immigrant labor, all of the foreign employees in the footwear industry could be classified as professional or managerial. On this assumption, 51 of 85 (or 60 percent) of the total

---

10. This percentage is less than that of the figure above which indicates that 70.4 percent of the net worth in the Nigerian urban footwear industry was held by foreigners. Over time, with the emphasis upon the establishment of large Nigerian private and public footwear firms, and the pressure for foreign private firms to sell ownership shares to Nigerians, the percentage of foreign ownership would be expected to fall. However, probably the major reasons for the discrepancy in percentages are not the differences in years, but the variations in the method of acquiring information and the definition of ownership. Foreigners, subject to government approval for capital transfers and taxation for property ownership, had a particular inducement to understate capital ownership. A discreet businessman may be more likely to understate capital ownership on a written questionnaire under the auspices of an office of the Nigerian government than in response to an interview with a foreign scholar. Nigeria, Office of Statistics, *Industrial Survey, 1964 and 1965* (Lagos, 1968), p. 21, indicates some of the inaccuracies associated with data on capital ownership. In addition, the concept used to measure ownership, paid-up capital, measures only initial capital contributions, not capital originating from retained earnings. Since the large foreign enterprises were, on the whole, more profitable than the large indigenous enterprises, undistributed profits would be a larger percentage of capital stock in foreign firms than in indigenous firms.

Table 5.7

Employment[a], Net Worth[b] and Value of Output of Footwear Firms with an Employment of Thirty or More, 1964

Firm, Location[c]	Year of First Output	Major Types of Output[d]	Employment	Net Worth (£N)	Value of Output (£N)
Ikeja Manufacturing Co. (Lagos Met)[efg]	1960	P,R	560	800,000	620,000
Kano Shoe Co.[e]	1959	P,R	250	150,000	340,000
Midwestern Manufacturing Co.	1963	R	250	250,000	210,000
Southeastern Shoe Co.	1964	L,B	115	110,000	14,800[h]
Lagos Plastics Co.[e]	1962	P	80	120,000	120,000
Northern Shoe Manufacturing Co.	1963	L,S,B	72	26,000	22,000
Metro Plastics Co. (Lagos Met)[g]	1962	P	65	40,000	70,000
Lagos Supreme Company	1960	P	61	20,000	4,500
Ikeja Manufacturing Co. (Lagos Met)[efgi]	1964	L	60	100,000	300,000
Capital City Shoe Co. (Lagos Met)[eg]	1964	L	60	80,000	5,000
Kano Plastics Co.[e]	1963	P	56	80,000	80,000
Nigerian Plastics Co. (Lagos)[ej]	1964	P	55	40,000	180,000
Onitsha Shoe Company	1954	S	45	2,400	9,500
Circle Manufacturing Co. (Lagos Met)[eg]	1964	L	30	30,000	25,000

a. Concept of employment and net worth used for the firm is the average in 1964. Exceptions are that the average for firms operating only during part of 1964 is calculated only for the period of operation.

b. Purchase cost (with computations for amortization) is used instead of replacement cost.

c. The location of the firm is indicated in parentheses except where the pseudonym specifies the location.

d. P indicates plastic footwear; L - leather shoes; R - rubber and canvas shoes; S - sandals; B - boots; and M - footwear repairs.

e. Foreign firm.

f. Operating same plant, though registered separately. In aggregation, the two are considered one firm.

g. The Lagos metropolitan area includes all territory within present-day Lagos state, but not inside Lagos city.

h. Operated only the last 3½ months in 1964.

i. Initial output in July 1964.

j. Operating same plant as another firm with twenty-five employed, producing rubber footwear.

Sources: Same as those cited in tables 5.1 and 5.2.

---

professional and managerial employees in footwear manufacturing in 1965 were foreigners.[11]

As detailed in chapter 10, the policy of the Federal government has been to set quotas on the amount of foreign managerial and technical personnel brought in by a firm, but these "expatriate quotas" have not been vigorously applied. In 1965, only one of the nineteen management officials, in the four foreign footwear firms that had been established for at least three years, was a Nigerian. The official, a personnel manager, although involved in routine matters of hiring, dismissal and discipline of workers, had no major decision-making responsibility. Only one of the nine foreign footwear firms indicated any concrete plans for recruiting and/or training Nigerians for eventual management positions.

However, it would be wrong to assume that appointing Nigerians to a substantial majority of the managerial positions in foreign firms would mean they had significant control in the firms. Since these firms are subsidiaries, major decisions are made at headquarters abroad, and only day-to-day decision-making is entrusted to management officials in Nigeria.

---

11. Ibid. p. 32. Cf. J.O. Odufalu, "Indigenous Enterprise in Nigerian Manufacturing," *The Journal of Modern African Studies*, IX, No. 4 (1971), 600. That this high percentage of foreigners is accurate is reinforced by data indicating that wages and salaries of non-Nigerians as a percentage of total wages and salaries, at 29.2 percent, in the industry, was ten times as high as the number of non-Nigerians employed as a percentage of the total employed, 2.9 percent (see table 2.8). This suggests that foreigners, who monopolize much of the technical skills associated with large-scale manufacturing, were disproportionately represented among high-level personnel in footwear enterprises.

In an economy with little large-scale modern manufacturing in the indigenous sector, foreign dominance is associated with a high concentration rate in manufacturing. The concentration rate refers to the percentage share of the largest four firms in the industry. Table 2.9 suggests the nature of the differences between the impact of a few (say, five or six) large-scale modern manufacturing establishments on concentration in Nigeria as compared to concentration in the U.S. When added to foreign private and Nigerian public joint enterprises, subsidiaries of multinational corporations have a much more substantial relative impact on total output on the industry than in the west, even though these may be much smaller than parent companies in absolute size. For example, computations from tables 5.2, 5.3 and 5.7, pp. 114-115, and p. 122, indicate that one foreign firm, Ikeja Manufacturing Company, produced about one-third of the value of footwear output in Nigeria, i.e. £N920,000 of £N2,722,290. Three firms, Ikeja, Kano Shoe, and Midwestern Manufacturing, produced £N1,470,000, over one-half the value of footwear output in Nigeria in 1964.

Data from the *Industrial Survey* reinforce this. The total value-added of the four largest footwear firms in Nigeria as a percentage of the total value-added in 1965 was 58.7 percent compared to a similar concentration rate of only 10.2 percent for the U.S. in 1947. The concentration rate for employment for the largest four firms was 56.6 percent for Nigeria, compared to 8.4 percent in the U.S. in 1947 (see table 2.9). Finally, in 1965, the concentration rates for total receipts, total net capital expenditures, and wages and salaries in the Nigerian urban footwear industry were 57.2 percent, 65.9 percent, and 67.1 percent respectively.[12]

Summary

The processes of production within the footwear industry vary from the highly-automated production of plastic footwear to the one-man leather and rubber footwear establishment using hammer, pliers, anvil, rasp, knife and other simple tools. There were 3,000 firms with 8,000 to 10,000 workers employed in the urban footwear industry in 1964. The Lagos metropolitan area accounted for more than one-half of the value of footwear output in Nigeria. The domestic output of footwear in urban firms with ten or more employed increased by 49.1 percent per annum from 1956 to 1971, when over 20 million pairs were produced. The Nigerian footwear manufacturing industry has been characterized by a high rate of concentration in output, and domination by foreign firms.

---

12. *Industrial Survey, 1964 and 1965*, pp. 39, 42, 43.

Chapter 6

Case Studies of Entrepreneurs and Firms

Nigeria's post-Independence strategy in manufacturing, as has been described previously, was to follow the pattern of large-scale capital-intensive industrialization in contemporary western economies. This strategy, together with the legacy of foreign companies and existing commitments and regulations favorable to the entry of foreign capital, resulted in a large foreign sector relative to the indigenous sector in the footwear industry in the early 1960s. The case studies of large enterprises given in this chapter show the extent to which the viability of the indigenous sector in 1964-65 was still dependent, by and large, on the acquisition of foreign technology. They indicate the scarcity of high-level technical and managerial skills available in the indigenous population, a scarcity perpetrated by the domination of the industrial sector by foreigners, and also reveal the difficulty in coordinating local skills and foreign expertness, even when the firm is under local control. Furthermore, an examination of small establishments suggests their weakness and vulnerability in an industry with a high degree of concentration.

A chapter on case studies of individual establishments could focus on one or more of a number of variables which influence the record of firms - e.g. capital formation, labor relations, input acquisition, and entrepreneurship. Here we emphasize the influence of the entrepreneur on firm performance, without trying to demonstrate that entrepreneurship is the most important factor explaining success or failure of the firm. Since aspects of the entrepreneurial history, structure and behavior found in sample firms are representative of a number of other firms in Nigeria, this analysis has general relevance.[1]

---

1. The appendix gives some indication how representative sample firms are.

Table 6.1 Selected Data on Sample Firms

Firm, Location,[a] Size,[b] Major Type(s) of Production[c]	Date of Origin	1964 ave. W^d (in £N)	1964 ave. N^e	1964 X^f (in £N)	1964 r^g	1965 ave. W^d (in £N)	1965 ave. N^e	1965 X^f (in £N)	1965 r^g
Metro (Lagos Met[h]) P	1962	40,000	65	70,000	14	50,000	90	70,000	8
Midwestern R	1963	250,000	250	210,000	-12	350,000	200	90,000	< -7
Southeastern L,B	1964	110,000	115	14,800[i]	-56	112,000	115	112,000	<-30
Lagos P	1960	20,000	61	4,500	-100[n]	[j]	16	1,500	
Northern L,S,B[k]	1963	26,000	90	22,000[m]	-215[n]	26,000	52	23,000	-122[n]
Aba S	1959		14			3,000	22	6,300	47
United (Aba) S	1963	550	13	3,600	31	700	26	4,800	
Market City (Onitsha) S	1960	270	8	6,300	29	880	9	10,500	38
Maiduguri M,L,S	1947	700	10	2,670		1,000	9	3,320	22
Royal (Aba)[l] S	1955	375	8	750	20	400	11	2,500	
Onitsha[k] S	1954	2,000	40	8,250	13	2,930	52	11,250	
Umuahia S	1958		25			850	20	6,250	11
Western (Ibadan) M,S,L	1953	2,650	12	1,020	6	2,350	12	1,020	7
Benin City M	1947	80	17	1,700	-4		17		
Quality (Aba) S	1948	225	15	1,600	-7		13	2,100	
Liberty (Aba) S	1960		24			1,000	26	800	-8
Cosmopolitan (Aba)[k] M,S	1963		8			850	8	370	-34
Southern (Aba) S	1951	3,000	10	320	-37	1,035	11	1,200	
Crossroads (Onitsha) S	1961		12			300	13	6,500	
Federal (Lagos) S,L	1959	1,200	13	5,200		1,400	15	5,800	
Dugbe (Ibadan) S	1962	650	12	4,850		600	12	4,600	
Enugu S,M	1962	750	10	3,900		850	12	4,250	
Capital (Lagos)[k] S	1958		14			600	11	2,100	
Port Harcourt S	1957		14			1,200	14	1,450	
Golden (Aba) M,S	1955		9			250	10	600	

a. The location of the firm is indicated in parentheses except where the firm pseudonym specifies the location. To protect their identity, only the region of large firms and the city of small firms are given.

b. Large firms are in italics; small firms in roman print.

c. P indicates plastic footwear; L - leather shoes; R - rubber and canvas shoes; S - sandals; B - boots; and M - footwear repairs.

d. Average net worth of the enterprise. An exception is that the average for firms operating only during part of the year is calculated only for the period of operation.

e. N indicates average employment.

f. X indicates value of output of footwear manufacturing and repairs.

g. r indicates percentage rate of profit.

h. This refers to the Lagos metropolitan area outside of the Federal Territory.

i. Operating only 3½ months in 1964 after initial production.

j. Blank space indicates information not available. Net worth for Lagos firm is difficult to define because of deterioration of this position due to losses.

k. Since accounting year t begins on 1 July $t-1$, and ends 30 June t, figures for the firms do not correspond with table 5.7.

l. Since accounting year 1964 ends 31 March 1964, figures do not correspond to table 5.7.

m. Estimate.

n. See p. 128.

A secondary theme is the impact of government policy on the entrepreneur and firm.

Quantitative Data on Sample Firms

Table 6.1, p. 126, sets forth 1964-65 data on average net worth, employment, value of output and rate of profit.[2] Where data are available, both large and small firms are ranked according to their percentage rate of profit in 1964 (or 1965 if 1964 figures are not available).

The figures on losses for the Lagos Supreme and Northern Leather Works firms imply that variable costs exceed total revenue. In 1964, the Lagos firm suspended production after it became clear that operating cost exceeded revenue. In the fiscal year 1964 the principals of Northern Shoe were not aware of the large loss, since the firm kept only cursory data on cost and revenue[3] and the entrepreneurs lacked experience. Because regional politicians exercised much of the control over the firm in the fiscal year 1965, the decision to continue some production was a political decision.

Even if the two firms with losses of 100 percent or more are excluded from the analysis, in 1964 and 1965, profit rates varied a minimum of about 70-80 percentage points among both sub-samples of large and small firms. Among other things, this study attempts to indicate some of the ways in which entrepreneurship helped to account for these differences.

Large Firms

The following five case studies of large indigenous footwear firms and their entrepreneurs were selected with the objective of shedding light upon more general issues and providing a concrete base for subsequent analysis.

Lagos Supreme Company

About £N900 thousand of the £N2.2 million estimated 1964 value of manufacturing output in urban footwear firms with ten

---

2. Chapter 4 defines rates of profit as profit/net worth. In the computation of profit, costs include, *inter alia*, implicit interest charges and wages of management.

3. Data on losses for the firm were based on the decrease in net worth shown in the balance sheet.

or more employed was plastic footwear (see table 6.2). This output was produced by eight firms, each of which had at least an employment of twenty-five and assets of £N20,000. About 8 percent of the value of Nigeria's plastic footwear output was produced by the two indigenous firms, Metro Plastics and Lagos Supreme.

Table 6.2

Estimated 1964 Value of Manufacturing Output in Urban Footwear Firms with an Employment of Ten or More by Type of Footwear Produced

Type of Footwear Produced	Output (in thousands of pairs)	Value of Output (£N'000)
Plastics footwear	3,600	900
Canvas-rubber footwear	2,000	480
Rubber sandals	500	120
Rubber shoes	500	120
Leather shoes	300	240
Leather sandals	1,000	340
TOTAL	7,900	2,200

The estimates are based partly on the work of Nigeria, Ministry of Commerce and Industry.

Lagos Supreme was started in 1960 by British capitalists engaged in manufacturing plastic products in the U.K. Under their leadership, the annual value of output and rate of loss in both 1960 and 1961 probably exceeded £N18,500 and 27 percent respectively, the figures for 1962.

The performance of these capitalists resembled that of a number of other foreigners, who succeeded at home but failed in Nigeria. The foreign entrepreneurs of Lagos Supreme were well acquainted with the industry in Europe, but had little conception of how to adapt to business mores, labor conventions, and marketing institutions in Nigeria. Except for a Nigerian in a sub-management position, Mr. M.E. Akitoye, the present entrepreneur in Metro Plastics, no one exercising managerial responsibility had a first-hand acquaintance with the Nigerian economy and culture. Furthermore, little prior business research on the industry in Nigeria was undertaken. Mr. L.G. Ade-Williams, the present entrepreneur, and sources outside the firm, report that these deficiencies helped contribute to an overextension of the enterprise, a mishandling of funds, an irregularity of accounts, and a lack of control of plant and marketing staff in the early years of the unit.

After the substantial losses of 1960-61, the control of the company reverted to three Nigerian directors of a Lagos bank,[4] which held a debenture on the assets and properties of the firm. In September 1961, one of the bank directors, Mr. Ade-Williams, a retired civil servant who was previously a self-employed accountant, assumed the top management position of the firm. Under his firm leadership, irregularities were eliminated, but losses continued. In retrospect one decision was crucial, and could have substantially affected the poor record of the enterprise. This was the bank directors' decision, perhaps because of their reluctance to hire foreigners and because of the scarcity of Nigerians with the relevant experience,[5] not to acquire someone, for a position of high-level responsibility, with general engineering or a specialized background in plastics technology.

Metro Plastics Company

The growth rate of the value of output of the Metro firm from 1962 to 1964 was 23.9 percent per annum,[6] and the 1964 profit rate was 14 percent (table 6.1), a considerable contrast to Lagos Supreme. The decline in profit rates and a levelling off in output in 1965 are not representative of the long run position of the firm. Metro, like other plastic footwear firms, produced virtually nothing for four and one-half months in 1965, because of the increase in the excise tax from one to three shillings on

---

4. The three bank directors were members of an elite group in Lagos descended from slaves emancipated in the early nineteenth century. This group has had a disproportionate representation in large business activity.

5. Mr. Akitoye was not considered for the position because of his identification with the discredited managerial regime of 1960-61.

6. The output for only part of the initial year, 1962, was adjusted to an annual basis.

each pair of plastic footwear produced.[7] The higher rate was virtually prohibitive for plastic footwear producers, who had previously been selling their products at an average ex-factory price of five shillings per pair.

At the beginning of 1962, only two firms - both foreign ventures - produced plastic footwear in Nigeria. The original shareholders in Metro were the principal, Mr. M.E. Akitoye, three other Nigerians, and two foreigners. By 1963, Mr. Akitoye had procured a majority of the equity holdings.

Mr. Akitoye's work experience, well-suited for an entrepreneurial position in the plastic footwear industry, included a sub-management position in an English plastic footwear firm for twelve months in 1959-60, the operation of a West African agency of this firm for ten months in 1960, and the highest-ranking Nigerian managerial post (and third highest altogether) in Lagos Supreme for nine months in 1961. With official pressure on foreign firms for progressive Nigerianization of management positions, it appeared to him that the chances for upward mobility in the Lagos firm, perhaps even to top resident manager, were good. It was a disappointment to Mr. Akitoye when he was passed over in favor of Mr. Ade-Williams when the new general manager was selected. Since Mr. Akitoye lacked sufficient capital to establish his own plastic footwear manufacturing firm, he continued a trading establishment he had been managing after his resignation from Lagos Supreme in the last quarter of 1961.

Mr. Akitoye had conceived the idea of a plastic footwear venture in 1960 when, as marketing agent, he observed that plastic shoes, because of their low unit cost, were well-suited to the Nigerian market, characterized by a low per capita income. The insights he gained from his experiences contributed to the success of Metro. He emphasized the recruitment of a relatively competent staff so that, from the beginnings of the operation, he always had at least one (foreign) specialist in plastics engineering. From time to time, an expert from Europe was brought in to assist in training the workers in machine operation, main-

---

7. For example, the Nigerian Plastics Company, a foreign plastic footwear firm, produced only 40 dozen pairs in April 1965, after the excise duty of three shillings per pair had been levied. In March 1965, when the duty was only one shilling per pair, production was 2,900 dozen.

tenance and repair. Since the strength of Akitoye lay in management, the specialists in engineering and labor training complemented his skills. Furthermore, the six Nigerian members of senior staff, quite capable in their specialties, were used rather effectively as an input into M.E. Akitoye's decision-making.

However, the firm had difficulty meeting its obligations to creditors in 1963, when expansion was too rapid, and in 1965, when the rapid expansion in investment was combined with the production stoppage caused by the unexpected prohibitive excise tax levy, and a financial crisis ensued.

Northern Leather Works

The Southeastern Shoe Company and the Northern Leather Works are the only two indigenous firms among five producers in Nigeria with *assets* of at least £N30,000 in leather footwear manufacturing plant and equipment. Among the five firms in Nigeria with assets of at least £N30,000 in rubber and/or rubber-canvas footwear manufacturing, two, Southeastern and Midwestern, are indigenous.[8]

Although thirty Northern traders had each contributed a fraction of the initial equity capital of £N48,000, the major impetus for the establishment of Northern came from Alhaji N.R. Shetima, a top administrative officer in the Native Authority for over twenty years.[9] Sources of initial loan capital were a regional statutory development corporation, Northern Nigeria Development Corporation (N.N.D.C.), with £N100,000, and the Federal Loans Board, with £N50,000. Alhaji Shetima, chairman of the board of directors and chief formulator of general policies, hired as general manager (in charge of day-to-day operations) a Greek-Cypriot, who had been manager of a long-established Lebanese retail store in Lagos; a production manager from a German firm supplying the machines; and a chief engineer who had been a

---

8. Two firms, Southeastern and Ikeja Manufacturing, had assets of at least £N30,000 in both leather footwear manufacturing, on the one hand, and rubber and rubber-canvas footwear manufacturing, on the other hand.

9. The Native Authorities, the local governmental units in the North until 1968, were developed by the British on the basis of the pre-colonial political system. Richard L. Sklar, *Nigerian Political Parties: Power in an Emergent African Nation* (Princeton, N.J.: Princeton University Press, 1963), pp. 26-7.

skilled industrial worker in Greece.

An audit demanded by the firm's major creditor, N.N.D.C., in July 1964, revealed a loss of £N56,000 for the first fiscal year. Immediately following the audit, N.N.D.C. exercised its option to convert £N50,000 bonds to stocks. The first decision of N.N.D.C., the majority shareholder, was to close the firm for the four months following August 1964.

In the last quarter of 1964, the statutory corporation made several changes in the firm's entrepreneurial and managerial structure. Alhaji Shetima was relieved of his entrepreneurial responsibility and his position on the board, while N.N.D.C.'s director of operations, an Englishman, conducted the over-all policy-making. This director delegated much of the responsibility for day-to-day management to another Englishman, an accountant with the development corporation. In early 1965, the general manager, whose influence was waning, resigned; the engineer followed suit. N.N.D.C.'s accountant, though not working full-time, became in effect the acting general manager. By November 1965, it became clear to the principals of Northern, which recorded losses of over 100 percent in both 1964 and 1965, that further reorganization of the capital structure of the firm would be necessary to avert liquidation.

A highly-placed official in N.N.D.C. contended that the initial entrepreneurs (namely, the shareholders) lacked an awareness of the intricate planning and timing involved in bringing together managers, supervisors, laborers, materials and machines to manufacture a commodity; as a result of this misconception, Alhaji Shetima and his colleagues had little notion of minimal qualifications for management officials. Secondly, the entrepreneurs did not comprehend the market research, sales effort and organization demanded in order to sell even 25 percent of the estimated capacity output of 1,000 pairs per day. Thirdly, it seemed unlikely that they were aware of the long gestation period investment in manufacturing required.

A review of the major errors of the early principals of the firm tends to reinforce the N.N.D.C. official's view that they were cognizant with few of the minimal requirements for managing a large manufacturing enterprise. The three top management and technical personnel had been hired on the basis of recommendations by machinery suppliers and the manager of a chain of Lebanese retail shops in Nigeria. The general manager had had no experience or training related to an initial venture in manufacturing; the chief engineer had never held a managerial, supervisory or engineering position, and finally, the German production manager, though perhaps competent, lacked the ability to communicate in either of the two major languages in the North, English or Hausa.[10] It seems clear, therefore, that the principals were far from efficient in their appraisal of personnel recommended for management positions.

Also, records of cost and revenue were meager. The acting general manager-accountant in 1965 claimed that, on the basis of the scanty records, the management in 1963-64 was under the impression that revenue exceeded operating costs. The audit in July 1964, however, revealed that operating cost had exceeded revenue by over £N1 for each pair of shoes produced. Furthermore, there is little evidence of marketing research prior to the establishment of the firm. It was not until a backlog of unsold footwear had accumulated that the firm attempted to organize a network of salesmen, agencies and supply depots. Finally, nepotism and favoritism in hiring proved to be a barrier to labor discipline and effectiveness. A 1965 management official complained that a member of the office staff, a close relative of Alhaji Shetima, could not be dismissed, despite evidence of his fraud and incompetence.

The establishment of the Northern company depended upon a title to the land granted by the Northern Ministry of Land and Survey, which routinely allowed the Northern Ministry of Trade and Industry to veto such titles where prospective manufacturing firms were involved. But, in spite of the views of some officials that the firm was ill-conceived, its establishment was permitted by the N.N.D.C. and the Northern economic ministries.

Restraint by the N.N.D.C. could have sharply curtailed Northern's initial access to capital, since the Federal Loans Board loan of £N50,000 was made contingent on the N.N.D.C. loan of £N100,000. This £N150,000 comprised about three-fourths of the initial loan and equity capital of the business.

Officials in the ministries and statutory corporation, subject to potential political pressures of Northern's initial entrepreneurs,[11] did not impose conditions upon the existence of

---

10. Finally, a 1965 management official reported that there were major personality conflicts between the general manager and engineer, on the one hand, and the production manager, on the other.

11. Henry L. Bretton, *Power and Stability in Nigeria* (New York: Frederick A. Praeger, 1962), p. 87, states that, "Nigerian politicians expect the bureaucracy to be a tool in the pow-

the business, even though the firm failed to obtain adequate management and technical expertness. The positions of foreign staff in statutory corporations were especially politically vulnerable. On the other hand, Nigerian civil servants faced uncertainties concerning promotion in position and rank, and perhaps even tenure. Thus officials had an incentive to acquiesce to the wishes of the oligarchy of ministers, politicians, legislators, indigenous rulers and administrators, and superiors in the government service in the North.

One of the top officials of the N.N.D.C. indicated that the process of loaning to Northern Shoe had parallels with others establishing manufacturing enterprises who also held political power in the North. In essence, the N.N.D.C. officers' remarks were as follows:

> Many N.N.D.C. industrial loan applicants have no concept of how a large manufacturing enterprise should be run. Yet if, as in the case of the Northern Leather Works, the applicants have political power, they are able to procure loans from the N.N.D.C. Few of these applicants comprehend the returns necessary to make a profit while the loan is being paid off. Many never even expect to have to pay back the loan.
>
> There is little that we can do to impose business-like standards, until the firm is close to bankruptcy. Even at that stage, there will still be pressure in the regional government for N.N.D.C. to "bail the firm out." But at least the principals of the firm are likely to be sufficiently embarrassed, so that conditions can be imposed that were politically unfeasible before. In return for our assistance, we can demand control of the firm. Among other things, we can require the business to obtain the proper managerial and technical personnel.
>
> One can understand why we continue in our practice

---

er processes, including those outside the limits of legality, propriety, and legitimacy. . . . The bureaucracy is expected to be instrumental - or, at least, not to be an obstacle - in the acquisition of individual power or of group power. Objectivity or impartiality by the bureaucracy in the power processes is not appreciated under those circumstances."

See also Eme O. Awa, *Federal Government in Nigeria* (Berkeley and Los Angeles: University of California Press, 1964), p. 166; and Sklar, *Nigerian Political Parties*, pp. 497-8.

> of approving loans to firms that have little chance of being viable. We can only hope that in time Northern Nigerians in positions of leadership, including our colleagues in the N.N.D.C., will be able to grasp what some of the requirements of modern manufacturing are.[12]

Southeastern Shoe Company

Although the rate of loss of Southeastern Shoe Company exceeded 50 percent in 1964, the date of initial operation, and 1965, the 1965 value of output of the firm exceeded all other indigenous footwear establishments in Nigeria. According to Jerome N. Afuba, the firm produced 83,000 pairs of shoes and boots in 1965, compared to a capacity output per annum, assuming two eight-hour shifts for 175 days, of 210,000 pairs.[13] Philip C. Packard, on the basis of Afuba's figures, indicates that the firm would still have lost even if capacity output had been reached.[14]

After the Eastern Ministry of Commerce originated the idea for the firm, the Eastern Nigeria Development Corporation (E.N.D.C.), a development corporation responsible to the Ministry, was enlisted to provide 80 percent of the initial £N120,000 share capital and four of the six directors. Arrangements were made for a European shoe firm to contribute technical and managerial expertness, in addition to supplying the remainder of the equity capital and directors.

One important choice made by the initial entrepreneurs of the firm, personnel in the E.N.D.C. and the Ministry, was the decision of plant location. This location proved to have almost no economic advantage over Eastern cities like Aba, Port Harcourt and Onitsha. There were major local market places in the three other Eastern cities, while the market in the city of the firm was small.[15] In the East, the port of entry for machinery and

---

12. See also "Politics in Development," *West Africa*, No. 2581 (19 November 1966), p. 1315, and No. 2582 (26 November 1966), p. 1360.

13. "A Feasibility Study of an Eastern Shoe Firm" (Economic Development Institute Working Paper No. 1, University of Nigeria, Enugu, March 1965), p. 8.

14. "The Need for Product Market Analysis: A Case Study of the Feasibility of Import Substitution in Nigeria," *Journal of Industrial Economics*, XVI, No. 1 (November 1967), 64-9.

15. Nigeria, Ministry of Commerce and Industry, *Handbook of Commerce and Industry in Nigeria* (Lagos, 1962), pp. 331-2,

materials has been Port Harcourt, with Aba being closer to the port than the city in question. The supply of water and electricity in the city was not adequate or regular, and the cost was high.[16] Finally, banking facilities were not available locally until several months after the business was established.

Afuba, a 1965 postgraduate fellow in economics at the University of Nigeria, who had formerly been personal secretary to the premier of the Eastern Region, argued that the major reasons for choosing the site were political instead of economic.

> The preponderate factor leading to the [location of] the firm would appear to be political. [Partly because of its population, the division where the firm is located has much political power.] Since [a petroleum producer] transferred its headquarters to Port Harcourt, there has been persistent agitation for an industry to fill the gap. The pressure from the community more than anything else contributed to the siting of the shoe firm.[17]

A major error made by the initial entrepreneurs was the poor coordination of high-level manpower. The primary problem was not the formal organizational structure (shown in figure 3, p. 138), which is quite common, but the actual working relationships between foreign and indigenous personnel, whose skills might have been expected to be complementary. None of the indigenous directors or managers had prior technical and managerial experience in footwear or industrial production. The foreigners were capable of providing skills which the firm needed in the early years, especially in production management; but they were not in a position to make judgments concerning the objectives of the firm. In addition, they were unfamiliar with the local *modus operandi* between labor and management, and between producer and wholesale buyer.

The knowledge of the Nigerian managers might have been expected to make up for the deficiencies of the foreigners. Yet, although the foreign and indigenous managers were indispensable to each other, dissension occurred between them.

---

and Afuba, "A Feasibility Study," p. 3.

As indicated in chapter 9, the footwear distributive network centered in Onitsha.

16. Ibid. Information was also obtained from Nigeria, *Handbook of Commerce and Industry*, pp. 72, 74-5, 347.

17. Afuba, "A Feasibility Study," p. 3.

Independent sources report that the Nigerian management officials demanded the replacement of all foreign managerial officials in August 1965, at the time the European managing director departed from the firm. Frequently Nigerian lower management officials had the power to reverse the decisions of the foreign managing director and general manager.

The European general manager indicated his dissatisfaction

Figure 3

Managerial Organizational Chart of Southeastern Shoe Company

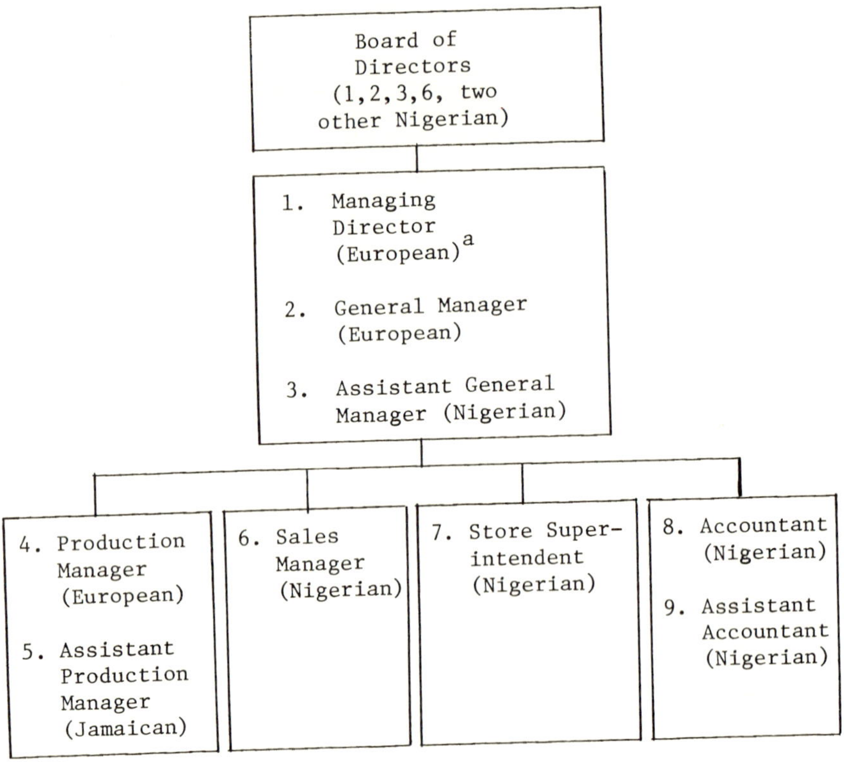

a. The managing director left his management position in August 1965. His position was left vacant. According to the organizational chart, the general manager then assumed the top management position.

with the Nigerian staff members in the following words:

> The Nigerians [in management] had little experience in business. They had no experience in shoes. We had to train them ourselves. . . .
>
> We had little to say about the people we have here [in management positions]. Politics has been very important. We had to use the people they [Eastern government officials] wanted us to use. It would have been better if we had chosen them [the Nigerian managers]. If we could "sack" the people we have and employ different ones, we'd be better off.
>
> . . . We cannot let the Nigerians make the decision. . . . [In fact, often] they cannot even follow orders.

The disaccord stemmed largely from the deficiency in the *de facto* organization of management in the firm, a deficiency which contributed to the inefficiency of management and the poor record of the firm. As Frederick Harbison and Charles A. Myers state, "The efficiency of management as a resource is related not only to the individuals within the hierarchy but also to the system of authority which binds them together. The methods of leadership, the structure of organization, and art of delegation of authority are crucial to successful industrial development."[18] Responsibility at Southeastern was not well-defined, and the system of decision-making was not structured to bring together and utilize the particular specialties of the foreign and Nigerian groups within the management organization.

Four of the six directors of the firm represented E.N.D.C. One of its directors, Mr. S.E. Dindu, who was also sales manager, was the major decision-maker within the management hierarchy. Although, as a member of the board, he would be expected to have a voice in the making of general policy, his role relative to the managing director and general manager should have been more explicitly delineated. This is especially true in technical matters, where Mr. Dindu had little competence. Essentially, technical expertness as an input into decision-making in Southeastern was little better than in Northern, where technical personnel were lacking.

---

18. *Management in the Industrial World: An International Analysis* (New York: McGraw-Hill Book Company, Inc., 1959), p. 47.

Midwestern Manufacturing Company

In all three years of its operation, Midwestern Manufacturing, a rubber footwear firm, incurred losses. Value of output rose from £N63,000 (adjusted to an annual rate) in 1963 to £N210,000 in 1964, but dropped substantially in 1965 due to problems arising from plant reorganization.

For Mr. M.W. Ejor, a Nigerian who had founded a rubber export firm in 1948 and an enterprise to process sheet and crepe rubber in 1958, the establishment of Midwestern was merely a further step in the vertical growth of his enterprises. His other business interests included four private schools, a cement enterprise and a plastics manufacturing firm. In addition to his wide experience in entrepreneurial positions, Mr. Ejor had had fourteen years' experience in management positions with a foreign footwear firm. While in the employ of this firm, he spent four years studying business administration in Europe, but had little chance to get acquainted with the technology of footwear production.

In 1964, a holding company dominated by M.W. Ejor increased its shareholdings in the firm from 60 percent to 100 percent. The six top management posts (except for Ejor and the personnel manager) were filled by foreigners. Turnover of senior staff personnel was rapid, with three people holding the top day-to-day management position of general manager in three years.

The major reason for the drop in sales in 1965 was that a number of shoe traders stopped purchasing Midwestern's shoes, because of complaints from consumers as to their lack of durability. This was thought to have resulted from the poor quality of rubber used. Ironically, the major inducement for establishing the footwear firm had been the economies expected from the rubber procured at Mr. Ejor's nearby processing plant.

Unlike Alhaji Shetima, Mr. Ejor was aware, to a certain extent, of his own technical inadequacies, and of the personnel required in the firm to compensate for this. He also understood, to a greater extent than the officials who established Southeastern, the need to utilize the skills of subordinate technicians and managers. Although from the beginning, Midwestern acquired skills from two production managers and an engineer from abroad, it is evident that Mr. Ejor was still not satisfied that the technical gap was being filled. The discussion of these technical problems serves to underscore the nature of the scarcity of both foreign and indigenous high-level manpower (see chapter 3).

It should be mentioned that Mr. Ejor had a dual role as a

leading entrepreneur and as a member of the Federal Council of Ministers, where he was a major economic policy-maker, with substantial influence on excise tax, tariff, pioneer company and other measures. Footwear manufacturers - especially those of plastic shoes and leather sandals - complained that differential excise tax levies in the middle of 1965 favored Midwestern. As the appendix to this chapter demonstrates, the excise duty indeed bore much less heavily on Midwestern and other rubber-canvas footwear producers than on plastic footwear and leather sandal manufacturers.

Small Firms

This section presents synopses of four small firms, including two in the East, the region with the largest value of output of indigenous footwear firms. Particular emphasis is placed on firms in Onitsha, the largest entrepôt in West Africa, and Aba, both of which are noted for their very large indigenous open-air market places.[19] The Ibo footwear distributive system (see chapter 9), the largest one in Nigeria, centered in the Onitsha and Aba markets, and handled mostly leather and rubber sandals made primarily in the East, and especially in Onitsha and Aba. The three footwear firms with 25-99 employed and over 20 of the estimated 32 firms with an employment of 10-24 in the East were Onitsha and Aba sandal producers (see table 5.1).

Central Shoe Firm (Aba)[20]

Central, which is somewhat representative of Eastern footwear firms with 6-10 workers employed, has, like most firms of its size, never kept records.[21] Interviews indicate that the firm has, since its beginnings in 1945, remained close to the margin of survival with a long run rate of profit close to zero. The author estimates that average net worth in 1965 was £N400, value of output - £N550, and the average employment - eight.

The entrepreneur, Mr. C.N. Ekenta, completed six years in

19. P.T. Bauer, *West African Trade* (London: Routledge & Kegan Paul Ltd., 1963), p. 29. According to Nigeria, *Handbook of Commerce and Industry*, pp. 331-2, Onitsha and Aba had two of the eleven "very large" indigenous open-air markets in Nigeria.

20. The firm is not a part of the sample.

21. Peter Kilby estimated that no more than 10 percent of the East's small manufacturing firms had minimally adequate bookkeeping systems. *The Development of Small Industries in Eastern Nigeria* (Enugu: Eastern Ministry of Information, 1963), p. 15.

primary school in the East, but did not receive his school-leaving certificate. In 1941, at the age of fourteen, Ekenta, like most other Ibos learning the shoemaking trade at that time, left the East to become an apprentice to a Hausa shoemaker in the North, since there were very few skilled shoemakers outside Hausaland.[22] At that time, there were only about 15 shoemakers in Aba compared with more than 400 in 1961.[23]

In 1944, after completing his apprenticeship in Kaduna, Mr. Ekenta opened a shoe repair business in the *Sabon Gari* district[24] of the Northern city. Two years later he moved to Aba, where he began producing sandals and doing repairs. Without additional formal training, he was able to produce a close imitation of the imported styles popular in the south, although consumer tastes differed from those in the North.

In 1946, when the enterprise was established in Aba, the entrepreneur had five apprentices, two journeymen, one clerk, and no machines. The work space consisted of an eight by twelve foot shop in the entrepreneur's house, together with sixteen square feet available in an open-air annex with a corrugated metal roof.

There were still eight persons employed in the firm in 1965 - the entrepreneur, four apprentices, one journeyman and two clerks. They were working in a fifteen by twenty-five foot shop that the firm had been renting for the past three years. The only machines in use were three sewing machines, which had been purchased by the entrepreneur in the past six years.

The volume of manufactured output of the firm in 1965 was about double that of 1946, while repair output had probably not changed in nineteen years. Manufacturing and repair output each comprised about one-half of the total value of output of the firm. Virtually all production was sold directly to the final consumer.

---

22. This was verified by G.U. Alisigwe, postgraduate fellow in economics at the Economic Development Institute, University of Nigeria, Enugu.

In 1965, the communal group with the largest number of skilled shoemakers was the Ibo.

23. The 1941 figure was based on interviews with Mr. C.N. Ekenta and another Aba shoemaker. Kilby, *The Development of Small Industries*, p. 15, was the source for the 1961 figure.

24. This was the area in Northern Hausa-Fulani cities set aside for the residence of "aliens" from southern Nigeria.

Other than the adaptation of design to southern tastes in 1946 and the shift in sewing from manual to machine techniques, there have been few improvements or changes in product design, organization or technology in the firm. Without the rapid long run increase in the demand for Nigerian-produced footwear, the firm would have probably incurred a long-run loss, and been forced to close down.

Onitsha Shoe Company

Onitsha ranked first among small footwear firms and fifth among all indigenous footwear firms in Nigerian in 1964 value of output (see table 6.1). Before the 1964/65 fiscal year, the rate of profit was high - probably averaging well above the 13 percent rate of profit in 1964.[25] In 1964/65, the firm suffered a high rate of loss, due largely to the fact that it was among three of an estimated 600 Eastern urban leather sandal producers subject to the steep excise tax levy.[26] If the 1965 excise tax had not been levied, Onitsha would have had a rate of profit comparable to that of 1963/64.

From the establishment of the firm in 1954 to 1963, the annual value of output increased about 400 percent, or at a relatively rapid rate of 16 percent per annum. If the two years following the early 1964 merger of another Onitsha firm with the Onitsha Shoe Company are included, output has increased 1,400 percent since the founding of the firm, or at a rate of 28 percent per annum.

Before the initial proprietor, Mr. O.N. Ozomeie, a primary graduate, established the firm, his only experience in business had been three years training as an apprentice with an Enugu supervisor. The rapid growth of the firm required that the plant, initially an eight by twelve foot shop, be enlarged twice

---

25. Despite the excise tax of two shillings per unit levied on leather sandals selling for ten shillings during one-third of the 1964 fiscal year, the rate of the firm was 13 percent.

Although the firm kept no record before 1963, the fact that the enterprise was able to expand rapidly on the basis of reinvested earnings and the fact that twelve persons were fully supported on income received by the entrepreneur from footwear indicate that profits were high.

26. A Federal government document was the source for the list of exciseable footwear firms in 1965.

and finally replaced in 1963 by a twenty-eight by seventy-two foot factory at a new site.

The major reasons for the rapid growth of the firm were the development of a good reputation with wholesale buyers, the utilization of technical assistance from the Industrial Development Centre in Owerri, and the high rate of business saving. For example, in 1964 all (business) profits were reinvested, except for £N15 per month to support twelve dependents.

Like many small sandal firms, Onitsha initially sold all its output directly to final consumers. However, firms selling at retail encountered an upper sales limit of about forty pairs per week. In order to grow beyond this sales level, and take advantage of economies of scale from the use of specialized labor and machinery, and a routinized assembly line, it was essential that a producer develop a steady wholesale market. This threshold, dependent partly upon the cost of time and travel of the wholesale distributor, was reached at about seventy-five pairs of sandals per week. The gap between the maximum level of retail sandal sales and the threshold level of wholesale sandal sales of the firm frequently corresponded to a discontinuity in the supply of technique and capital stock. Small firms encountered difficulties in insuring that the requisite development of wholesale marketing channels and the necessary creation of productive capacity were synchronized properly.

Because of the good reputation of its product with Onitsha shoe merchants, the Onitsha Shoe Company was able to attract additional wholesale buyers to correspond with the expansion of its productive capacity. The firm had several factors in its favor in attracting marketing outlets: the high quality of design of the product, the proximity of the firm to major commercial markets, the personality and selling techniques of the entrepreneur, and his connections with merchants.

By 1963, Onitsha had reached the point where further expansion necessitated technical and managerial training beyond the apprentice training Mr. Ozomeie had received. Additional expansion required that management change from direct supervision of the production process to a coordination of a relatively complex arrangement of factors of production. Ozomeie received technical assistance from the Industrial Development Centre (I.D.C.) in Owerri, where the footwear training program corresponded closely to the model for post-apprentice training indicated in chapter 10. The footwear specialist at the I.D.C. advised on machinery procurement, assisted in ordering machines, helped in designing production lines, gave technical assistance on machine repairing and maintenance, and counselled on management problems. Without the improvement in the managerial and technical input arising from I.D.C. assistance, Onitsha, like the Market City, Aba and Royal footwear firms in the sample, would not have been able to expand profitably beyond the 1963 level of output of the firm.[27]

Western Shoe Firm (Ibadan)

Ibadan ranked second in the Federation in the value of total sales in the open-air market places,[28] which have been major centers for the sale of footwear. However, since most imports of footwear entered through Lagos, and over one-half of the domestic output of footwear originated in the Lagos metropolitan area, it was difficult for small footwear firms in southwestern Nigeria to compete. Ibadan, for example, had only two footwear firms with a 1964 value of output over £N900.

Western Shoe, the largest footwear firm in Ibadan, was established in Lagos in 1953 by Mr. W.N. Akintoya, a former apprentice engineer, army officer and school clerk who had completed four years of secondary school. After Nigeria was federated in 1954, there was a major influx of civil servants and government officials into Ibadan, the capital of the newly formed Western Region. Mr. Akintoya, who perceived that the influx meant an increase in the potential shoe consumers, transferred his firm to the Western capital city in 1956. From that year through 1963, Western Shoe was the largest footwear producer in the city. However, the value of footwear output of the firm has declined steadily from about £N2,500 in 1957 to about £N1,020 in 1965, and this has only been partially offset by increases in the output of auxiliary goods.

In the early and middle 1950s, most of the sales of the firm were individual orders by consumers outside the Lagos-Western-Mid-Western area. Even though Mr. Akintoya was himself a superb craftsman, the brisk demand for his products throughout

---

27. The annual expansion of the Onitsha, Market City, Aba, and Royal firms from 1963 to 1965 was about 77, 62, 93 and 89 percent respectively compared to about 28, 62, 22 and 26 respectively from the initial year to 1965.

The success of the entrepreneurs of these four firms is not discredited by the crucial role of the I.D.C. shoe expert, since the ability to be able to utilize services and resources available to the firm is to the credit of the entrepreneur.

28. See Nigeria, *Handbook of Commerce and Industry*, pp. 333-4.

the Federation probably stemmed largely from the long reputation of his father for shoe craftsmanship. However, by the late 1950s, the increased competition by footwear firms with mass production techniques and wholesale marketing outlets curtailed the sales of Western Shoe. Relatively high-quality shoes and sandals could be produced and distributed in Nigeria at a rather low cost. Thus, in 1965, only 5 to 10 percent of the firm's sales were outside the Lagos-Western-Mid-Western area. The individual consumer outside the Western Region, who in 1956 might have ordered a pair of shoes from Western Shoe, found in 1965 that, because of the rapid rise in domestic production, a satisfactory pair could be purchased at a lower price in his own region.

Western Shoe's fall in output was due largely to the failure of the entrepreneur to develop wholesale marketing channels in the face of a new competitive situation. Although the firm had the capacity to produce the rate of output necessary to meet the threshold level essential to sell in volume to merchants, Akintoya did not sell to wholesale buyers for several reasons. First, wholesale distributors could frequently buy only on credit, which he was reluctant to extend.[29] Secondly, he may have feared that the craftsmanship learned from his father would be sacrificed for greater volume of output. Finally, Akintoya probably did not fully comprehend the change in supply factors in the industry that placed the craftsman selling at retail in a poor competitive position. He still maintained, "A good product needs no promotion. The design of my work serves as an advertisement." However, despite his economic decline, Mr. Akintoya apparently received a satisfaction from his work that few other Nigerian businessmen attained.

Maiduguri Shoe Firm

Maiduguri Shoe Firm is the fourth largest footwear producer in the North, and the largest footwear producer among firms with less than £N5,000 net worth in the region. The firm was established in 1947, closed in the second half of 1955 when the entrepreneur went to England for training, and reopened in late 1957, shortly after his return. The author estimates that the annual rate of production before 1955 ranged from one-half to two-thirds of 1958 production, with rates of profits modest, if above zero. After 1958, profit rates were high and the output of the firm grew steadily.

---

29. See chapter 9 for a discussion of the role of credit extension in the expansion of a firm.

A major factor explaining the success of the entrepreneur since 1958 was the training he received on a government scholarship in England in 1955-57 at a cordwainers' college. Mallam M.D. Sanusi, the entrepreneur, insisted that the college itself was of practically no value to him because of its lack of relevance for the Nigerian small industrial sector, but that his extracurricular training and experience as an unpaid learner in a London shoe factory was of considerable value. At this factory, Sanusi received practical training on the operation, maintenance and repair of machines, and was even allowed to assemble and dismantle machines.

This mechanical and technical ability, which is scarce in Nigeria, is necessary to plan the purchase of machines, to organize and supervise a production line, and to evaluate the competence of applicants or employees in positions requiring mechanical ability. Yet in small enterprises like Maiduguri Shoe, the wage of a *hired* mechanic would probably exceed his productivity.

In addition to his technical competence, M.D. Sanusi was also a competent manager and diligent worker. In many shoe firms the size of Maiduguri Shoe, bottlenecks developed when the majority of the labor force had to wait to last and assemble the shoes while the initial steps of cutting and fitting were finished by the one or two skilled operators. In this firm, the proprietor tried to determine in the evening whether enough cutting and fitting had been prepared to utilize all workers fully at the beginning of the following day. If enough had not been prepared, the entrepreneur undertook this himself.

As indicated in chapter 9, a major weakness of the firm was the failure to develop any wholesale outlets.

Conclusion

In large firms, the lack of technical and managerial experience by the entrepreneurs stands out as a major barrier to success. One of the chief costs of inadequate experience was the initiating entrepreneurs' inability to select personnel who could direct and manage the firm after its establishment.

An important problem for many large firms, especially parastal enterprises like Southeastern Shoe, was the coordination of foreign and Nigerian managerial resources. A.H. Hansen's charge that statutory corporations frequently fail to utilize foreign personnel was still valid in the early 1960s. Indigenous board members lacking technical knowledge about the industry often place undue restrictions on the day-to-day authority and administration of competent foreign managing directors or general managers. In other cases, foreign managers may be incompetent, in part as a result of recruitment "in a hole-and-corner fashion by Board Chairmen on their trips to Europe . . . of people to whom European firms would not have assigned very responsible positions."[30] Chapter 10 discusses possible policies for enhancing the quality of foreign personnel obtained.

All the large firms with a rate of loss exceeding 25 percent built plants with a capacity output far in excess of profitable sales value. In the cases of Northern and Southeastern, the excess capacity resulted from the fact that the initial entrepreneurs were unaware of the marketing research and organization necessary to sell footwear in volume. Finally, the surveys of Midwestern, Southeastern and Northern and the analysis in the appendix to this chapter suggest how important the role of political power may be in determining factors such as the tax rate and access to capital by the firm.

Success among small entrepreneurs depended partly on the ability of the entrepreneur to acquire wholesale buyers. Since economies of scale accrued to firms with a sandal output which exceeded the lower limit for selling wholesale, firms with regular wholesale outlets were more likely to be profitable than firms selling at retail. Six of the eight sample small sandal firms with a positive rate of profit sold most of their footwear wholesale in 1965, while only one of the five sample small sandal firms with a negative rate of profit did so.

A number of points alluded to in the analysis of individual firms are discussed in subsequent chapters from the perspective of the industry as a whole.

---

30. Hansen, "Public Enterprise in Nigeria," *Public Administration*, XXXV (Winter 1958), 375, and XXXVI (Spring 1959), 37.

Appendix: The Impact of Differential Excise Levies in 1965 on Sample Firms

Generally an entrepreneur with access to political power benefited his firm, even though it was neither necessary nor sufficient for business success. This political strength could be used to facilitate the acquisition of capital from public agencies; the procurement of pioneer status, land titles and rent permits; and, as indicated subsequently, the eliciting of favorable tax legislation.

A number of footwear entrepreneurs complained that the profits of their firms were hampered by the discriminatory use of political power by entrepreneurs also in government. One such complaint was that differential excise levies in the middle of 1965 favored Midwestern, the rubber footwear firm of a federal cabinet minister. A concept crucial to an examination of this charge is λ, the ratio of excise tax per pair (April-August 1965) to the average ex factory price per pair (immediately prior to April 1965)[31] (see table 6.3, p. 150, for excise tax rates.) λ was about 1s/5s or 20 percent for rubber and/or canvas footwear. The ratio for low-quality leather sandals, a close competitor of rubber-canvas footwear, stood at about 3s/7s or 43 percent. For another competitor to rubber-canvas footwear, plastic footwear, λ was near 3s/5s or 60 percent.

What would the long run general equilibrium effect of this structure of excise duties have been? There would have been a shift from the consumption of plastic footwear and leather sandals to that of rubber-canvas footwear of excisable firms, and footwear repairs and leather footwear produced by non-excisable (i.e. very small) footwear firms. All plastic footwear producers and most leather sandal producers would have had to close down. Rubber footwear producers, including Midwestern Manufacturing, would clearly have benefited from the steep tax on the competitors (plastic footwear and leather sandals), which in 1964 had accounted for 4.6 million of the 7.9 million pairs of footwear produced.[32]

---

31. The denominator of the ratio, based on pre-April ex factory prices, was not entirely independent of the (pre-April) level of excise taxes. Yet this fact does not change the rankings of the three types of footwear by their values of λ.

32. See table 6.2. Of course, the excise tax would not only have induced a substitute of rubber-canvas footwear for plastic footwear and leather sandals. It would also have led to

Table 6.3

Excise Duties on Footwear in Nigeria
1964-5 (per pair)

Type of Footwear	1 Jan. 1964- 8 Mar. 1964	9 Mar. 1964- 2 Aug. 1964	3 Aug. 1964- 31 Mar. 1965	1 Apr. 1965- 18 Aug. 1965	19 Aug. 1965- 31 Dec. 1965
Leather	0	2s[a]	3s	3s	0
Rubber and canvas	0	6d	1s	1s	0
Plastic	0	6d	1s	3s	0

a. 12d = 1s; 20s = £N1.

Sources: Joseph C. Miller, "Nigerian Tax Legislation: An Outline" (report to the Economic Development Institute, University of Nigeria, Enugu, 1965); and Nigeria, *Supplement to Official Gazette Extraordinary, L.N. 46*, Vol. LII, No. 29 (1 April 1965), B509-B510.

Because of the clear advantage of the structure of excise duties to Midwestern, its entrepreneur, Mr. M.W. Ejor, was accused by a number of legislators and entrepreneurs of using the power of his cabinet office to further the interests of his firm. Mr. Ejor's retort was that the purpose of the excise duties in footwear was to benefit rubber, produced in Nigeria, at the expense of an imported product, plastic.[33] However, if one considers the many alternative uses of rubber and plastic, a tariff would have more effectively achieved Mr. Ejor's stated purpose.

Regardless of the motivation for the structure of excise tax

---

a substitution of other commodities for footwear. This effect would have been disadvantageous to rubber-canvas producers. But this detrimental effect on rubber-canvas footwear manufacturers would have been more than countered by the substitution of rubber-canvas footwear for other footwear.

33. This is based on a quotation from Nigeria, House of Representatives, *Parliamentary Debates 1965*.

levies, it was clear that the fact that the levies benefited the footwear firm of Mr. Ejor undermined the confidence of footwear entrepreneurs in the soundness and fairness of government policy. The morale of both indigenous and foreign footwear entrepreneurs was impaired. Even more importantly, the frequent and substantial changes in excise duties made it difficult for entrepreneurs to plan investment projects and firm policy rationally.

Another inequity resulted from the fact that a large percentage of small footwear firms were not subject to any excise duty, since they were unknown to the Federal Board of Customs and Excise. Out of approximately 3,000 small urban footwear firms in Nigeria, only five paid an excise tax.[34] Thus firms like Market City with a 1965 output of £N10,500; Crossroads Shoe with an output of £N6,500; Aba Shoe with an output of £N6,300; Umuahia Shoe with an output of £N6,250; Federal Shoe with an output of £N5,800; and two Onitsha firms each with an output of around £N6,000, were not paying any excise tax. On the other hand, Maiduguri Shoe with an output of £N3,320 and Southern Shoe with an output of £N1,200 were forced to pay the duty.

On 18 August 1965, the excise tax was abolished.[35] What factors led to the repeal? Independent sources indicate that the principals of Southeastern Shoe and Northern Shoe had sufficient political power to bring some pressure to bear upon the leaders of N.N.A.-U.P.G.A. coalition. Others suggest that entrepreneurs of two Lebanese firms in the North had enough influence with leaders in the dominant party of the region, the Northern People's Congress, to be instrumental in bringing about a change in duty. Since other industries were affected by a significant rise in excise duties in April 1965, entrepreneurs in other industries, such as the singlet industry, may have joined with footwear entrepreneurs in pressing for a revision in the overall excise tax structure. Finally, some observers contend that government leaders were motivated by a fear that the concern of foreign advisors in the Federal Ministry of Commerce and Industry over the impact of the excise taxes on entrepreneurship would be conveyed to businesmen in the home country - resulting perhaps

---

34. Nigeria, Parliament, *Parliamentary Debates* (House of Representatives), Vol. XVIII, No. 10 (5 April 1965).

35. At the same time, import duties on shoe materials such as leather and rubber were increased. Nigeria, *Supplement to Official Gazette Extraordinary, L.N. 92*, Vol. LII, No. 65 (18 August 1965), B509. This ended the discrimination against firms on the Board of Customs and Excise list of excisable firms.

in a decrease in foreign investment. It is difficult to assess the validity of these conjectures, but observers generally agree that little influence was brought to bear on excise tax policy by the delegations from small footwear firms.

Chapter 7

The Origin and Background of the Entrepreneurs

Hypotheses on Entrepreneurship and Education

Theoretical studies on the economics of education[1] and empirical studies on entrepreneurship in less developed countries[2] indicate a higher level of education among entrepreneurs than for the population as a whole, and a direct relationship between the education of the entrepreneur and firm success. For Nigeria the following hypotheses are presented:

---

1. Burton A. Weisbrod, "Education and Investment in Human Capital," *Journal of Political Economy*, LXXX, No. 5, Part 2 (October 1962), 108; Mary Jean Bowman and C. Arnold Anderson, *Development of Emerging Countries: An Agenda for Research* (Washington, D.C.: The Brookings Institution, 1962), pp. 155-60; Neil J. Smelser and Seymour Martin Lipset, ed., *Social Structure and Mobility in Economic Development* (Chicago: Aldine Publishing Company, 1966), p. 34; Harvey Leibenstein, "Shortages and Surpluses in Education in Underdeveloped Countries: A Theoretical Foray," in *Education and Economic Development*, ed. by C. Arnold Anderson and Mary Jean Bowman (Chicago: Aldine Publishing Co., 1965), pp. 60-2; Frederick Harbison, "The Prime Movers of Innovation," in ibid., p. 231; Stephen Enke, *Economics for Development* (Englewood Cliffs, N.J.: Prentice-Hall, Inc., 1963), pp. 385-6; and Samuel Bowles, "The Efficient Allocation of Resources in Education," *Quarterly Journal of Economics*, LXXXI, No. 2 (May 1967), 189-219.

2. John J. Carroll, *The Filipino Manufacturing Entrepreneur* (Ithaca, N.Y.: Cornell University Press, 1965), pp. 106, 110-1; Alec P. Alexander, *Greek Industrialists* (Athens, Greece: Center of Planning and Economic Research, 1964), pp. 94-100; and Yusif A. Sayigh, *Entrepreneurs of Lebanon* (Cambridge, Mass.: Harvard University Press, 1962), pp. 55, 72.

1. The educational level of entrepreneurs will be higher than the educational level of the population as a whole.

2. The educational attainment of the entrepreneur will be positively related to the value of the firm's output.

3. The educational attainment of the entrepreneur will be positively related to the firm's rate of profit.

The three hypotheses seem very plausible. Persons with more education would be expected to have a larger body of knowledge available for making decisions. In addition, the verbal skills of the better educated person would assist him in acquiring new ideas and methods, corresponding and conversing in business relationships, and understanding instruction manuals and other routine written information. Finally, the mathematical ability of the entrepreneur with more education should facilitate the computation of transactions and the use of records as an instrument in firm analysis. Since some of the knowledge and skill acquired in school would be helpful in entrepreneurial activity, educational attainment would be expected to be positively related to entrepreneurial quantity and success.

However, some economists are beginning to question whether this direct relationship applies to Nigeria.[3] This section presents empirical evidence on relationships between entrepreneurial education and firm success in Nigeria and considers explanations for the relationships established.

Education and Entrepreneurial Quantity

An indication of the relationship between education and entrepreneurial quantity can be found by observing differences between the backgrounds of the entrepreneurs and the rest of the population. Since those exercising the entrepreneurial function form only a small minority of the population, educational characteristics of the rest of the population should approximate those of the population as a whole, for which data are available.

Educational attainment or level of education is measured by

---

3. Peter Kilby, *African Enterprise: The Nigerian Bread Industry* (Stanford, Calif.: Hoover Institution, 1965), pp. 92-7, and Gerald K. Helleiner, *Peasant Agriculture, Government and Economic Growth in Nigeria* (Homewood, Ill.: Richard D. Irwin, 1966), pp. 39-40, 144, 307-10.

the number of years of formal education successfully completed.[4] The educational level of sample entrepreneurs, which averages 7.1 years, was far above the educational level of the general population in Nigeria. Statistics on age structure and education[5] and figures on enrollment rates[6] indicate that around 1964-65 no more than 25 percent of the population (seven years of age or older) had a minimum of four years of schooling. Twenty-two of the twenty-five sample entrepreneurs - or 88 percent - had at least four years at school.

The relatively high educational attainment of major entrepreneurs in the sample can be seen more clearly if they are classified by age group and geographical area. The primary enrollment rate[7] in the south was about 18 percent in 1947.[8] All of the seventeen southern sample entrepreneurs, however, age nine in 1947 or before, attended[9] some primary school, and average 7.3 years of education. In the North, the primary enrollment rate in 1947 was about 2 percent.[10] However, two of the three Northern sample entrepreneurs who were nine years of age in 1947 or before attended some primary school.[11] The average number of years of education for the three Northern entrepreneurs is 6.3.[12]

---

4. For Elementary VI, Form V (11 years of education) and Upper Form VI (13 years of education), successful completion implies the earning of a certificate.

5. Nigeria, Office of Statistics, *Annual Abstract of Statistics, 1964* (Lagos, 1965), pp. 13-4.

6. Peter Kilby, "Technical Education in Nigeria," *Bulletin of the Oxford University Institute of Economics and Statistics*, XXVI (May 1964), 182; and Nigeria, Office of Statistics, *Annual Abstract of Statistics, 1963* (Lagos, August 1963), p. 25.

7. To be more precise, the primary enrollment rate is primary school enrollment divided by the population in the age group, 6-12.

8. Gerald K. Helleiner, *Peasant Agriculture, Government and Economic Growth in Nigeria* (Homewood, Ill.: Richard D. Irwin, Inc., 1966), pp. 305-6.

9. Southern entrepreneurs are those in southern firms. All of the seventeen attended southern primary schools. There are twenty-two southern entrepreneurs in the sample.

10. Helleiner, *Peasant Agriculture, Government and Economic Growth*, pp. 205-6.

11. Both Northern sample entrepreneurs attended Northern primary schools.

12. Since educated businessmen are more likely to keep records, the sample may contain a disproportionate number of edu-

These findings, together with the results of Peter Kilby[13] and John R. Harris,[14] indicate that the average educational attainment of Nigerian entrepreneurs in firms with eight or more employed is more than that of the population at large.

If entrepreneurs from smaller firms are included in a sample, the differences between the average educational attainment of Nigerian entrepreneurs and the population at large diminish. Archibald Callaway's study of 5,135 small indigenous industrial firms in Ibadan, most with an employment of less than ten, indicates that only 36 percent of the entrepreneurs had some primary education[15] compared to about 30-35 percent of the population of the Western Region with the same age distribution.[16]

If entrepreneurs from firms with less than eight employed are included in a sample, the educational level of Nigerian entrepreneurs may not be greater than the population at large. For example, in the footwear industry, over 95 percent of urban entrepreneurs were in firms with an employment of five or less. In addition, rural firms, which virtually all have less than five persons working, outnumber urban firms by over four to one.[17] A

---

cated entrepreneurs. Nevertheless, the findings indicate that even if the extreme assumption were made that none of the non-sample entrepreneurs of the statistical universe of forty-one firms had attended primary school, the percentage of entrepreneurs from the universe who have attended primary school would be higher than the percentage for the population at large.

13. Twenty-four of the forty-five entrepreneurs in the Kilby study completed primary school while an additional eleven had some primary education. The firms are about the same size as those in this study. *African Enterprise*, p. 94.

14. Harris, in a study of the sawmilling, furniture, printing, rubber-processing and garment-making industries, found that 234 of 268 entrepreneurs (87 percent) had attended primary school. The average size of the firms in the Harris sample exceeds the size of the firms in this study. "Industrial Entrepreneurship in Nigeria" (unpublished Ph.D. dissertation, Northwestern University, 1967), p. 270.

15. "From Traditional Crafts to Modern Industries," *Odu: University of Ife Journal of African Studies*, II, No. 1 (July 1965), 36.

16. Kilby, *Oxford Bulletin*, XXVI, 182; Nigeria, *Annual Abstract, 1964*, pp. 12, 14; Helleiner, *Peasant Agriculture, Government and Economic Growth*, pp. 305-6; and Callaway, *Odu*, II, No. 1, 36.

17. See tables 5.1-5.3.

large proportion of entrepreneurs from firms with less than eight workers employed had no formal education.[18] In most industries, like the footwear industry, a very large percentage of the firms had an employment of less than eight. If entrepreneurs from all sizes of industrial firms are considered, it seems very likely that the average education of entrepreneurs was no higher than that of the population in general.

Education is positively correlated with the quantity of entrepreneurs, when those in firms with no more than eight employed are considered. However, if the definition of entrepreneurs is broadened to include those in firms with an employment of less than eight, there is probably no relationship between education and entrepreneurial quantity.

Education and Firm Output

There is a positive relationship between entrepreneurial education and the value of output of the firm (see table 7.1).[19]

Table 7.1

The Relationship between Entrepreneurial Education and the Value of Output of the Firm

Size Class (by value of output of the firm)	Number of Firms	Average Level of Education of the Entrepreneur (in number of years completed)
£N20,000 or more	4	10.5
£N10,000-19,999	2	6.0
£N5,000-9,999	4	8.8
£N2,500-4,999	5	6.0
£N1,000-2,499	7	5.6
£N999 or less	3	6.7
TOTAL	25	7.1

18. See "Does 'Universal' Education Work?" *West Africa*, No. 2647 (24 February 1968), pp. 225-6.

19. If X equals the number of years of formal education of

Entrepreneurs in large complex firms need the ability to communicate in writing within and outside the firm, the possibilities of obtaining access to new ideas and developments through reading and other forms of communication, and the ability to make computations for management control and firm analysis. Large complex firms usually acquire entrepreneurs with some secondary education; firms with entrepreneurs lacking in education are limited in the growth of complexity of the firm.

Education and Profit Rate of the Firm

There is a significant negative relationship between entrepreneurial education and profit rate among the eighteen sample firms with data on profit rate (see table 7.2, p. 159).[20]

It has often been suggested that primary education in Ni-

---

the entrepreneur and Y the 1965 value of output (in pounds), Y = -101,596 + 35,232X. If the *t*-test is used, the regression coefficient is significant at the 5 percent level (t = 2.32).

This finding is reinforced by two other studies of Nigerian firms where there is a wide dispersion of firm size. Harris, "Industrial Entrepreneurship," pp. 270-1, and Theodore Geiger and Winifred Armstrong, *The Development of African Private Enterprise* (Washington, D.C.: National Planning Association, 1964), p. 130. The sample of Geiger and Armstrong consists of sixty-four Lagos entrepreneurs in manufacturing, construction, trading, transportation and services.

20. If X indicates the number of years of formal education of the entrepreneur and Y the 1964 percentage rate of profit, Y = 69.8 - 9.5X. If the *t*-test is used, the regression coefficient is significant at the ½ percent level (t = 3.21).

The negative relationship does not result from a situation where older more-experienced entrepreneurs, with less opportunity for education, are more successful than younger entrepreneurs. If X is the age of the entrepreneur and Y his years of formal education, Y = 2.93 + 0.12X. The regression coefficient is not significant at the 5 percent level (t = 0.17).

Unlike the findings of Kilby, *African Enterprise*, pp. 92-7, there is no tendency for better educated entrepreneurs in the sample to be engaged in more entrepreneurial activities than the less educated entrepreneurs. The eight entrepreneurs with entrepreneurial interests outside of footwear have an average education of 7.25 compared to 7.50 for entrepreneurs in the other ten sample firms with data on profit rate.

Table 7.2

The Relationship between Entrepreneurial Education and the Profit Rate of the Firm

Profit Rate Classification (by percentage)	Number of Firms	Average Level of Education of the Entrepreneur (by number of years completed)
13 or more	7	6.0
0 to 12	2	8.0
-1 to -17	4	5.0
-18 or less	5	13.5
TOTAL	18	7.3

geria, by increasing job aspirations[21] without significantly increasing labor proficiency,[22] may have a negative effect on economic growth and the development of skilled manpower, including entrepreneurs.[23] Empirical data are lacking to support the contention. In fact, the meager data available on the returns to primary education in Nigeria would seem to contradict the contention.[24] Other explanations for the negative relationship be-

---

21. Ibid. p. 96; Frederick Harbison, "Human Resources and Economic Development in Nigeria," in *The Nigerian Political Scene*, ed. by Robert O. Tilman and Taylor Cole (Durham, N.C.: Duke University Press, 1962), pp. 213-4; and Helleiner, *Peasant Agriculture, Government and Economic Growth*, pp. 39, 308.

22. Helleiner, *Peasant Agriculture, Government and Economic Growth*, pp. 305-10; and Geiger and Armstrong, *African Private Enterprise*, p. 96. See also Kilby, *Oxford Bulletin*, XXVI, 182-3.

23. Helleiner, *Peasant Agriculture, Government and Economic Growth*, p. 308. See also James S. Coleman, *Nigeria: Background to Nationalism* (Berkeley and Los Angeles: University of California Press, 1958), p. 122; and Henry L. Bretton, *Power and Stability in Nigeria* (New York: Frederick A. Praeger, 1962), p. 163.

24. Samuel Bowles, "The Efficient Allocation of Resources

tween entrepreneurial education and firm success seem more plausible.

First, time and money spent in obtaining a formal education, particularly secondary academic education, may mean foregoing technical or vocational training, such as an apprenticeship. This training was a virtual necessity for success in a small footwear enterprise, as indicated in a subsequent section of this chapter. Furthermore, the level of education is inversely related to the number of years of experience in footwear manufacturing,[25] and the number of years of entrepreneurial and management experience,[26] both measures of which are positively correlated with the size of the firm and the success of the entrepreneur (see below).

Secondly, the remuneration of entrepreneurial pursuits divided by the remuneration in alternative endeavors is inversely related to the educational level of the person. Assume that in each educational class there is a positive relationship between the individual's competence and his remuneration. Thus, whereas in low educational classes entrepreneurs are more likely to be among the more competent, in high educational classes entrepreneurs are more likely to be among the less competent.

Consider the market for manpower in high educational classes. Because of high salaries, foreign enterprises and government attract most of the highly competent university and secondary

---

in Education," *Quarterly Journal of Economics*, LXXXI, No. 2 (May 1967), 189-219, and "The Efficient Allocation of Resources in Education: A Planning Model with Application to Northern Nigeria" (unpublished Ph.D. dissertation, Harvard University, 1965).

25. If X is the level of educational attainment of the entrepreneur, and Y_1 the number of years the entrepreneur has been in the footwear industry prior to 1965, $Y_1 = 23.5 - 1.4X$. If the t-test is used, the regression coefficient is significant at the ½ percent level ($t = 3.57$). The number of years in the industry includes those as an apprentice, trainee, employee, manager or entrepreneur in a footwear manufacturing or trading firm.

26. If X, educational attainment, is defined as in the previous footnote, and Y_2 is the number of years the entrepreneur has held an entrepreneurial or managerial position in a manufacturing or trading firm with an employment of at least three (prior to 1965), $Y_2 = 16.6 - 0.9X$. If the t-test is used, the regression coefficient is significant at the 2 percent level ($t = 2.63$).

graduates. Graduates unable to obtain the more lucrative positions with foreign firms or government are more likely to become entrepreneurs.

The demand for (and salary of) indigenous managers in foreign firms is increased as a result of public and political pressure to obtain Nigerian managers. Salaries, additional allowances, fringe benefits, and working conditions are quite attractive for government officials and high-ranking civil servants.[27] In addition, the civil servant enjoys much more job security than the entrepreneur. The 1965 salaries of selected civil servants and government officials are shown in table 3.2. Median income for entrepreneurs (from all sources, including returns to capital) in the Harris sample, where median employment size was twenty-three,[28] was about £N1,100 per year.[29] However, if entrepreneurs from firms which had failed had been included in the sample, median income would have been much lower.[30] It is not surprising that, as Harris states it, the "graduate turns to the high and certain salary, immediate prestige, and other perquisites offered by the civil service or expatriate [foreign] corporations rather than to entrepreneurial activity with its relatively low mean and high variance of expected earnings."[31]

A disproportionately large number of highly educated persons who become entrepreneurs of small firms have either failed in other occupations or have low alternative wages. Consider the case of small entrepreneurs from firms with an employment of 8-12. In 1965 modal (economic) profits of firms of this size were about zero, and modal wages to management £N15 per month. The 1965 prevailing wage of persons with several years of secondary education was higher than this.[32] Consequently, entrepreneurs

---

27. See "The Civil Service," *Nigerian Opinion*, I (August 1965), 3-4; and Richard Burghart, "Ministerial Emoluments in Nigeria," *Nigerian Opinion*, I (August 1965), 10-2.

28. Harris, "Industrial Entrepreneurship," p. 8.

29. Ibid. p. 278.

30. Ibid. p. 279, and Sayre P. Schatz, *Development Bank Lending in Nigeria* (Ibadan: Oxford University Press, 1964).

31. Harris, "Industrial Entrepreneurship," p. 279.

32. Nigeria, Ministry of Commerce and Industry, *Industrial Labor - An Introductory Guide for Prospective Investors* (Lagos, 1962), pp. 10-4, x-xiii; Nigeria, Ministry of Commerce and Industry, *Handbook of Commerce and Industry in Nigeria* (Lagos, 1962), pp. 339-40; and the sources cited in table 3.2. As examples of 1965 wage rates in Nigeria, secondary graduates hired as a Grade

with a secondary education who establish small enterprises were likely to be persons with low opportunity costs. For example, Mr. C.S. Akpabio, the entrepreneur of the Cosmopolitan Shoe firm, which had a £N370 output and a 34 percent rate of loss in 1965, was the only secondary graduate among small entrepreneurs in the sample. His dissatisfaction with a job as an unskilled operative in a Lagos shipping firm had led him to train for a managerial position in the footwear industry.

Experience of the Entrepreneur

The previous chapter indicated that the lack of technical, managerial and marketing experience in business was one of the major barriers to entrepreneurial success in the five large indigenous footwear firms in Nigeria. Most entrepreneurs did not have the network of relationships with business-oriented friends and relatives to obtain access to trustworthy management personnel or even to acquire a reliable evaluation of the ability and integrity of prospective managers. In addition, those with greater experience in business had more time to acquire retained earnings to increase the capital available for their initial venture in manufacturing. Thus, there was a significant positive relationship between the entrepreneurial and managerial experience of the entrepreneur and the percentage rate of profit of the five large firms.[33] Of these, the two in the firms with the two

---

I stenographer, Grade I social worker and laboratory technician received £N39, £N37 and £N30 per month respectively. Nigeria, Ministry of Information, *Estimates of the Government of the Federal Republic of Nigeria, 1965-66 (Approved)* (Lagos, 1965), pp. 67, 257, 285, 287. The wages of a starting mechanic, employed by a large Northern footwear firm after three and one-half years of training at a post-primary government technical school, were £N30 per month in 1965.

33. If X_1 is entrepreneurial and managerial experience (see the full definition of the variable, then Y_2, p. 160, n. 26) and Y percentage rate of profit of the firm, $Y = -180.6 + 7.3X_1$. If the t-test is used, the regression coefficient is significant at the 1/10 percent level ($t = 12.68$). There is also a significant positive relationship (at the 5 percent level) between X_1, on the one hand, and either value of output or net worth, on the other, among the five large firms.

However, there is no significant relationship between the number of years the entrepreneur has been working in the footwear industry (X_2) and the percentage rate of profit of the firm (Y) among large firms. $Y = -149.4 + 14.5X_2$ ($t = 2.27$). The relationship between Y and X_2 is, however, significant among these firms (at the 5 percent level) when Y is net worth or employment.

highest 1964 profit rates had previous entrepreneurial or managerial experience in manufacturing. However, for small firms, the relationship is not significant.[34]

Except for an apprenticeship, the experience of the entrepreneur in small firms, where the management of production is not complex, has less importance for success than in large firms. The entrepreneur in a firm with a net worth less than £N6,000-7,000 per annum is required primarily to teach and supervise the labor force, and to design and construct footwear; other production problems are more routine.

Occupational Background

All of the entrepreneurs of the five large firms were in government service at some time prior to taking an entrepreneurial position in the footwear industry. A strategic government position was usually beneficial to the entrepreneur in his business activity.[35] In addition, for four of the five entrepreneurs, the relatively high government remuneration facilitated the accumulation of money capital for later entrepreneurial ventures (table 7.3, p. 164).

Other studies indicate that although persons with experience in government service are well-represented in entrepreneurial activity in large manufacturing firms, persons with a trading background comprise a plurality of the entrepreneurs.[36] It is not surprising that the two large footwear entrepreneurs whose firms had the best profit rate in 1964 had been entrepreneurs in large trading firms prior to entrance into manufacturing. The fact that traders may possess business experience, capital resources and a knowledge of the market may explain why in Nigeria, as in many other newly industrialized countries,[37] a high percentage of manufacturers have a background in trade.

---

34. If Y is percentage rate of profit, and the other variables are defined as in the previous footnote, $Y = -1.1 + 1.0X_1$ ($t = 0.71$), and $Y = -4.8 + .9X_2$ ($t = 0.75$). Neither regression coefficient is significant at the 5 percent level.

35. See chapter 6 and its appendix.

36. Kilby, *African Enterprise*, p. 93; and Harris, "Industrial Entrepreneurship," pp. 272-4, where apparently former traders comprise the largest group, when the "self-employed" are divided into craftsmen, contractors and transporters.

37. Alexander, *Greek Industrialists*, pp. 49-51; and Carroll, *The Filipino Manufacturing Entrepreneur*, p. 73.

Table 7.3

Occupations of Entrepreneurs of Large Footwear Firms prior to Entrepreneurial Positions in the Footwear Firms[a]

Firm of Entrepreneur	Occupation of Entrepreneur
Metro	Government service, trading, skilled industrial labor, management in manufacturing, sales
Midwestern	Accountancy, trading, entrepreneurship in manufacturing, government service
Southeastern	Government service, sales
Lagos	Government service, accountancy
Northern	Government service

a. In some cases, the person remained in these occupations while holding an entrepreneurial position in a footwear firm.

In many cases, the perception of the opportunity for profits in a manufacturing industry arises from experience in a previous business activity, such as trade. The entrepreneurs in the two large firms with the highest profits, the Metro Plastics Company and the Midwestern Manufacturing Company, both conceived the idea for their footwear manufacturing firms during an earlier business endeavor. Mr. M.E. Akitoye's observations as the West African agent for an English plastic shoe firm in 1960 gave rise to the idea of establishing Metro Plastics. Mr. M.W. Ejor, the founder of the Midwestern Manufacturing Company, entered rubber footwear manufacturing both because he saw increased opportunities for profits in industry relative to trade, and because of the linkages with his existing rubber-processing and rubber wholesale enterprises. The major catalyst for the enhanced attractiveness of industry was deliberate post-Independence government policy encouraging import substitution in manufacturing through higher tariffs (e.g., on rubber and rubber footwear).

In general, like the five entrepreneurs in question,[38] Nige-

38. See Kilby, *African Enterprise*, p. 93, and Bauer, *West African Trade*, pp. 11-3.

Table 7.4

Occupations of Sample Small Footwear Entrepreneurs prior to Entrepreneurial Positions in the Footwear Firms[a]

Percentage Rate of Profit of Firms	Trading	Government Service	Management of Handicrafts	Manual Labor	Domestic Service	No Other Occupation	Total
13 or more	-	-	-	-	1	5	6
0 - 12	1	1	-	-	-	-	2
-1 - -17	-	-	1	-	-	2	3
-18 or less	1	-	-	1	-	-	2
	2	1	1	1	1	7	13

a. Work as an apprentice, journeyman or employee in a footwear firm is not included as a separate occupation.

rian large entrepreneurs displayed a large amount of occupational mobility. However, this fluidity was not characteristic of the sample small footwear entrepreneurs (see table 7.4). Fourteen of the nineteen major entrepreneurs in the sample with apprentice training had not been engaged in any other occupation before they began their entrepreneurial activities in their present firms.[39] Even more noteworthy, five of the six entrepreneurs in the high-

39. The imperfect occupational specialization of many Nigerians makes it necessary to explain in more detail what is meant by the prior occupations of the entrepreneurs. Bauer, *West African Trade*, p. 11, states that "Africans frequently do not regard trade as an occupation (especially when carried on by dependents), and would not refer to it as such." The author tried, with little success, to obtain information on the extent to which the entrepreneurs in the sample had engaged in farming or petty trading either when as young boys or as a subsidiary economic

est profit rate category had not been engaged in any occupation prior to their entrance into entrepreneurial positions in their present firm. The occupation of the sixth entrepreneur - domestic service - is of little value as preparation for an entrepreneurial position.

The reason for the occupational immobility of small footwear entrepreneurs was the lengthy apprenticeship necessary to learn the craft of shoemaking. In virtually all cases, someone within the apprentice's extended family sponsored his training.[40] The apprenticeship usually began within two or three years of the apprentice leaving school to insure that he was contributing to the family income by the time he was about twenty-one.[41] Since an apprenticeship could last from two to five years, followed perhaps by one or two years as a journeyman, the small shoe entrepreneur would establish a firm between the ages of eighteen and twenty-three.[42]

A person who became dissatisfied with, or failed in, an occupation for which he trained was unlikely to receive financial support from the extended family for training in another craft;[43] and probably lacked the resources to do so himself. Thus it was unusual for a small footwear entrepreneur to have spent several years in another occupation.

---

activity, though most had probably obtained some income from doing so. Prior occupations, therefore, do not include occupations at the time when the person was a dependent, or subsidiary economic activities accounting for less than one-fourth of the person's income.

40. See chapter 8, on "Apprentice Training for Prospective Entrepreneurs."

41. Typically, primary school is completed between the ages of twelve and fourteen.

42. Four of the nineteen small entrepreneurs with apprentice training started their entrepreneurial responsibilities in the footwear industry after the age of twenty-three. None attained an entrepreneurial position in footwear before the age of eighteen. The median age at which they began entrepreneurial activity in footwear was twenty-two.

43. In many respects, expenditure on training or education of family members can be viewed as an investment for the family. The young person usually has no formal obligation to repay the money expended on his training, but he is expected to contribute to the training and subsistence of other family members when it is completed.

The entrepreneur of the small shoe firm with apprentice training is a specialized resource. While the demand for footwear and the derived demand for its entrepreneurship remained relatively brisk, small shoe entrepreneurs had an alternative price in 1965 of around £N15-25 per month. But if the industry were to become depressed, apprentice-trained shoemakers would have had a very low alternative cost. A large part of the relatively high wages of small footwear entrepreneurs in 1965 stemmed from knowledge and skills which were not transferrable to other industries. Much of the scarcity value of these entrepreneurs was due to skill in shoe design and craft rather than management skills.

Apprentice Training

To facilitate discussion, small firms are here divided into Type II firms - those with a 1964 average net worth of £N3,000 or less, and Type I firms - those with a 1964 average net worth of more than £N3,000. This boundary between categories is meant to correspond roughly to a distinction between entrepreneurs of Type II firms, where apprentice training is necessary and probably sufficient training, and those of Type I firms, where an apprenticeship may be necessary but certainly not sufficient training.

Most entrepreneurs of Type II firms are trained in the indigenous apprentice system. Under this system, a youth, usually fourteen to eighteen years old, enrolls for a two to five year course with a proprietor of a Type II firm. Over a period of a few years, the youth learns the craft on the job.

The supply of entrepreneurs of new Type II firms is basically a function of the supply of apprentice course graduates. It is very rare for a Type II firm to survive for more than three years if the entrepreneur lacks apprentice training. For example, all the initial entrepreneurs of the sixteen sample Type II firms more than three years old (on 1 January 1966) had been trained in the apprentice system.[44] As Callaway indicates, "Almost all the proprietors of the few Nigerian-owned and managed [Type II] firms . . . began their business lives [as appren-

---

44. Mr. C.S. Akpabio is the only initial entrepreneur in a sample Type II firm three years old or less who was not trained in the apprentice system. His firm, Cosmopolitan Shoe, recorded a 34 percent loss (on a net worth of £N850) in 1965.

tices.]"[45]

The entrepreneurial success and teaching skill of the master (generally a firm proprietor) were closely related to the subsequent entrepreneurial success of the apprentice. The proprietors of the footwear firms ranking first and fourth in 1965 value of output in Enugu, a city with approximately eighty footwear firms, were two former students of Mr. E.N. Ezienyi, entrepreneur of Enugu Fine Shoes, the firm ranking second in value of footwear output.[46] In Onitsha, Messrs. O.N. Ozomeie and C.R. Emeadi, the entrepreneurs of the Onitsha Shoe and Crossroads Shoe Firms - probably ranking first and fifth respectively in 1965 value of footwear output among 500 footwear firms in the city[47] - were trained by an entrepreneur[48] of the firm in which footwear output probably ranked third in the city.

Advanced Training

The entrepreneur of a Type II firm who wished to expand his firm to a Type I firm usually required an upgrading of technical and entrepreneurial skills beyond that acquired in the apprentice course. Whereas Type II firms are relatively labor-intensive, the greater size and complexity of Type I firms demand that they be more management and technical-skill intensive.[49]

If the entrepreneur planning the expansion chooses a labor-intensive technology, he can no longer rely on supervising the production process on an *ad hoc* basis. The organization of the firm needs to be more complex than before, with a greater neces-

---

45. Archibald Callaway, "Nigeria's Indigenous Education: The Apprentice System," *Odu: University of Ife Journal of African Studies*, I, No. 1 (July 1964), 4.

46. Mr. Ezienyi had seven apprentices in 1965, while the rest of the Enugu footwear firms would be expected to have had a total of at least eighty apprentices. See Peter Kilby, *The Development of Small Industries in Eastern Nigeria* (Enugu: Eastern Ministry of Information, 1963), p. 3.

47. See table 6.1.

48. This entrepreneur had 13 apprentices in 1965. On the basis of our field work and Kilby, *Development of Small Industries*, p. 41, one would have expected that Onitsha footwear firms would have had at least 300 apprentices in 1965.

49. Frederick Harbison and Charles A. Myers, *Management in the Industrial World: An International Analysis* (New York: McGraw-Hill Book Company, Inc., 1959), pp. 21-2.

sity for delegation of responsibility, advanced planning of work tasks, and a system of communication. The entrepreneur with a more capital-intensive technology requires further technical skill or the ability to supervise it, in addition to the obvious need for more skill to organize and coordinate increased and more specialized capital and labor. The emphasis of the apprenticeship on designing skills and craftsmanship does not prepare the entrepreneur for such management and organizational problems.

Although other resources of production tend to be substitutable for each other, entrepreneurship is a complementary factor. The more capital, labor, and natural resources a firm has, the more entrepreneurship is needed to combine these productive factors. Frequently, especially where there is a discontinuity in its production function, a Type II firm may reach a point in its growth where it is unable to absorb additional capital efficiently without a substantial increase in the input of entrepreneurial skills. In many cases, expansion is not feasible without training of the entrepreneur beyond his apprentice training. However, as more entrepreneurs receive advanced training, the apprentice training offered by entrepreneurs may also become more advanced.

The importance of advanced training for expansion is illustrated by the case of the Crossroads Shoe firm, representative of three other footwear firms in Onitsha which produced about £N6,000 per annum with a very labor-intensive technology. The profit rate of the firm was probably over 20 percent. But instead of using the funds generated from profits for the expansion of the enterprise, the top entrepreneur was investing the funds in his hotel business, despite the fact that he admitted that his footwear firm was "more profitable" than his hotel.

The explanation for his pattern of investment is not difficult. First, when the entrepreneur used the term "profitable," he was speaking in terms of an average concept rather than a marginal concept. While the average productivity of capital in the footwear enterprise was undoubtedly high, the marginal efficiency of investment in the firm was low. The firm had reached a point where there was a discontinuity in the production function, arising from deficiencies in footwear entrepreneurial and technical skills. Growth of the firm to an output exceeding £N7,000-8,000 per annum required an upgrading of the skills of the entrepreneur beyond that acquired in apprentice training.[50]

---

50. Despite its high profit rate, the firm did not qualify for intensive assistance from the Eastern Region's training center for shoemakers, the Industrial Development Centre in Owerri,

Thus, an increase in entrepreneurial and technical skills was necessary to increase the marginal efficiency of investment in the firm.

Socio-economic Class and Mobility

Many of the studies on entrepreneurship and economic development, when they are not apologetics for ruthless capitalist exploitation, as Baran suggests,[51] extol the achievements of the capitalist entrepreneur without examining class origins and monopoly advantage. Schumpeter sees entrepreneurs, irrespective of class origin, as heroic figures, with the dream and will to found a private kingdom, to conquer adversity, to achieve success for its own sake, and to experience the joy of creation.[52] McClelland, in a scheme, labelled a moral theory by one critic,[53] conceives the efforts of the entrepreneur, in his exercise of control over production in both capitalist and socialist econo-mies, as largely responsible for the global association between a high need for achievement (a psychological measure of the urge to improve) and rapid economic growth. The entrepreneurial role is assumed to be characterized by moderate risk-taking as a function of skill rather than chance, energetic and/or novel instrumental activity, individual responsibility, inner satisfaction that arises from having done well, an interest in money primarily as a measure of achievement, and long-range planning and organizational abilities.[54] For Papanek, the private entrepreneur, frugal, hard-working, far-sighted, remarkably able, and willing to take political risks, is in large part responsible for the "success" of Pakistan in achieving rapid industrialization.[55]

---

since the entrepreneur ranked low in one of the major criteria of the center, the quality of the design of the footwear.

51. Paul A. Baran, *The Political Economy of Growth* (New York: Monthly Review Press, 1957), pp. 254-7.

52. Joseph A. Schumpeter, *The Theory of Economic Development: An Inquiry into Profits, Capital, Credit, Interest, and the Business Cycle*, trans. by Redvers Opie (New York: Oxford University Press, 1961), pp. 78-9, 93-4.

53. Henry Bernstein, "Modernization Theory and the Sociological Study of Development," *Journal of Development Studies*, VII, No. 2 (January 1971), 148.

54. David C. McClelland, *The Achieving Society* (Princeton: D. Van Nostrand Company, 1961), pp. 36-239.

55. Gustav F. Papanek, *Pakistan's Development: Social Goals and Private Incentives* (Cambridge: Harvard University Press, 1967), pp. 2, 25-36, 199.

Carroll has characterized Filipino entrepreneurs as exhibiting "a desire for independence; drive, energy, and stamina which lead them to continue innovating and expanding even after their original goals have been achieved; a high level of intelligence, and the willingness to take calculated risks."[56]

Three recent empirical studies of the socio-economic mobility of the entrepreneur have reinforced this conception of the heroic entrepreneur. Collins, Moore, and Unwalla found that most of the entrepreneurs in medium manufacturing firms in Michigan "clearly moved a long way from the somewhat impoverished economic level of their childhoods."[57] Both Nigerian and Greek industrialists were considered highly upwardly mobile by Harris and Alexander, respectively.[58] This view is consistent with the paradigm of neoclassical economics, which, in its analysis of entrepreneurship, tends either to abstract from considerations of conflict and political power,[59] or to assume relatively open competition in a polity characterized by the balancing of independent interests. Below, I hope to demonstrate that it is the particular way in which the authors asked the question in these empirical studies that led to their conclusions of substantial upward socio-economic mobility, and that the data can be interpreted as corroborating the low degree of vertical mobility found in my sample of Nigerian entrepreneurs.

A period of rapid industrial growth and economic modernization, as in the post-World War II period in Nigeria, did not remove the advantages of ascribed status, even in entrepreneurial activity in manufacturing. The traditional Nigerian upper classes - chiefs, emirs and administrators - whose strength was a legacy of the feudal and colonial periods, have allied, and in some cases overlapped, with the capitalist, political and bureau-

---

56. John J. Carroll, *The Filipino Manufacturing Entrepreneur: Agent and Product of Change* (Ithaca: Cornell University Press, 1965), p. 136.

57. Orvis F. Collins, David G. Moore, and Darab B. Unwalla, *The Enterprising Man* (East Lansing: MSU Business Studies, 1964), p. 238.

58. John R. Harris, "Nigerian Entrepreneurship in Industry," in *Entrepreneurship and Economic Development*, ed. by Peter Kilby (New York: Free Press, 1971), pp. 336-7, and Alec P. Alexander, *Greek Industrialists* (Athens: Center of Planning and Economic Development, 1964), pp. 80-95.

59. Benjamin Higgins, *Economic Development - Problems, Principals, and Policies* (New York: W.W. Norton and Company, 1968), p. 227.

cratic elites, most of whom originated from high-income families, to control much of the access to key business positions. Families and clans with wealth and position used the monopoly advantage resulting from ready access to capital, greater information and mobility, superior education and training, privileged access to concessions from government, and a low discount of future income, to become industrial entrepreneurs in disproportional numbers.

In this section of the chapter, data on the distribution of entrepreneurs by class (paternal economic status) are compared with information on the population at large. The median personal income of entrepreneurs (profits, returns to capital, and wages to management in the footwear enterprise plus income from other economic endeavors) was £N450 per annum in fiscal year 1964/65, which divided by the median number of persons dependent upon the entrepreneur's income, 6.5 (substantially higher than the median number of dependents of income-earners in Nigeria), gives a median per capita income of £N69, much above the 1964/65 all-Nigerian average per capita GNP of £N26 (itself higher than the median figure). The paternal economic status of the entrepreneurs (especially those from large firms) was high compared to that of the population of Nigeria as a whole. The fathers of the five large entrepreneurs consisted of one large trader, two government servants (both above average in rank) and two members of the traditional aristocracy (i.e. a traditional title-holder in a Northern emirate, and a southern chief). Both of the indigenous rulers held their positions with the acquiescence of the British colonial government. An entrepreneur, whose father was a civil servant, was a member of a ruling family in the West, and the great-grandson of an oba (or chief) in the pre-colonial period. Major occupations of the fathers of the small entrepreneurs were government service for three, trading for three, shoemaking for three, large farming for eight, small farming for two, and unknown for one (table 7.5, p. 175). The high status is reinforced by the fact that 58 percent (14 of 24) of the fathers was in the non-agricultural sector (with a much higher income per capita than the agricultural sector), compared to 21 percent of Nigerian males, according to the 1952-3 census (table 7.6, p. 176).

Although Harris does classify the socio-economic status of the entrepreneurs into highest, upper, middle, lower, and lowest, this information is used to correlate the status of the entrepreneurs and their fathers,[60] and cannot be utilized to compare the

---

60. There is a significant positive correlation between the statuses of the entrepreneur and his father. (The value of Good-

socio-economic class background of entrepreneurs to the general population.[61] Furthermore, the information available on the highly contrasting socio-economic class between entrepreneurs and the general population is not discussed by Harris. However, the fact that 56 percent (147 of 262) of the fathers of entrepreneurs in the Harris sample was in the non-agricultural sector (table 7.6) augments my position that the socio-economic class of Nigerian industrial entrepreneurs was far above that of the population at large (chi-square = 193.512, $p. < 0.001$).

The economic status of fathers was classified by the author on the basis of information about their occupation and income. Fathers who were subsistence farmers (where more than 50 percent of farm output was for the family or clan), farm workers, or unskilled workers were considered of low economic status. The author estimates that these three groups comprised about 75 percent of the male working population in 1952-53. The fact that only two sample fathers (8 percent of the total - both subsistance farmers - were of low economic rank provides further evidence for the contention that class status of the entrepreneurs was substan-

---

man-Krushkal's Gamma is significant at the $p < 0.001$ level). "Nevertheless, entrepreneurial activity has been an avenue of upward status mobility for many entrepreneurs. . . . It is quite clear that entrepreneurial activity is a means of moving one or two 'notches up the ladder.'" Harris, "Nigerian Entrepreneurship in Industry," in *Entrepreneurship and Economic Development*, ed. by Kilby, p. 336.

61. Harris indicates that a rough index - one that "is necessarily subjective" - was constructed on the basis of "occupation, income, and positions of leadership within society." "Industrial Entrepreneurship," pp. 256, 363. The ranking of occupations are based on prestige ratings by Nigerian economics and medical students at the University of Ibadan, as reported by Robert W. Morgen, Jr., "Occupational Prestige Ratings by Nigerian Students," *Nigerian Journal of Economic and Social Studies*, VII, No. 3 (November 1965), 325-32 (Harris, "Industrial Entrepreneurship," p. 363.) It also appears that the socio-economic status of fathers who were unskilled laborers was "lower" or "lowest" (categories which comprised 22.8 percent of the 254 fathers). This is not substantially inconsistent with the class rankings of these workers in western countries, or with my discussion in the next paragraph. However, it should be pointed out that the incomes of unskilled workers in the 1940s and 1950s in Nigeria were above average, as about four-fifths of the population were engaged in the low-income agricultural sector.

tially higher than the general population. High-status fathers included two members of the ruling aristocracy, three of the five civil servants,[62] and two plantation farm owners. All others were classified in the medium category.

There was a close relationship between economic status of the father, and certain measures of entrepreneurial success. Entrepreneurs with a higher paternal economic status tended to be associated with firms with a higher value of output (chi-square = 17.11810, 8 d.f., p = 0.0289), a greater net worth (chi-square = 14.81725, 6 d.f., p = 0.022), a greater employment (chi-square = 12.79870, 6 d.f., p = 0.046), and a higher rate of profit, although the last relationship was not significant (chi-square = 9.25170, 6 d.f., p = 0.160).[63] A high economic status of the father assists the prospective entrepreneur in obtaining the appropriate business experience, and acquiring resources for investment in education,[64] training, and plant and equipment.[65] In addition, businessmen with a greater paternal economic status, because of more education and erudition, a more extensive network of influential acquaintances, and more resources available to acquire information, were more likely to be successful in receiving government assistance.

Comparative Data on Socio-economic Class Mobility

An analysis of Nigerian industrialists in Harris's and the author's samples indicates that entrepreneurs with a high socio-economic status were more highly represented and more successful than other entrepreneurs. This finding is true not only in Nigeria but, contrary to a widely-held viewpoint, also in most of

---

62. Omitted from high economic status were a policeman and a clerk.

63. For purposes of the chi-square test I used the following categories: value of output - 20,000 and more, 6,000 - 19,999, 3,000 - 5,999, 1,000 - 2,999, and 999 and less; net worth - 10,000 or more, 1,000 - 9,999, 500 - 999, and 499 and less; employment - 50 and more, 15 - 49, 11 - 14, and 8 - 10; and rate of profit - +0.13 or more, 0 to +0.12, -0.01 to -0.12, and -0.13 or less.

64. There is a significant positive correlation between the economic status of the fathers and the education of the entrepreneurs (chi-square = 16.83521, 8 d.f., p. < 0.05).

65. There is a significant positive correlation between the economic status of the fathers and the median initial capital of the firms (chi-square = 16.632, 8 d.f., $p < 0.05$).

Table 7.5

Major Occupation of the Father

Percentage Rate of Profit of Firms	Number of Entrepreneurs	Traditional Aristocracy[a]	Government Service	Trading	Shoemaking	Large farming[c]	Small farming[c]	Not Known
<u>Large</u>								
13 or more	1	-	-	1	-	-	-	-
-1 - -17	1	1	-	-	-	-	-	-
-18 or less	3	1	2[b]	-	-	-	-	-
TOTAL	5	2	2	1	0	0	0	0
<u>Small</u>								
13 or more	6	-	-	-	2	3	1	-
0 - 12	2	-	-	-	1	1	-	-
-1 - -17	3	-	1	-	-	1	1	-
-18 or less	2	-	1	-	-	1	-	-
Unknown	7	-	1	3	-	2	-	1
TOTAL	20	0	3	3	3	8	2	1

a. Examples of this category are two fathers of sample entrepreneurs: a traditional title-holder in a Northern emirate, and a southern chief.

b. One father whose occupation was a civil servant was a member of a ruling family in the West.

c. Those engaged in small farming include hired farm laborers, and subsistence farmers - those who produce more than 50 percent of their output for the family or clan. All other farmers are engaged in large farming.

Table 7.6

Percentage Distribution of the Occupational Category of the Fathers of Sample Industrialists Compared to the Working Population (Nigeria)

Occupational Category	Major Occupation of the Fathers of the Entrepreneurs (Harris Sample)	Major Occupation of the Fathers of the Entrepreneurs (Nafziger Sample)	Primary Occupations of Nigerian Males, 1952/53 Census
Agriculture, forestry, animal-husbandry, fishing and hunting	44	42	79
Craftsman, skilled and semi-skilled workers engaged in producing articles	21	12	6
Traders and employees engaged in commerce	22	17	6
All government and local government and professional workers	10	29	3
Other occupations	3	0	7
TOTAL	100%	100%	101%[a]

a. Column may not add up to 100 percent because of rounding.

Sources: Harris, "Nigerian Entrepreneurship in Industry," in *Entrepreneurship and Economic Development*, ed. by Kilby, p. 335; my field research; and Nigeria, Office of Statistics, *Annual Abstract of Statistics, 1964* (Lagos, 1964), p. 13.

the rest of the non-socialist world, at least if evidence is based upon empirical studies of entrepreneurs. The proportion of fathers of Filipino manufacturing entrepreneurs from an upper socio-economic position was thirty-six times that of the population. Opportunities for industrial enterprise were available chiefly to those who were already well established financially. A highly disproportionate number of the fathers of manufacturing entrepreneurs in Pakistan were from high-caste business communities while a low percentage of fathers were in wage employment or agriculture. This pattern would suggest, contrary to Papanek's interpretation, that the socio-economic class status of entrepreneurs was high when compared to the population.[66] My study of south Indian entrepreneurs indicated that a disproportional number of entrepreneurs (especially successful ones) were from twice-born (i.e., high) castes and from families with a high economic status.[67] Similarly, the analysis above of the data from the Harris sample, and the fact that in Alexander's study of Greek industrialists, 54 percent (282 of 522) of their fathers was big merchants, industrialists, professional men or business executives compared to 2 percent of the working population[68] support the contention that the socio-economic class of the entrepreneurs was far above that of the population at large (table 7.7, p. 178).

Those for whom today's "modernized" societies present an image of the future of "traditional societies"[69] envisage a movement in history from a "rigid" social structure and underdeveloped economy to a fluid social structure and developed economy, whose archetype is the U.S. and Western Europe.[70] But if studies

---

66. Carroll, *The Filipino Manufacturing Entrepreneur*, pp. 100, 126, and Gustav Papanek, "The Development of Entrepreneurship," *American Economic Review*, LII, No. 2 (May 1962), 50-8.

67. E. Wayne Nafziger, "Class, Caste and Community of South Indian Industrialists: An Examination of the Horatio Alger Model," *Journal of Development Studies*, XI, No. 2, (January 1975), 131-48.

68. Chi-square = 7,394.722, $p < 0.001$.

69. Stephen Enke, *Economics for Development* (Englewood Cliffs: Prentice-Hall, Inc., 1963), p. 65; Benjamin Higgins, *Economic Development: Problems, Principles and Policies* (New York: W.W. Norton, 1968), pp. 55, 175, 188; Walter W. Rostow, *The Stages of Economic Growth: A Non-Communist Manifesto* (2nd ed., Cambridge: Cambridge University Press, 1971), pp. 143-7.

70. Neil J. Smelser and Seymour Martin Lipset, ed., *Social Structure and Mobility in Economic Development* (Chicago: Aldine Publishing Co., 1966), pp. 9, 44; Alexander, *Greek Industrial-*

Table 7.7

Percentage Distribution of the Occupational Category of the Fathers of Sample Industrialists Compared to the Working Population (Greece and the U.S.)

Greece - c. 1961 (Alexander)

Economic Occupational Activity	Major Activities of the Fathers of Sample Industrialists	Working Population, Greece, Early 1950's
Craftsman	17	8
Big merchant	16	1
Small merchant	13	4
Industrialist	34	b
Professional man	3	1
Business executive	1	b
Farmer	11	50
Other activities	5	36[c]
TOTAL	100%	100%

U.S. (Michigan) - 1960-2 (Collins, Moore, and Unwala)

Occupation	Major Occupation of the Fathers of Sample Industrialists	Employed Labor Force, U.S., 1940
Unskilled or semi-skilled worker (including farm worker)	18	44
Skilled worker	12	11
Farmer or farm manager	19	11
Clerk, salesman and kindred worker	6	17
Businessman, executive, manager, and official	28	8
Professional worker	10	7
Other	6	1
TOTAL	99%[a]	99%[a]

a. Columns may not add up to 100 percent because of rounding.

b. Less than 0.5 percent.

c. Consists of 13 percent white collar worker, 12 percent worker, 10 percent civil servant, and 1 percent miscellaneous.

Sources: Alexander, *Greek Industrialists*, pp. 45, 87; Collins, Moore and Unwalla, *The Enterprising Man*, pp. 238-9; and U.S. Department of Commerce, Bureau of the Census, *Sixteenth Census of the United States: 1940*, Vol. III, *The Labor Force: Occupation, Industry, Employment and Income*, Part I, *U.S. Summary* (Washington: Government Printing Office, 1943), 87.

---

of businessmen are any indication, the fluidity of the proto-typical modern country, the U.S., does not vary much from that of Nigeria. It is true that two-thirds of the sample entrepreneurs in Michigan studied by Collins, Moore, and Unwalla described their early family life as "poor" or "underprivileged." But the only other choices were "affluent" or "well off."[71] Given the lack of any choice corresponding to a middle-level category, respondents may have avoided designations implying higher income. Furthermore entrepreneurs may have evaluated parental family income in terms of contemporary standards (the 1960s) and in comparison with their own high level of economic well-being. The vast underrepresentation of Michigan sample fathers in unskilled, or semi-skilled work, clerical, sales and kindred work (24 percent from the sample and 61 percent from the general labor force), together with the disproportional representation of fathers in business, executive, managerial, and official, farm owner and managerial, and professional work (57 percent compared to 26 percent), points to median incomes substantially above the corresponding population of their period (table 7.7).

Executives in large U.S. joint-stock companies, who as a group enjoy higher remuneration and lower risk, are likely to originate from an economically more select portion of the population than medium-scale industrial entrepreneurs.[72] The U.S.

---

ists, p. 80; and Harris, "Nigerian Entrepreneurship in Industry," in *Entrepreneurship and Economic Development*, ed. by Kilby, p. 337.

71. Orvis F. Collins, David G. Moore, and Darab B. Unwalla, *The Enterprising Man* (East Lansing: MSU Business Studies, 1964), p. 238.

72. Ibid. p. 239.

business elite in 1952 was comprised largely of "the sons of men of relatively high occupational status, the sons of business and professional men." Among the fathers of this elite, the number of executives or owners of large businesses was eight times its proportion within the general population, while the number of unskilled or semiskilled laborers was one-sixth its percentage in the population.[73]

In India, indigenous managers of large public, foreign and private enterprises also originate from a highly-select portion of the population: as none of the fathers were laborers, only 10 percent were farmers (all of whom were small farm operators or large farm owners), and the rest were white-collar workers, government officials, business executives, professional men, and business owners.[74]

Entrepreneurs in Nigeria, Greece and Michigan underwent, in the aggregate, an inter-generational upward movement (i.e. from father to son) in occupational status and material level of living.[75] However, the fact that the socio-economic status of the entrepreneurs was higher than that of their fathers does not conflict with the evidence that the paternal economic status of entrepreneurs was higher than that of the population as a whole.[76]

---

73. W. Lloyd Warner and James C. Abegglen, *Occupational Mobility in American Business and Industry* (Minneapolis: University of Minnesota Press, 1955), pp. 41-2. The figures of Mable Newcomer, *The Big Business Executive: The Factors that Made Him, 1900-1950* (New York: Columbia University Press, 1955), p. 55, reinforce these findings.

74. S.B. Prasad and A.R. Negandhi, *Managerialism for Economic Development: Essays on India* (The Hague: Martinue Nijhoff, 1968), p. 27.

75. Harris, "Nigerian Entrepreneurship in Industry," in *Entrepreneurship and Economic Development*, ed. by Kilby, p. 337; Alec P. Alexander, *Greek Industrialists*, pp. 80-95; and Collins, Moore and Unwalla, *The Enterprising Man*, p. 238.

76. In this study, in order to determine inter-generational mobility, sample entrepreneurs were asked, "Are you better off economically than your father was at your age?" If the replies of respondents can be considered valid, three of the five large entrepreneurs were upwardly mobile, one was not mobile in either direction, and one moved downward economically. All but six of the twenty small entrepreneurs were upwardly mobile economically. In light of the general upward movement of the level of living in Nigeria, it is not surprising that most of the entrepreneurs were upwardly mobile.

The foregoing discussion should make clear that the heroic model of the entrepreneur presented by previous empirical studies resulted from the types of questions posed. Although the data indicating the upward social and economic mobility of industrialists compared to their fathers are useful, this exclusive focus detracts from the considerable contrast between the socio-economic class backgrounds of entrepreneurs and that of the general population.

It is perhaps not surprising that despite the readily available data, U.S. business scholars and development economists, who tend to assume a harmony of interests between the goals of the businessmen and the community at large, do not generally consider it important to raise questions about the relative economic class origin of the entrepreneurs. The findings here, however, suggest that industrial business activity, rather than being a path for substantial upward socio-economic mobility, is a way of maintaining or defending privileged status, and enhancing or consolidating the high economic position of the family.[77]

Communal Origin

A majority of sample entrepreneurs (i.e. fourteen of twenty-five) were members of the Ibo community.[78] Could it be that Ibo entrepreneurship in footwear manufacturing was a part of a general pattern suggested by LeVine in which Ibos, with a high need for achievement (n Ach), have a high propensity to enter entrepreneurial positions?[79]

It is doubtful that the representation of Ibos among indigenous industrial entrepreneurs in general was substantially greater than the representation of their community in the popula-

---

77. See Nafziger, *Journal of Development Studies*, XI, No. 2, 137, for evidence to suggest that the paternal socio-economic status of Soviet business executives is substantially higher than that of the general population.

78. The distribution of sample entrepreneurs by ethnic community is: Ibo - 14, Yoruba - 6, Efik - 1, Urhobo - 1, Beni - 1, Hausa-Fulani - 1, and Kanuri - 1.

79. Robert A. LeVine and others, *Dreams and Deeds: Achievement Motivation in Nigeria* (Chicago: University of Chicago Press, 1966), pp. 16, 71-5. See also Phoebe Ottenberg, "The Afikpo Ibo of Eastern Nigeria," in *Peoples of Africa*, ed. by James L. Gibbs, Jr. (New York: Holt, Rinehart and Winston, Inc., 1965), p. 6.

tion as a whole. Since the majority of indigenous shoe firms,[80] and a majority of sample firms (i.e. fifteen of twenty-five) were located in the East, it was not surprising that most sample entrepreneurs were members of the dominant ethnic community in the East, the Ibos. Undoubtedly Ibo dominance in footwear trading in the East and most of the North was an advantage for Ibo footwear producers.[81] Secondly, as pointed out below, unlike Northern entrepreneurs, Ibo (and other southern) entrepreneurs had access to an inexpensive source of labor - apprentice labor.[82] Thirdly, footwear producers in Iboland encountered less competition than those in Yorubaland from imported footwear and footwear produced by large foreign firms in the Lagos area.

Harris's study of the sawmilling, furniture, rubber processing, printing, garment making, and baking industries indicated only a very slight overrepresentation of Ibo entrepreneurs. Yoruba entrepreneurs were substantially overrepresented, but this appeared to result from the fact that 168 of the 269 firms were from Greater Lagos in contrast to less than 300 of 929 in the 1965 *Industrial Survey*.[83] Lagos is a metropolitan area where about 70 percent of the population was Yoruba, according to the 1952-53 census.

The only study of Nigerian entrepreneurs known to the author which utilized measures of achievement motivation, that by E.O. Akeredolu-Ale, found no relationship between n Ach, on the one hand, and either entrepreneurial activity or communal origin, on the other. Instead the initial concentration of entrepreneurship by ethnic communities resulted from an opportune geographical location, or from unfavorable economic alternatives to entrepreneurial activity.[84] Until further evidence is available, I would

---

80. See table 5.1.

81. See chapter 9 for a more detailed discussion of this point.

82. As pointed out in chapter 9, a higher discount of the future by Northerners may explain the short supply of apprentice labor in the North.

83. Harris, "Nigerian Entrepreneurship in Industry" in *Entrepreneurship and Economic Development*, ed. by Kilby, pp. 333, 337-8, and Nigeria, Office of Statistics, *Industrial Survey of Nigeria, 1964 and 1965* (Lagos, 1968), p. 2.

84. E.O. Akeredolu-Ale, "A Sociohistorical Study of the Development of Entrepreneurship among the Ijebu of Western Nigeria," *African Studies Review*, XVI, No. 3 (December 1973), 358-60.

attribute the disproportional representation of Ibos among footwear entrepreneurs to favorable locational factors, and the lack of options available in the East, an over-populated region with poor agricultural land.[85]

Summary

The educational level of entrepreneurs in firms with eight or more employed is more than the population at large. However, if entrepreneurs from all sizes of firms are considered, the average education of entrepreneurs is probably no higher than that of the population in general. This relationship differs from that hypothesized. More education can not only increase the supply of entrepreneurs by making available more skills which are suitable to entrepreneurial endeavors; it can also decrease the supply of entrepreneurs by raising the opportunity costs of providing entrepreneurial services.

As expected, there is a positive relationship between entrepreneurial education and the value of output of the firm. Education and literacy of the entrepreneur set a limit to the size and complexity of the firm.

Contrary to the relationship hypothesized, entrepreneurial education is negatively correlated with the profit rate of the firm. Time and money spent in formal education represent opportunities foregone in training more closely related to entrepreneurial occupations. In addition, the higher the educational level of the entrepreneur, the more likely it is that he may have chosen an entrepreneurial pursuit because of failure in another occupation or low opportunity costs.

On the basis of evidence from data on Nigerian footwear firms, entrepreneurial education is probably no higher than that of the population as a whole, is positively related to value of output of the firm and is negatively related to the rate of profit of the firm.

The lack of previous entrepreneurial or managerial experience was a major barrier to success among large entrepreneurs. Apprentice training appears to be virtually necessary for the success of small entrepreneurs.

---

85. E. Wayne Nafziger, "The Political Economy of Disintegration in Nigeria," *The Journal of Modern African Studies*, XI, No. 4 (1973), 525.

The paternal economic status of entrepreneurs was substantially higher than that of the population as a whole. There was a close positive relationship between the economic status of the father and the entrepreneurial success of the son. These findings, together with comparative information from other countries, suggest that industrial business activity, rather than being a path for substantial upward socio-economic mobility, is a way of maintaining and defending a relatively high class status.

Although a majority of sample entrepreneurs were Ibo, there is not enough evidence to indicate that Ibos are disproportionately represented among indigenous manufacturing entrepreneurs in general.

Chapter 8

The Acquisition and Management of Capital and Labor

This chapter discusses certain aspects of the markets for inputs (capital and labor) encountered by the entrepreneur, including the availability and acquisition of these inputs, the management of the labor force, and the relationship between the market for inputs and the quantity and success of entrepreneurs. Particular emphasis is placed upon the role of the extended family in hampering or facilitating the acquisition of capital.

Initial Sources of Capital for Large Firms

The major source of initial capital in large firms was loan capital. In two cases, the source of loan capital was a bank; in one case - a government loan organization; and in another case - a private individual. The second major source of original capital was equity capital from individuals other than the initial entrepreneur. The personal savings of the entrepreneur was the major source in only one firm (table 8.1, p. 186).

Sources of Additional Capital for Large Firms

Profits were not a significant source of additional capital for large firms, since only one firm made a (business) profit.[1] Loans were the most important sources of additional capital (see table 8.2, p. 186). Despite large losses in their first year of operation, both the Lagos Supreme and Northern Leather Works firms obtained loans when the firms were about a year old.[2]

---

1. Implicit interest and wages of management are not included as expenses when business profits are computed.

2. Due to the political power of its entrepreneur, Northern Leather Works was able to obtain further loans from N.N.D.C. A Lagos bank, which regarded losses of the Lagos Manufacturing Company in its initial year as temporary, loaned the firm further capital.

Table 8.1

Initial Sources of Capital of Large Footwear Firms (ranked according to pound value)[a]

Sources	Metro	Mid-western	South-eastern	Lagos	Northern	Total
Loan capital	1	2	2		*1*[b]	1
Equity capital[c]	3	3	3	*1*	2	2
Savings[d]	2	1		2	3	3
Government statutory corporation			*1*			4

a. The largest source is indicated by "1;" the second largest by "2;" and so forth. If the "1" is in italics, it indicates that the source accounted for over 50 percent of the initial capital.

b. Government loan.

c. Equity capital from sources other than the initial entrepreneur.

d. Equity capital of the initial entrepreneur obtained from previous savings.

Table 8.2

Sources of Additional Capital of Large Footwear Firms (ranked according to pound value)[a]

Sources	Metro	Mid-western	South-eastern	Lagos	Northern	Total
Loan capital	3	2	2	*1*	*1*[b]	1
Equity capital[c]	2		*1*			2
Savings[d]		*1*				3
Profits	*1*					4

a. See table 8.1, n. a.

b. Government loan.

c. Equity capital from sources other than the major entrepreneur.

d. Equity capital of the entrepreneur obtained from previous savings.

Entrepreneurship and the Extended Family

Security against economic loss resulting from sickness, accidents, death, old age, poverty and unemployment is valued highly by most societies. Social security, provident funds, old age pensions, life insurance, unemployment insurance, accident insurance, medical insurance and welfare programs instituted by government (and business) provide much of this security in economically advanced countries; in contrast, in many less developed countries such as Nigeria, this function is assumed by the extended family.

It would be useful, though difficult, to compare the costs and benefits of providing the security through government on the one hand, and the extended family on the other. However, the problem under consideration is more specific - the effect of the extended family on entrepreneurial activity in small firms.

Development economists generally contend that the institution of the extended family is a major barrier to entrepreneurial activity.[3] The joint family is thought to dampen incentives to achieve, deter risk-taking and impede the mobilization of capital. For example, Wolf writes:

> The joint or extended family system provides another example of institutions deterring economic growth. . . . The joint family . . . involves a system of shared rights and obligations encompassing a large number of near and distant relatives. One characteristic of these relationships is that the individual family member receives the right of support and security from the group in return for the obligation to share his wealth to provide support and security for other members of the group. Where an individual member of the group contemplates a wealth-increasing activity, e.g., through investment in a productive asset that will yield future returns, he must bear all of the costs associated

---

3. Charles Wolf, Jr., "Institutions and Economic Development," *American Economic Review*, XLV (December 1955), 872-3; Adamantios Papelasis, Leon Mears and Irma Adelman, *Economic Development: Analysis and Case Studies* (New York: Harper and Brothers, Publishers, 1961), p. 170; Benjamin Higgins, *Economic Development: Principles, Problems and Policies* (New York: W.W. Norton Co., 1959), pp. 255-6; and Charles P. Kindleberger, *Economic Development* (New York: McGraw-Hill Book Company, 1965), pp. 21-2.

> therewith. Such costs are not a levy on the group since they are not essential to the individual's support or security. However the fruits or returns from his investment are subject to sharing among the other members of the extended family. Because of the differentiation between responsible and benefitting economic units, what may appear objectively to be strong incentives to invest are not subjectively so regarded by the potential entrepreneur.[4]

Here I plan to examine the effects of the extended family on capital formation and entrepreneurial activity in small footwear firms in Nigeria.

Definitions

The smallest family unit, the nuclear family, consists of the father, mother and offspring.[5] The joint or extended family consists of two or more nuclear families in which the resources of its members are pooled for consumption.[6]

Apprentice Training for Prospective Entrepreneurs

As indicated in chapter 7, the supply of entrepreneurs of new small firms is largely dependent upon the number of apprentice course graduates. Because of the scarcity of capital and highly-skilled manpower in Nigeria, small firms can compete in a number of industries by using very intensively the abundant factor, labor - especially unskilled apprentice labor, where the receipts from apprentice fees may exceed wages. However, these labor-intensive techniques demand designing skills and craftsmanship on the part of the prospective supervisor-entrepreneur that can only be acquired from a long period of training, supervision, observation and practice.

Consider the expenditures required for apprentice training

---

4. *American Economic Review*, XLV, pp. 872-3.

5. For an elaboration of the concept of the nuclear family, see M.F. Nimkoff, *Comparative Family Systems* (Boston: Houghton Mifflin Co., 1965), pp. 14-7.

6. A two-generation polygamous household would not be considered an extended family, while a consumption unit consisting of a father and mother with a married son, wife and children would. Cf. Ibid. p. 19.

for prospective entrepreneurs of small firms. Total apprentice fees for a two to four year course usually ranged from about £N17 to £N40 in 1965. In addition, subsistence costs in Onitsha, for example, amounted to about £N25 to £N30 a year. Since individual youths could rarely obtain access to credit or raise the funds themselves, the resources of the extended family were probably required.

Callaway's study of apprentices in 5,135 Nigerian firms found that 96 percent of the apprentice sponsors were members of the extended family.[7] In addition, family members provided or financed the apprentice's room and board.

Moreover, the prospective apprentice was likely to be dependent upon the extended family for initial contacts with capable apprentice instructors.

In rare cases, the extended family may prevent a youth from obtaining apprentice training.[8] The person who might otherwise be able to afford apprentice training may have to forego it as a result of the demands on his income by the extended family.

The Establishment of the Firm

Raising the initial capital of the firm was one of its major problems. The outlay needed for the establishment of even a very small firm was £N25 at a minimum, and perhaps more than £N150.[9] Most prospective small entrepreneurs in Nigeria did not have access to funds from organized financial institutions.

The extended family, because of its age composition and size, may have been able to mobilize funds that the prospective entrepreneur would not have had available especially if he were young. When asked for the sources of initial capital for the firm, fourteen of the twenty small entrepreneurs in the sample indicated that at least part was raised from other members of the extended family (see table 8.3, p. 190). Even though the median initial investment was no more than £N200, only five of the

---

7. Archibald Callaway, "Nigeria's Indigenous Education: The Apprentice System," *Odu: University of Ife Journal of African Studies*, I, No. 1 (July 1964), 8. This is the most comprehensive treatment of the apprentice system in Nigeria.

8. A part of the next section explains why these cases are rare.

9. See Peter Kilby, *The Development of Small Industries in Eastern Nigeria* (Enugu: Ministry of Information, 1963), p. 9.

Table 8.3

Initial Sources of Capital for Small Sample Firms

Source	Total
Personal savings[a]	5
Family savings[b]	11
Personal and family savings	2
Inheritance of business	1
Government loan	1
TOTAL	20

a. One entrepreneur received part of his capital from the master of his apprentice course.
b. Extended family savings.

twenty entrepreneurs obtained all the initial capital from their own resources.

On the basis of evidence from our sample and other studies,[10] it seems reasonable to conclude that small Nigerian industrial entrepreneurs were very dependent upon the extended family for their initial capital.

Usually the entrepreneur had no formal obligation to repay family members the money expended on his training and the establishment of his firm. The lack of formal repayments was likely to be very advantageous to the enterprise in its early years when liquid funds were frequently scarce. However, as funds permitted, the businessman was expected to contribute to the subsistence, education, training and establishment of firms of other family members.

---

10. Archibald Callaway, "From Traditional Crafts to Modern Industries," *Odu: University of Ife Journal of African Studies*, II, No. 1 (July 1965), 42-5; and John R. Harris, "Industrial Entrepreneurship in Nigeria," (unpublished Ph.D. dissertation, Northwestern University, 1967), p. 230.

The extended family may have reduced the entrepreneur's initial outlays in other ways. Family members often provided room and board, and/or building space and tools needed for the enterprise.

The family also sometimes helped the initial entrepreneur to obtain access to suppliers, merchants, creditors, market authorities, local officials and persons with economic power and influence. For example, suppliers tended to extend credit to the entrepreneur only if a member of the extended family guaranteed payment.

In a few cases, however, the extended family may have impeded the establishment of a firm. Income which a person might have otherwise used for investment in training or in the establishment of an enterprise might have been allotted by the family for other purposes, such as consumption expenditures.[11] On the other hand, the family may have allotted the funds for investment in the training, education or enterprise of another family member whose investment project was expected to yield higher returns. This transfer of funds to other family members by prospective entrepreneurs occurred only rarely, however, since most of them were young and unlikely to have income and wealth to divert.

Finally, the associations of the extended family in the home village affected the businessman's acquisition of labor and apprentices. Most small firms obtained more than half of their labor force from the entrepreneur's home city or village, even when the firm was located in a different city.

It is not surprising that a large percentage of the labor force of the firm was drawn from the entrepreneur's home district. Over a period of years the extended family of the entrepreneur had incurred a number of (social) claims and obligations which could be satisfied in part when selecting a labor force. In some instances, the entrepreneur was pressed to hire a laborer or train an apprentice from some family to whom his family was obligated. On the other hand, it may have been difficult for the entrepreneur to find persons to evaluate applicants outside his home village.

Frequently workers from the village took their positions for granted and did not work as hard. However, it was sometimes easier to instill a high *esprit de corps* in the work force if the

---

11. See the next section.

Table 8.4

Sources of Expansion Capital for Small Sample Firms

Source	Total
Profits[a]	10
Profits and savings[b]	1
Profits and government loans	1
Profits and loans other than government	2
Savings[b]	2
No additional capital	5
TOTAL	20

a. Profits include those realized from the enterprise in question.

b. Savings include those from income of the major entrepreneur realized outside of the footwear firm.

entrepreneur and most of the laborers were from the same district.[12] Thus, on balance, the entrepreneur probably benefited at least as much as he lost from the fact that a large percentage of his labor force was drawn from his home district.

The Growth of the Firm

Entrepreneurs from eleven of the fifteen firms acquiring additional capital raised at least 50 percent of the funds from profits retained in the enterprise. Part of the expansion of two other firms was financed through profits. In no case did the entrepreneurs report that new capital had been received from members of the extended family (see table 8.4).

In fact, the demands of the extended family curtailed the

12. Theodore Geiger and Winifred Armstrong, *The Development of African Private Enterprise* (Washington, D.C.: National Planning Association, 1964), p. 134.

use of profits for the expansion of sample firms. As the income of the entrepreneur increased, the number of dependents he was required to support also increased.[13] Among thirteen sample firms on which reliable data on profit were available, there is a strong positive relationship between the profit of the firm and the number of dependents[14] of the top entrepreneur.[15]

This evidence is reinforced by a finding of the Harris study.

> It seems clear that family obligations [on the part of entrepreneurs] require substantial amounts of current consumption expenditure, some of which might otherwise be saved and reinvested . . . . The number of dependents is positively correlated with income.[16]

It seems reasonable to believe, though, that the prestige and power afforded the successful entrepreneur by the extended family may provide an important incentive for entrepreneurial activity which may at least partially offset the disincentive effects of sharing income and wealth.[17]

Finally, as indicated in the discussion of the establishment of the firm, the extended family can affect the acquisition of labor and apprentice supply, and assist in obtaining useful contacts with businessmen and persons with economic power.[18]

---

13. In some cases, relatives of the entrepreneur would withdraw funds from the enterprise exceeding its profits.

14. A person who receives more than one-half his support from an entrepreneur is a dependent of the entrepreneur.

15. If X equals the 1964 profit of the firm (in pounds) and Y the number of dependents of the entrepreneur in 1964, $Y = 8.12 + 0.0039X$. If the *t*-test is used, the regression coeffi- is significant at the ½ percent level.

16. Harris, "Industrial Entrepreneurship in Nigeria," p. 284.

17. This point was mentioned to the author by John R. Harris.

18. The effect of the extended family on entrepreneurial activity probably varies from region to region. Several social scientists lend support to the view that the Ibo families (mostly from Eastern Nigeria) have a higher percentage of income invested in physical and human capital than families from other Nigerian socio-ethnic groups. Peter Kilby, "Nigerian Industry in

Investments outside the Firm

A part of the earnings diverted from the expansion of the firm was invested in other projects. In four cases the other projects of the entrepreneur had vertical linkages with the shoe firm. For example, two Aba firms began selling imported leather and rubber to other local shoemakers in order to obtain economies in purchasing materials. In another instance of vertical expansion, the Maiduguri Shoe firm established a small leather tanning firm in 1962 for the purpose of procuring an inexpensive source of leather.

For small entrepreneurs, the major form of investment outside footwear was in education and training. In 1965, seven of the twenty small entrepreneurs were supporting students in secondary school.[19]

One frequent pattern of investment can be found in Nigerian families. The family invests in the apprentice training and the initial business venture of the eldest son. The earnings of the eldest son, in addition to providing subsistence for himself and several other family members, are used to finance secondary education for a younger brother or relative. When the younger brother or relative completes his education, a large part of his earnings may be used to finance other forms of investment considered to be in the interest of the family as a whole.

The Shortage of Capital

Most Nigerian businessmen mention lack of capital as one of their major problems.[20] For example, most sample entrepreneurs

---

the Northern Region," (unpublished report submitted to the United States International Cooperation Administration, April 1961), p. 8; Robert A. LeVine and others, *Dreams and Deeds: Achievement Motivation in Nigeria* (Chicago: University of Chicago Press, 1966), pp. 12, 74, 78-9; Peter T. Bauer, *West African Trade* (London: Routledge and Kegan Paul Ltd., 1963), pp. 30-1; James S. Coleman, *Nigeria: Background to Nationalism* (Berkeley and Los Angeles: University of California Press, 1958), p. 333; Victor C. Uchendu, *The Igbo of Southeast Nigeria* (New York: Holt, Rinehart and Winston, 1966), pp. 36-7; and Callaway, *Odu*, I, No. 1, 12.

19. In 1965, the median tuition cost for a secondary student in a private school was about £N65 per year. This expenditure can definitely be considered as an investment. Other expenses of the student may be more than £N200 per annum.

20. Sayre P. Schatz and S.J. Edokpayi, "Economic Attitudes

indicated that the output and profit of the firm would increase if they could acquire more capital. Some indicated an interest in borrowing money from government loan agencies.

As Schatz indicates, the desire for additional capital by the entrepreneur does not necessarily represent an effective demand for it.[21] A number of the entrepreneurs wishing to acquire additional capital were probably over-optimistic, as some were making losses and many had a low rate of capacity utilization.[22] However, even if entrepreneurs with a desire for capital but a lack of effective demand are eliminated from the analysis, there may be an excess demand for capital resulting from government loan agencies charging a rate of interest below the market rate.[23]

---

of Nigerian Businessmen," *Nigerian Journal of Economic and Social Studies*, IV, No. 3 (December 1962), 266.

Thirteen of the twenty small entrepreneurs in our sample and most of the other entrepreneurs interviewed reported that one of their major problems was a shortage of capital.

21. *Development Bank Lending in Nigeria: The Federal Loans Board* (Ibadan: Oxford University Press, 1964), and "The Capital Shortage Illusion: Government Lending in Nigeria," *Oxford Economic Papers*, XVII, No. 2 (July 1965), 309-16. See E. Wayne Nafziger, "A Reconsideration of 'Capital Surplus' in Nigeria," *Nigerian Journal of Economic and Social Studies*, X, No. 1 (March 1968), 111-6, for an evaluation of Schatz's analysis.

22. A series of questions was devised to arrive at an estimate of capacity utilization of the firm. At one point in the interview the entrepreneur was asked for an estimate of present sales in pairs of footwear per unit of time. At another point he was asked for an estimate of the number of pairs the firm could produce per unit of time (with the same plant and equipment). In a number of instances the entrepreneur complained about the lack of capital when other statements in the interview indicated low capacity utilization of the firm.

23. See Gerald K. Helleiner, *Peasant Agriculture, Government, and Economic Growth in Nigeria* (Homewood, Ill.: Richard D. Irwin, Inc., 1966), pp. 265-6.

The financial advisor to the Fund for Agricultural and Industrial Development, the Eastern Region small loan board (F.A.I.D.), indicated in a personal interview, 16 March 1965, that frequently the explicit labor cost of officials and advisors of government agencies who appraise prospective F.A.I.D. loan projects exceeds the interest charges on the loan. The 9 percent interest rate charged by F.A.I.D. was only 2 percentage points above the modal Lagos bond rate and the bank rate to prime lenders.

Managing Apprentice Labor[24]

Apprentices, enrolled in the two to five year course in a small labor-intensive firm, frequently average about fifty hours per week on the job. In the footwear firm, most of the steps in the construction of a shoe are relatively arduous and meticulous. Much practice and observation is needed to master the arts of designing, fitting, stitching and lasting. The first stage is to learn routine sewing and stitching on repairs, and the apprentice may wait a long time after mastering this before he is instructed in and subsequently assigned to the next stage. Such delays may be due to fears, on the part of the master-proprietor that the inexperienced apprentice may ruin the fairly expensive materials - costing about one-fourth to one-third the final price of the shoe.

Although apprentice fees and wages were not standardized in 1965, they varied from £N17 to £N40 - frequently paid in annual installments, with the first payment at the beginning of the course. This initial payment may be a boon for the entrepreneur lacking working capital in the early stages of the enterprise. The highest fees are usually charged for the two to three year courses, since apprentices make very little contribution to output in such a relatively short time. In some instances, especially after the apprentice has been with the firm for more than a year, the master may pay the apprentice 10s (£N½) to £N1 per month.

Apprentices who are relatives of the master frequently pay no fees, and the master may in fact provide room and board for them. However, since the support of close relatives is frequently an accepted obligation, little marginal outlay is required.

Small firms depend heavily on apprentice labor. For example, most firms with ten workers employed do not usually have more than three persons working for an explicit wage. The rest are usually apprentices of the proprietor. As the size of the firm increases, the proportion of the labor force consisting of apprentice labor decreases. Among sample firms with value of output less than £N1,500, the percentage of workers employed as apprentices is 96; among firms with £N1,500-5,999 the percentage is 89; among those with £N6,000-12,000 the percentage is 73; and

---

24. For more information on the apprentice system, see chapter 7 above.

among large firms, the percentage is zero (see table 8.5). The increased division of labor accompanying increments in the size of firm necessitates lesser dependence upon apprentice labor. The broad training demanded by apprentice labor is not possible with the highly specialized production lines in large firms.[25]

Table 8.5

Apprentices as a Percentage of Workers Employed in Small Sample Firms, 1965[a]

Size of Firm by Per Annum Output in 1965	Number of Firms	Total Employment[b]	Total Number of Apprentices	Apprentices as a Percentage of Workers Employed
£N6,000-12,000	6	145	106	73
£N1,500-5,999	6	92	82	89
£N0-1,499	8	96	92	96
TOTAL	20	333	280	84

a. The figures for number of apprentices and number of employees are the *average* for 1965.

b. Working proprietors and partners not paid an explicit wage are not included.

Determinants of Apprentice Quantity

Most footwear apprentices train to be footwear entrepreneurs. Thus the supply of apprentices depends on long run expectations concerning the demand for footwear entrepreneurs, derived from the demand for footwear.

The extent of apprentice training is much greater in the

25. In some instances, large firms may refer to trainees as "apprentices." But as used in this study, the term "apprentice" excludes persons being trained in programs intended to prepare employees for positions within the firm.

south than in the North. In part, this results from the fact that in the North there are fewer small firms, which do most of the training of apprentices.[26] However, supply factors are also involved; Northern businessmen, charging comparable fees to those in the south, can find few apprentices available from their own region; and cannot attract southerners unless they offer more favorable terms. Northerners appear to have, for various socio-historical reasons, a higher discount of future earnings.[27] The Northerners' shorter time horizon, then, probably explains their paucity of investment in education and training - including apprentice training. However, without further data, generalizations about differential regional discount rates must be considered conjectural.

Apprentice Quantity and Future Population of Firms

A small entrepreneur, in training an apprentice or journeyman, is frequently training a prospective competitor, and the disadvantages in this system for the proprietor-teacher should be examined.

About one-eighth of the footwear *consumed* in Nigeria in 1964 (in terms of pound value) was produced in small urban domestic firms, which accounted for an ex factory output of £N670,000.[28] Footwear produced by small Onitsha firms comprised about 2 percent of total domestic consumption.

An Onitsha footwear firm with six apprentices engaged is likely to graduate two apprentices per annum, one of which, on the average, would establish his own firm. If the new firm produces £N500 footwear per annum, double the 1964 mean value of output of small Eastern firms, the firm would have no perceptible impact upon the price of footwear received by the old firm.

Yet it is possible that the increase in entrepreneurs from among the six to eight apprentice graduates per annum of firms like the United Shoe, the Liberty Footwear and Umuahia Shoe firms could have a perceptible effect on the price of footwear

26. See Callaway, *Odu*, I, No. 1, 12.

27. See Kilby, "Nigerian Industry in the Northern Region," p. 8; LeVine and others, *Dreams and Deeds*, pp. 12, 73-5, 78-9; Bauer, *West African Trade*, pp. 30-1; and Coleman, *Nigeria*, p. 333.

28. Cf. tables 5.2 and 5.3, which, however, measure different concepts.

of the firm over a period of a few years. This is especially possible if apprentices learning the trade from entrepreneurs in firms with a high output tend to develop the capability of producing a high level of output themselves. For example, if three Umuahia firms run by apprentice graduates of the Umuahia Shoe enterprise each produced one-half the output of the master's firm, the price of footwear in the city would undoubtedly be depressed.

But even if a firm's output of apprentices is expected to have an adverse effect on competition in the area, the entrepreneur may not restrict the number of apprentices trained. For it is highly probable that if the entrepreneur does not engage the apprentice, some competing entrepreneur will. Thus, restricting the number of apprentice trainees of the firm may reduce the inexpensive labor available to the firm, without reducing the number of prospective competitors.[29]

In the long run a problem of over-production of apprentice-trained footwear entrepreneurs is self-correcting. The increase in supply and decrease in the price of footwear resulting from a surplus of apprentice-trained entrepreneurs makes apprenticing in preparation for a footwear entrepreneurial position less attractive. A decrease in the number of apprentices together with the exit of some entrepreneurs will consequently eliminate the surplus of footwear entrepreneurs. However, due to the length of the apprentice course, there may be a several-year lag before price signals in the footwear market affect the supply of footwear apprentice graduates.[30] In the medium run, before the effects of the adjustment mechanism are completed, remuneration of footwear entrepreneurs would be very low.

Wage Rates of Unskilled Labor

Soon after the two-week general strike of June 1964, the

---

29. However there is a limit to the number of apprentices an entrepreneur will engage. But this limit is imposed not so much by the fear of producing increased competitors as by the difficulty of maintaining an effective organization while still providing apprentices with the broad individualized training expected.

30. Potential apprentices and their sponsors may be able to anticipate long run movements in industries in which the youths are considering training. If the long run expectations of apprentices are accurate, the over-production of apprentice-trained entrepreneurs would not take place.

Table 8.6

Government Minimum Monthly Wage Rates for Selected Nigerian Cities after July 1964

	£N.s.d.[a]
Lagos metropolitan area[b]	10.0.0
Ibadan, Benin, Sapele, Warri	8.2.6
Port Harcourt, Enugu, Aba, Onitsha, Umuahia, Owerri	8.2.6
Kano, Kaduna	6.18.8
Jos, Zaria	6.7.10
Maiduguri	5.4.0

a. 12d = 1s; 20s = £N1.

b. This zone covers a radius of sixteen miles from Tinibu Square in the city of Lagos.

Source: Lagos Chamber of Commerce, Economic Sub-Committee, *Economic Trends in Nigeria*, (August 1964), p. 9.

minimum monthly wage for government employees was increased (table 8.6 lists the minimum wages for selected cities in Nigeria). Although non-government employers were not legally bound to pay the minimum wages, pressure was brought to bear on large firms to do so.[31] In March 1965, the lowest wages in the Southeastern Shoe Company were £N7 per month. This is close to the 1965 prevailing wage for unskilled workers in urban areas in the south, except for the Lagos metropolitan area where wages were higher. In the North wages were lower.

Small firms usually paid less for labor. A journeyman in an Eastern firm with about £N2,000-10,000 output per annum was paid £N4-5 per month. The wage for a journeyman was relatively

---

31. See Lagos Chamber of Commerce, Economic Sub-committee, "The Morgan Report and its Aftermath," *Economic Trends in Nigeria*, 4th issue (August 1964), p. 10.

low, since the position was usually expected to be interim employment between apprentice training and establishing a business.

By and large, the following description of the Nigerian labor market by Gerald K. Helleiner was correct.

> Wage rates in the government sector and to a great extent in large-scale private industry, are pushed to artificially high levels through a variety of non-economic pressures. The market-clearing wage for unskilled and semi-skilled labor is, and in recent years, always has been far below the prevailing government-established minima. The lower wages paid in small industry are clearly far nearer the market-clearing rate. They probably usually approximate subsistence wages, although with the institution of the extended family system, which always ensures that family members will be provided for, it is quite possible for the wages to fall below subsistence. Thus there exists a considerable spread between the high "institutionally" established wage rate paid by some employers and the subsistence or even sub-subsistence wage paid for equivalent labor by others.[32]

> One can say . . . that if labor mobility were such as to permit the spreading of the available labor over the entire country, Nigeria would certainly not be a labor-surplus economy, and probably could be classified as a land-surplus economy . . . In most of Nigerian agriculture, labor (even of the unskilled sort) was and is a scarce factor of production. It carries a price (the wage rate) which, unlike that in labor surplus economies, probably roughly approximates its marginal productivity.[33]

---

32. *Peasant Agriculture, Government, and Economic Growth in Nigeria* (Homewood, Ill.: Richard D. Irwin, Inc., 1966), p. 324.

33. Ibid. pp. 55, 143. Helleiner observes that many young people in the labor force remain as unemployed applicants in urban areas rather than return to the rural areas where marginal productivity is positive. "To the universal primary education schemes must be ascribed a large share of the blame for the rising levels of unemployed youth in the urban areas of Southern

Thus, in the main, the labor hired by Nigerian manufacturing firms has had a positive opportunity cost.

Labor Relations and Discipline[34]

In the initial years of production by the firm, most entrepreneurs of large footwear enterprises reported some problems in labor adapting to the rigors of an industrial production line. Yet voluntary absence and voluntary turnover among Nigerian workers was relatively low.[35]

Indigenous footwear firms were adversely affected to a limited extent by strikes. The two-week general striks in Nigeria in June 1964 did not affect the small firms, where unions had virtually no power. However the labor force went on strike in the four large footwear firms established before this date; and the resultant rise in the *government* minimum wage rate led to pressure on large industrial firms to raise wages also.[36]

Nigeria," he contends. "The growth of urban unemployment . . . was, apparently, the result of an acceleration in the rural-urban flow of labor which found its roots partly in the spread of primary education and the consequent dissatisfaction among young people with farming as a way of life . . . The semi-educated young people turned out by the schools left the rural areas in droves to seek the sophistication, the 'bright lights,' and the higher-status jobs of the cities." Ibid. pp. 308, 39.

It is more helpful to view the decision to remain an unemployed applicant in the urban area from the perspective of the extended family instead of the individual. Unemployed youths are dependent upon the extended family for subsistence and security. Thus it is unlikely that the young unemployed applicant would remain in the city without the acquiescence of the extended family, who, given that individual family members are provided for, may view the applicant's status in terms of long run rather than short run maximization. A high probability of the youth finding remunerative employment in the city may be valued more than the certainty of his obtaining a relatively low income on the farm. But in addition, employment of the youth in the city diversifies the sources of family income and provides a more reliable and steady source of income.

34. Because of the nature of the study, labor relations are viewed in terms of their effect on entrepreneurship instead of from a wider perspective.

35. Kilby, "African Labour Productivity Reconsidered," *Economic Journal*, LXXI (June 1961), 278.

36. The pressure for higher wages and other long run ef-

Small firms encountered some problems in labor discipline, even though the requirements for laborers were not as rigorous as in large firms. Irregular attendance among apprentices for reasons other than poor health was frequent. In 1965 at the Western Shoe firm, a five-month apprentice attendant chart showed about a 25 percent absentee rate among the eleven apprentices. An Aba entrepreneur, who complained about idolence, poor discipline and irregular attendance among his apprentices, found it necessary to suspend or release apprentices. Yet few apprentices left before their apprentice period expired.

The Onitsha Shoe firm probably had the highest worker attendance rates among small sample firms. An independent source attributed the strong discipline in the firm to the decision to release its six most skilled journeymen when, in February 1964, they refused to transfer to a new plant unless they received higher wages.

As indicated in chapter 4, workers were not interviewed systematically since it was feared that this might damage rapport with entrepreneurs. However it appeared that entrepreneurs, especially in small firms, were frequently paternalistic towards unskilled workers and apprentices, and, in adopting policies with regard to wages, hours, working conditions, and fringe benefits, took advantage of the workers' limited alternative employment opportunities.

Labor Utilization in Small Firms

The author, like Callaway in his study of apprentices in Nigeria, observed much low productivity and underemployment in the apprentice system.[37] Low utilization of labor is understandable where the wage is low, particularly in the apprentice system where fees generally exceed wages. Even if the apprentice is diligent, his marginal net revenue productivity is probably negative in the early months of the course.[38] It is rational, therefore, for the entrepreneur to continue to engage apprentice labor until the *decrement* in the value of output from an additional apprentice equals the apprentice fee minus the wage (the sight of a proprietor and fifteen apprentices in a shop so small

---

fects of the general strike are discussed from the perspective of the businessman in Lagos Chamber of Commerce, *Economic Trends in Nigeria* (August 1964), pp. 8-12.

37. *Odu*, I, No. 1, 12-3.

38. See Ibid. p. 12.

that they hindered each other was a common scene).

Callaway's description of the activity of apprentices could be applied satisfactorily to small footwear firms also. "Sewing machines were quiet. Some apprentices were reading the daily papers; others were peacefully asleep at their tables."[39] But since the entrepreneur receives income from apprentice fees as well as sales of commodities, it may be advantageous for the entrepreneur to engage apprentices even if work cannot be provided for them.

J.I. Roper indicates that low productivity among small firms arises from the lack of specialization and division of labor in the work force. He notes that "in West Africa, handicraft production shows no marked tendency towards the division of labour in larger workshops and factories. The individual handicraftsman remains dominant. This is true even in shoemaking, for example, which is suitable for team work."[40]

In Nigeria, at least, the lack of division of labor among small footwear firms can be attributed, to a large extent, to the requirements of the apprentice system. Where apprentice labor is used, the necessity that the apprentice be broadly trained prevents a highly specialized production line.

Labor Productivity in Large Firms

Foreign entrepreneurs and managers in large manufacturing firms frequently complain about the low quality of the labor force in Nigeria. Whether or not the complaints are well founded, it is clear that where low labor productivity does exist in southern Nigeria it is due more to lack of experience or deficiency in supervision[41] rather than cultural impediments.

Conclusion

For large firms, the major sources of initial and expansion capital were loans. The extended family was instrumental in the acquisition of initial capital for small firms.

Small firms depended heavily on apprentice labor. Since

---

39. Ibid. p. 13.
40. *Labour Problems in West Africa* (London: Penguin Books Ltd., 1958), p. 7.
41. See Kilby, *Economic Journal*, LXXI, 273-91.

most footwear apprentices trained to be footwear entrepreneurs, there was some risk that, in the short run, a small entrepreneur would train so many apprentices that the price of footwear in the city might be depressed.

Although labor hired by Nigerian manufacturing firms did have a positive opportunity cost, official minimum wage rates were only £N10 per month in the Lagos metropolitan area. Voluntary absence was low among large firms, but attendance was irregular among apprentice laborers in several small firms.

Almost all prospective entrepreneurs in small firms have been students in an apprentice course, which in virtually all cases is sponsored by members of the extended family. Only rarely does a potential entrepreneur forego the necessary apprentice training as a result of demands on his income by the extended family. Clearly the effect of the extended family is to augment the number of students taking apprentice courses, which increases the supply of entrepreneurs.

Small entrepreneurs are very dependent upon the extended family for capital to establish a firm. Only rarely is the income of a prospective entrepreneur diverted from the establishment of a firm to consumption expenditures of other family members. Thus, *in toto*, the extended family increases the establishment of firms by entrepreneurs.

Entrepreneurs wishing to expand their firms lose more than they benefit from the institution of the extended family. Although entrepreneurs rarely receive funds from the family for expansion of the firm, the family does require resources for current consumption which might otherwise have been reinvested in the business.

Many development economists have contended that the institution of the extended family is a major barrier to entrepreneurial activity. Among small Nigerian shoe firms, the extended family hinders the expansion of the firm by the entrepreneur, but facilitates the entrepreneur's training and establishment of a firm, and, without further evidence, would therefore not seem to have a negative effect on entrepreneurial activity. It is conceivable that the positive contribution of training and firm establishment may in many cases exceed the negative effect on firm expansion, but this requires further research.

Chapter 9

The Interregional Structure of Entrepreneurship

Little information is available on interregional economic relations within Nigeria, or for that matter within other African countries. This chapter focuses on patterns of interregional and socio-ethnic group migration and business relations[1] among footwear entrepreneurs. In addition to the entrepreneurs of footwear manufacturing firms, entrepreneurs of ninety indigenous footwear trading firms were interviewed.[2]

The Nigerian Footwear Distribution System

During 1964-65 there were three major networks, corresponding to the three major ethnic communities in Nigeria - Ibo, Yoruba, and Hausa[3] - for distributing the footwear produced by indigenous firms. Production for each network was centered in the ethnic group area, and was distributed nationally by members of that community. There was one major exception: few Ibo and Yoruba

---

1. For quantitative estimates of interregional commodity flows, see A.M. Hay and R.H.T. Smith, "Preliminary Estimates of Nigeria's Interregional Trade and Associated Money Flows," *Nigerian Journal of Economic and Social Studies*, VIII (March 1966), 9-35, and *Interregional Trade and Money Flows in Nigeria, 1964* (Ibadan: Oxford University Press, 1970), reviewed by this author in *The Journal of Modern African Studies*, No. 1 (1972), 162-3.

2. Of the 90 trading firms, 32 were in the North, 21 in the East, 15 each in Lagos and the West, and 7 in the Mid-West. See E. Wayne Nafziger, "Nigerian Entrepreneurship: A Study of Indigenous Businessmen in the Footwear Industry," (unpublished Ph.D. dissertation, University of Illinois, 1967), pp. 205-7, for a further discussion of procedures and methods.

3. Each of the three communities comprises about one-sixth to one-fifth of the population of Nigeria (table 2.7).

shoe merchants were located in each other's ethnic group area.

An Ibo distributive system was especially prominent, reflecting the significance of the East in the output of indigenous firms.[4] This system fanned out from Onitsha (and Aba) to the east of a straight north-south line going through Onitsha. The Ibo distributive network extended to the east and southeast, including, in addition to Iboland, Efik-speaking Calabar; reached into all non-Yoruba urban areas of the North; and penetrated somewhat into the Mid-West. The Yoruba distributive system ran northwards in roughly a straight line from Lagos to Ilorin. Furthermore, Yorubas comprised a small minority of traders in Ibo-dominated Jos, Kaduna, Zaria, and Kano. Yoruba traders in these northern cities generally bought their footwear in Lagos and Ibadan. In the Ibo and Yoruba distributive systems, sales to the final consumer were generally made in shops and stalls in or near the indigenous open-air market places.

The Hausa production of footwear was a small part of the output of firms making leather goods. Production was centered mainly in Kano and Sokoto, besides other major Hausa and Kanuri cities, in addition to output by the small Hausa population in Lagos. From these centers, itinerant Hausa traders took the leather goods to airports (such as Kano and Lagos), hotels, rest houses, and high-income residential areas, in addition to market shops and stalls.

There were not many business dealings between members of the different communal group systems. A few major exceptions were the occasional Yoruba merchants of Ibadan, who went to Onitsha to purchase shoes and sandals; the Ibo merchants of Onitsha, who might buy in the Yoruba-dominated Ibadan and Lagos markets; and the Ibo merchants in Ibadan, who comprised approximately one-fifth of the footwear merchants in that city.

Business Relations between Ethnic Group Areas

Barriers to inter-ethnic economic relations existed despite the fact that Nigerian businessmen had appeared to be highly responsive to pecuniary incentives.[5] The three separate foot-

---

4. See tables 5.1 and 5.2.

5. See Peter Kilby, "African Labour Productivity Reconsidered," *The Economic Journal*, LXXXI, No. 282 (June 1961), 283; and John R. Harris and Mary P. Rowe, "Entrepreneurial Patterns in the Nigerian Sawmilling Industry," *Nigerian Journal of Economic and Social Studies*, VII, No. 1 (March 1966), 87-8.

wear distributive systems were probably less a result of communal partisanship than other factors, especially language barriers and credit difficulties, which made it advantageous for the entrepreneur to transact business with a member of his own ethnic group. Because of the large number of language groups in Nigeria, many businessmen were only able to communicate effectively in their "tribal" language or the dominant language of the region. The lack of a common language frequently hampered business dealings.

Cultural and language barriers are illustrated by the experience of Mr. C.S. Akpabio, an Efik-speaking shoemaker in the Ibo city of Aba from 1963 to the early part of 1966, and one of the most highly skilled designers among the entrepreneurs of small footwear firms. In 1965 his firm, the Cosmopolitan Shoe firm, had a loss of £N290 (on £N850 net worth) and a value of output of only £N370, due in part to the cultural and language barriers encountered by Mr. Akpabio in marketing. Virtually all Aba wholesale buyers were Ibo-speaking, but, since the entrepreneur and his laborers spoke Ibo poorly, the firm had not been able to acquire wholesale outlets,[6] and had forfeited the economies of scale which would have resulted.

The three separate distributive systems arose, to a large extent, from the significance of credit in Nigerian trade and the lack of credit facilities between members of different ethnic communities.[7] Most Nigerian small businessmen, especially merchants, were operating on a margin of liquid capital which did not provide for the time lag between purchasing and selling even a small volume of goods.[8] Since the merchant rarely had access to loanable funds, he frequently needed to obtain credit from the producer, who, in turn, was often forced to seek credit from his domestic suppliers.[9] Thus the rate of output and sales of the

---

6. Even foreign firms in Nigeria, which as a group had been slow to Nigerianize on the production side, had virtually all recognized the necessity of appointing depot and agency managers who knew the language of the local buyer.

7. See P.T. Bauer, *West African Trade* (Cambridge: Cambridge University Press, 1954), pp. 61-2; and Henry L. Bretton, *Power and Stability in Nigeria* (New York: Praeger, 1962), p. 89.

8. At the levels of income of Nigerian merchants, liquidity above a bare minimum might be a luxury. In addition, the claims of the extended family might prevent the merchant from accumulating a margin of liquid capital for current transactions demands.

9. Producers who could purchase supplies in large quanti-

producer might depend upon the credit-worthiness of both the producer, *vis-à-vis* the domestic supplier, and the merchant, *vis-à-vis* the producer. Credit-worthiness depended upon a number of socio-cultural factors. A businessman would generally sell on credit only to those he could trust - in most cases, people whom he knew, whose home was nearby, whose system of customary laws and courts was common, and whose language and cultural traits were similar to his.

Margaret Katzin, in her study of the Onitsha market, found almost no instances of Ibos in Onitsha attempting to discriminate against other ethnic groups.[10] However, she indicated that Ibos were more likely to extend credit to other Ibos, since it was much easier to check their credit-worthiness and establish that they or their families would be responsible, than to do so for prospective buyers who lived far away. It should be noted that the Ibo footwear distributive system was larger than the Yoruba system, one reason being the fact that Ibos had a greater tendency to extend credit to stranger Ibos than Yorubas to stranger Yorubas. For example, Ibo merchants in Kano and Jos indicated that, after they had paid cash for two major purchases, they could generally secure partial credit from Ibo traders and producers in Onitsha, and would then pay on their next trip to Onitsha to purchase footwear. Despite this, Ibo footwear producers and merchants indicated a lower ratio of "bad debts" to sales than Yoruba firms. Among Ibos, relatives were more likely to take the responsibility for guaranteeing that the debt was paid, and sanctions against default were strong since Ibos feel strongly that individual failure reflects on the reputation of the lineage.[11]

---

ties could frequently economize by ordering materials directly from overseas firms. However, there was usually a time lag of at least two months between the order and receipt of the supplies. Also it was virtually impossible for a small Nigerian firm to procure credit from a foreign firm. Thus the average working capital of the firm needed to be high if the firm was to order supplies directly from overseas. Of course the problem of maintaining adequate liquidity could be very acute if the firm bought from foreign suppliers, and sold on credit.

10. Katzin attributes this to their fear that such discrimination would harm the reputation of this trade center.

11. See Victor C. Uchendu, *The Igbo of Southeast Nigeria* (New York: Holt, Rinehart and Winston, 1966), pp. 34, 64-6; and Phoebe Ottenberg, "The Afikpo Ibo of Eastern Nigeria" in *Peoples of Africa*, ed. by James L. Gibbs (New York: Holt, Rinehart and Winston, Inc., 1965), p. 6.

The barrier to inter-communal credit transactions can be illustrated by the case of the Maiduguri Shoe firm. As a result of the wide reputation of the firm for the production of suede shoes and mosquito boots, two-thirds of its manufacturing output was sold directly to final consumers more than fifty miles from Maiduguri. The 1965 manufacturing output of the firm was £N1,020, compared to a repair output of £N2,300. The enterprise had the capacity to increase its production of sandals from the 1965 level of about 600 pairs (or £N300) per annum to at least 4,000 pairs per annum - above the lower limit of output necessary to sell regularly to wholesale buyers. Given 1965 plant size, the entrepreneur, Mallam M.D. Sanusi, admitted that the production of sandals was more profitable than the repair business. He had in fact been approached in 1963 by local Ibo merchants who wished to order sandals wholesale, but, since the merchants could not deposit money in advance of production or pay cash in full at the time of purchase, no agreement was made. The Ibo merchants who sold footwear in their shops on the outskirts of Maiduguri market were at that time travelling to Jos or Onitsha every three weeks to buy 300-500 pairs of sandals.

In this example, credit-worthiness was determined by a number of socio-cultural factors. Mallam Sanusi, although prepared to extend credit to fellow Kanuris, considered the local Ibo footwear merchants to be poor credit risks, partly because they were highly mobile and partly because their "home villages" were over 700 miles from Maiduguri, which made it difficult to check their credit-worthiness and find relatives to guarantee payment.

Migration of the Entrepreneur

Although there was some *inter*-provincial and *intra*-regional migration among manufacturing entrepreneurs, there was almost no interregional or socio-ethnic group area migration. Among the eighty-one indigenous entrepreneurs interviewed, only three were operating businesses in a region other than that of their birth,[12] and only two were operating businesses in an area dominated by another ethnic community.[13]

---

12. For the purpose of this analysis, Lagos is included with the Western Region.

13. The author made a deliberate attempt to find entrepreneurs of sizable businesses among minority groups in a communal group area. In addition to utilizing sources of information already cited, producers with a yearly output exceeding £N1,500 were found by questioning footwear merchants in the open-air

Early in 1966 Mr. Akpabio, the Efik shoemaker in Aba, transferred his firm to his own ethnic group area. This was planned several months before the political upheaval of January 1966, and was partly because of the language and cultural barriers he encountered in the Ibo city.

In Jos, Kaduna, Zaria, Kano, and Maiduguri, the author found only one minority-group entrepreneur[14] whose output was worth more than £N1,500 in 1965. The actual figure was £N2,500, and the firm, located in Jos, ranked third among indigenous footwear firms in the North, although its average net worth in 1965 was less than £N200. The entrepreneur was an Ibo, Mr. J.S. Nwaisioji. Yet this firm is not a significant exception to the hypothesis that migration among footwear entrepreneurs is confined to their ethnic group areas. In the first place, Mr. Nwaisioji had only one laborer, a rented shop, ten by fifteen feet, and a few hand-tools. Secondly, he remained in Jos for less than two years, and was then forced to return to Iboland in November 1965 when the Jos market authorities revoked the rent permit for his enterprise. This revocation conformed to a pattern of general political pressure for "Northernization" of the private sector and government service in the North.

Thus, in the two major recent examples of footwear entrepreneurs who had migrated to another ethnic group area, the migration was only temporary. A large percentage of minority-group manufacturing entrepreneurs encountered pressures to leave the area as a result of cultural and language barriers, economic restrictions and discrimination by local authorities, or the direct physical threat arising from inter-communal conflict or political crisis.

---

markets who bought from large-scale producers. These merchants knew of no wholesale sellers of footwear belonging to minority ethnic groups, other than the two indicated. John R. Harris, in a study of the sawmill, furniture, printing, rubber-processing, and garment-making industries, found only 5 out of 101 entrepreneurs operating businesses outside the regions of their birth. "Industrial Entrepreneurship in Nigeria" (unpublished Ph.D. dissertation, Northwestern University, 1967), p. 252.

Among the entrepreneurs of sample firms, there was no interregional migration and only one case of communal group migration (i.e. the case of Mr. C.S. Akpabio discussed above).

14. Foreigners are not considered to be members of minority groups.

Differential Migration Patterns among Merchants, Manufacturers and Petty Industrialists

However, in 1965 the pressures on traders and merchants were not as great as those on the manufacturers. For example, an Ibo market merchant in the North was less likely to be compelled to leave than an Ibo manufacturer, even if the value-added by the former was larger. Unlike Ibo manufacturers, Ibo merchants in the North had made themselves essential for the effectual functioning of the Northern economy before the emphasis on Northernization.

More important is the fact that most entrepreneurs did not feel sufficiently confident of long run stability and safety to establish a manufacturing firm with a large amount of fixed capital in another socio-ethnic group area. Since the large manufacturer could not easily liquidate his assets each time there was a political crisis or a communal conflict, the most prudent course was to remain in his own region. Minority-group merchants and petty industrialists had a major advantage over minority-group manufacturers, since they had only a few capital assets, mostly inventories of footwear, which could be converted relatively quickly into cash in the case of a crisis.[15]

For most of 1964-65, economic opportunities for southerners as merchants and petty industrialists in the Jos-Kaduna-Zaria-Kano area were very favorable, even on a short term basis.[16] The demand for footwear, for example, was keen, but Northerners had been slow to exploit the economic opportunities in this and other industries where there was a brisk demand. Southerners were generally more responsive to economic incentives,[17] but they had been deterred by a concern for security and safety. The

---

15. Here firms with a net worth of less than £N200 are designated as "petty firms," and their entrepreneurs "petty industrialists."

16. Regardless of where he lived, a member of a southern ethnic group was called a "southerner."

17. See Peter Kilby, "Nigerian Industry in the Northern Region" (unpublished report to the United States Industrial Cooperation Administration, 19 April 1961), p. 8; Margaret Katzin, "The Role of the Small Entrepreneur," in *Economic Transition in Africa*, ed. by Melville J. Herskovits and Mitchell Harwitz (Evanston, Illinois: Northwestern University Press, 1964), p. 189; Robert A. LeVine and others, *Dreams and Deeds: Achievement Motivation in Nigeria* (Chicago: University of Chicago Press, 1966), pp. 12, 73-9; James S. Coleman, *Nigeria: Background to*

southern petty industrialist who was willing to take non-economic risks could frequently secure monopoly profits - in part because footwear merchants in northern markets were predominantly members of southern ethnic groups.

In conclusion, minority-group manufacturing entrepreneurs in Nigeria were rare, even in 1965, except possibly in the relatively cosmopolitan city of Lagos, where non-Yoruba entrepreneurs established firms in some sectors. Along with barriers of language, culture, and communal discrimination, a major reason was the lack of political and economic security for businessmen operating in another ethnic group area.[18]

Interregional Managerial Wage Differentials

In 1965, in footwear manufacturing firms with about £N3,000 net worth and twenty workers, the monthly wages of top managers were about £N15 in the East, £N20 in the West and Lagos, and £N25 in the North. The relative ranking of regions by monthly managerial salaries was similar in small firms of other sizes - and probably in other industries, as a result of inter-industry mobility within each region. The barriers to migration mentioned above explain the persistence of regional differentials. Without these barriers, many of which have been non-economic, more entrepreneurs and managers would have migrated from Iboland, where entrepreneurial resources were relatively abundant, to Hausaland, where entrepreneurship was relatively scarce.

Interregional differences in salaries for top managers in large footwear firms were not significant. The availability of foreigners, who have been more mobile between regions than Nigerians, has made this market less segmented.

It is more difficult to draw inferences concerning manageri-

Nationalism (Berkeley and Los Angeles: University of California Press, 1958), pp. 64, 333-6; P. Ottenberg, "The Afikpo Ibo," in *Peoples of Africa*, ed. by Gibbs, p. 6; and Bauer, *West African Trade*, pp. 30-1.

18. The situation differs from the economic development of Europe in the seventeenth through the nineteenth century, where in a number of cases, the dominant socio-political group allowed members of minority groups to enter low-status business occupations. Perhaps one of the reasons for the difference is that pecuniary achievements have been valued rather highly by majority groups in Nigeria - especially in the south.

al wages in trading firms than in manufacturing firms. The wages to management are difficult to identify precisely, where there are no hired managers; in footwear trading firms, most returns to management are implicit wages of persons who also provide other factor services. However, one would expect that 1965 interregional differentials in wages to managers in trade were less than in manufacturing, because of greater interregional migration by merchants and traders.

Conclusion

Even before 1966, interregional and inter-communal migration and business intercourse were meager, except in some branches of trade.[19] From 1966 to 1970, as a result of civil conflict, there was a sharp decline in the number of entrepreneurs operating outside their own communal group areas.[20] Although some Yoruba businessmen returned to the North during the civil war, and a number of Ibos went back to areas of the Federation outside the East after the war, the number of entrepreneurs outside the area of their ethnic community in the 1970s was substantially smaller than in the early 1960s.

The reduction of barriers to inter-communal business dealings needs to be viewed in terms of the long run process of nation-building. Interregional economic integration depends upon political integration and stability, or more specifically upon the renewal or development of a spirit of Nigerian nationalism, an army and police force with primary loyalty to the Federal

---

19. There is no reason to expect socio-cultural barriers to inter-communal and interregional economic relations to be less significant in commodities other than footwear. See Bauer, *West African Trade*, pp. 39-40, 389-90.

20. The conflict has had a permanent effect on the communal composition of entrepreneurs in the North. Development economists have pointed to instances where rapid socio-economic change, including the rise of indigenous entrepreneurs, has resulted from external shocks to traditional societies. Cf. W.W. Rostow, *The Stages of Economic Growth* (2nd ed.; Cambridge: Cambridge University Press, 1961), pp. 6, 26-7. Perhaps the withdrawal of southern entrepreneurs from trade, transport, and crafts in the North and the accompanying disruption of the Northern economy may have provided the economic incentive and socio-psychological challenge for a rise in entrepreneurship among Hausas and other Northerners. See "Exodus from the North", *West Africa*, No. 2581 (19 November 1966), p. 319.

government, safeguards and protection for minorities, and the learning of languages used in other regions as well as a common language (i.e. English), which should be one of the advantages of universal primary education now being planned for the whole country.

In Nigeria, major centripetal forces could be the potential pecuniary gains from regional specialization, interregional migration, and inter-communal business relations. Even in the 1970s, it is not clear whether these forces of economic inducement are as powerful as the centrifugal forces of social, political, communal, and linguistic differences.

Chapter 10

The Development of Entrepreneurship

In attempting in this chapter, to recommend a policy for the development of Nigerian industrial entrepreneurship, I have conceived entrepreneurship as an integral part of the whole economy, and not, as others have done, viewed entrepreneurship as the primary target. I start with the premise that programs should pay for themselves in the long run unless they create positive spillover effects or redistribute income in a more equable way. A program that does not pay for itself, i.e. where the recipient of the service is not charged an economic price, involves a subsidy to him. Since the alternative to a subsidy is the allocation of resources for other investment or consumption purposes, the burden of proof for a subsidy should fall on its advocate. One justification for subsidies is an instance where there are spillovers, or external economies (as defined in the broader sense by development economists such as Scitovsky), i.e. where social profitability of a project exceeds its commercial profitability as a result of divergences between money receipts and real benefits to society, and between money costs and social costs. However, since the "external economies" argument is convenient for planners to use to support projects that are economically untenable but politically favored, it is essential that the nature of the positive divergences be made explicit.[1] In my view, another justification for subsidies to a program or project might be to improve the distribution of income. This principle would be consistent with, e.g., subsidies to distribute rice or milk to low-income families, but not to provide automobile allowances for

---

1. Wolfgang F. Stolper, *Planning Without Facts: Lessons in Resource Allocation from Nigeria's Development* (Cambridge: Harvard University Press, 1966), pp. 166, 280; Sayre P. Schatz, "African Capitalism: Development Policy in Nigeria" (unpublished manuscript, Berkeley, Calif: 1976), chapter 6, and Tibor Scitovsky, "Two Concepts of External Economies," *Journal of Political Economy*, LXII (April 1954), 143-51.

senior civil servants, who are in the higher-income brackets.

Training Programs

The first few sections discuss programs for small entrepreneurs. As indicated in chapter 7, an entrepreneur of a Type II firm (one with a 1964 average net worth of £N3,000 or less) who wishes to expand to a Type I firm (an average net worth of more than £N3,000) usually requires training beyond the apprentice course. Few training programs in Nigeria are designed for prospective Type I entrepreneurs. One or two post-apprentice courses[2] - each of less than six months duration - are probably optimal in training Type II entrepreneurs to make the transition to a Type I firm. In offering the course, priority should be given to individuals with a current or prospective entrepreneurial position in a Type I firm. Both technical and managerial training need to be stressed. It is preferable that the institution and instructors offering the course be partially involved in rendering on-the-job technical and managerial assistance to firms.

To insure optimal return on investment in training, the course should usually not be offered to persons unlikely to attain entrepreneurial authority in a Type I or large firm. A person who has finished the course successfully is likely to have too high an alternative price for a Type II firm, which usually requires only apprentice training.

In addition, both individual and group instruction is more effective if the instructors are acquainted with the needs of the firms the students represent. This point especially needs to be underlined in Nigeria, where instructors are frequently either foreigners who are initially unacquainted with the small scale and lack of technical and managerial expertness of many manufacturing enterprises, or indigenes who have had little acquaintance with the operation of industrial firms.

For two reasons, the length of course should be shorter than six months. First, a firm of the size considered is likely to be dominated by one entrepreneur, whose removal from the firm for a

---

2. "Post-apprentice" does not mean that the course would be taken immediately upon completion of the apprentice course. It only indicates that the student normally will have completed only, but no more than, an apprentice course. In most cases, a few years lapse between the apprentice course and post-apprentice course would be preferable.

shorter course brings about less disruption in the development of the firm. Secondly, longer courses would have difficulty competing for students with post-primary management and technical training institutes.

If the choice of additional training is considered from the standpoint of an entrepreneur in a firm with an employment of ten to twenty-four, who has attained the modal educational level of his group (graduation from a six-year primary school), it is clear that the majority would prefer a one- to three-year post-primary management or technical education that would prepare them for a starting annual salary of £N360-480 as a technician or administrator in the civil service or a large industrial firm, to a one- to two-year post-primary training program preparing them to direct a risky venture where annual wages to management may be £N200-360.

Direct Entrepreneurial Assistance to Small Firms

There is much economic rationale for extension programs which provide direct entrepreneurial and technical assistance to small firms. The alternative wage of a person with high-level technical and entrepreneurial skills is too high for him to be utilized in a small firm. However, if an individual's scarce entrepreneurial and technical skills are used as an input for thirty or forty firms in a year, the economic cost per firm is low.

The experience of centers in Nigeria providing direct entrepreneurial and technical assistance to firms has shown that successful departments and programs are often tied closely to the skill and drive of one person. Where turnover of personnel is rapid, firm expansion launched under the direction of a competent advisor from an industrial development center may no longer be successful after the advisor departs.

Industrial Extension Centers

In Nigeria, the major industrial centers for industrial training and extension are the Industrial Development Centres (I.D.C.s). An I.D.C. was established in Owerri, Eastern Nigeria in 1963, and in Zaria, Northern Nigeria in 1966. By 1980, the end of the Third National Development Plan, there is to be an I.D.C. in each of the states.[3] The I.D.C. has four basic func-

3. Nigeria, Ministry of Economic Development, *Third National Development Plan 1975-80*, V. II, *Project Summary* (Lagos: Central Planning Office, 1975), 155.

tions: (1) the making of feasibility studies of projects for which loans for small manufacturing firms are sought, and the rendering of assistance in implementing such projects; (2) the development of prototype projects; (3) the provision of management and technical training facilities; and (4) advice to entrepreneurs in their firms.[4]

As indicated in chapter 7, an improvement in the technical and managerial skills of the entrepreneur is usually necessary for a small firm to undertake substantial expansion profitably. Because the enhancement of these skills tends to go hand in hand with capital expansion, it is important that loan agencies coordinate their operations closely with industrial extension centers engaged in upgrading the entrepreneur's capabilities. Furthermore, this coordination is crucial, since loan agencies, which lack high-level personnel to assess projects in more than a narrow range of industrial fields, need to depend upon experts in these centers to appraise the feasibility of manufacturing projects.

The activities of I.D.C.s in product development, and the demonstration and exhibition of prototype projects, are closely related to their work in providing technical and entrepreneurial advice and assistance to small industrialists. The Zaria I.D.C. has tried to develop products or implements well adapted to the requirements of the North, such as plows, ridgers, oxcarts and ox-yokes, groundnut lifters, and so forth. These developments have drawn on the work done by the Federal Institute of Industrial Research on industrial technology and raw materials.[5] The I.D.C. in Owerri can demonstrate sewing, tack lasting, pulling-over, and finishing machines to shoemakers who have expanded in output and capital stock or anticipate such an expansion. However, costs have been too prohibitive to provide machinery prototypes for more than a few of the numerous potential manufacturing industries, even when there were only two I.D.C.s. At the Zaria I.D.C. equipment was underutilized, either because of lack of clients, or because of missing spare parts, inadequate local repair skills, insufficient electrical power, inappropriate machine

---

4. John C. De Wilde, *The Development of African Private Enterprise*, V. II, *Country Annexes*, International Bank for Reconstruction and Development, and International Development Association Report No. AW-31, Washington, D.C., 10 December 1971, Annex VIII, 13-7. The views of the report do not represent those of the Bank Group.

5. Ibid. II, Annex VIII, 15.

technology for indigenous requirements, or a shortage of skilled technical personnel to undertake the demonstrations.

Since I.D.C. technical and extension personnel are acquainted with the capabilities of a wide range of small entrepreneurs, they should have a major role in identifying potentially feasible projects. Frequently, projects for the expansion of small-scale industry are not feasible without the array of services provided by the I.D.C. - technical and management training, advice on capital acquisition and plant organization, and assistance in obtaining financing (e.g., from Small Industry Credit schemes).

The Third Plan has allocated substantial funds for undertaking a small industries potential survey, with a feasibility analysis of industries in each state.[6] If I.D.C. personnel have access to these findings, it will facilitate their ability to aid in the development of feasible projects for small entrepreneurs.[7]

A small number of the I.D.C. training programs - most notably, that coordinated by the Footwear Specialist at Owerri, 1964-65 -conform to the recommendations for programs discussed in the first part of the chapter. Courses for footwear entrepreneurs are usually less than one week - short enough to avoid serious disruption in one-man operations. The instruction tends to range from a three- or four-day course for ten to twelve entrepreneurs in bookkeeping and management practices to an afternoon session on the use of machines. Instruction by the Footwear Specialist is individualized, specific, and based on an acquaintance with the setting of the firm. Managerial and technical assistance and advice are provided at the entrepreneur's plant, as well as on the Centre's premises. Because of frequent visits to footwear firms throughout the Eastern Region, the Footwear Advisor can often give individualized assistance on production line sequence, machinery acquisition, skill training, and management practices, even at the I. D. C. workshop.

A comprehensive program of technical advice and training for entrepreneurs is limited to a very small number of industries at

---

6. The total estimated expenditure for the survey and feasibility analysis, together with the exhibitions, seminars and workshops for small industrialists, is £N1 million (i.e. two million Naira). Nigeria, *Third Plan*, II, 157.

7. Past experience suggests the difficulty of coordinating information between departments and agencies of the states and Federal government.

I.D.C.-Owerri or I.D.C.-Zaria. Most small manfuacturers have no access to an industrial extension advisor knowledgeable in their industry either in their own state or indeed in the country as a whole. The major impediment to industrial extension and training programs is the lack of high-level technical skills in Nigeria. The few Nigerians with both practical industrial skills and instructional competence are difficult to obtain because of their high opportunity costs in public firms, foreign private firms, and the civil service. In the past, a few gaps have been filled by personnel from the International Labour Organization, the United Nations Industrial Development Organization, and U.S. and other aid agencies at nominal costs to the Nigerian governments. Although Nigeria will be able to afford a larger number of foreign advisors as a result of the substantial number of foreign exchange reserves acquired from oil exports, it will no longer be able to obtain these advisors at concessionary rates.

A specialist in marketing, purchasing, labor relations, finance, management, cost accounting, or another field can probably be afforded by a single I.D.C., or at least two or three I.D.C.s in cooperation. However, the alternative cost of an instructor-extension worker in each state for each of the thirty to forty major small industries in the state would be prohibitive. Substantial economies can be achieved, though, if an extension agent is used in several industries (e.g., tanneries, leather products, and footwear), several states (e.g., the northern states), or even the whole country.

In some instances, the capabilities of extension agents can be enhanced through training provided by skilled personnel in foreign and government enterprises and other I.D.C.s in Nigeria, and foreigners on short-term contracts. The training may vary from individualized instruction to fill a gap in the background or experience of an I.D.C. worker to a one- to two-year course intended to provide him with comprehensive training. Since a number of training programs in western countries are geared for large corporations, it is important that the instruction be appropriate for techniques that are optimal for small industry in less developed countries. India, with a well-developed Small-Scale Industries Service, is a particularly good source for instructors, since the average size of manufacturing firms closely approximates that of Nigeria.

It is probably not feasible administratively to charge each industrial entrepreneur who utilizes management and technical assistance from the I.D.C.s. Yet there are sufficient grounds for the program, even though an implicit subsidy to the recipients may be involved. The assistance generates positive externalities such as the development of managerial, supervisory, technical, and mechanical skills in the entrepreneurs and high-level employees, and an enhancement of the abilities of these persons to transmit the skills to others. Normally, not all the benefits from this skill will be captured by the existing firm, but some will spill over into other endeavors.[8]

Industrial Estates

An industrial estate is "a tract of land which is subdivided and developed according to a comprehensive plan for the use of a community of industrial enterprises."[9] About 50 to 100 industrial estates will have been established by 1980, according to the Third Development Plan. None of the sample firms was located on an industrial estate. For this reason, the analysis is based on the literature on these estates in Nigeria and other countries.

Most of the literature on Nigeria focuses on the first estate for indigenous enterprises, the Yaba Industrial Estate, opened in November 1958. It provides land, factory buildings, showers, toilets, garage, canteen facilities, kitchen, accounting and other technical assistance, and access to an engineering workshop.

Several problems encountered in the Yaba Estate are of importance in discussing the general question of policy towards industrial estates in Nigeria. The Yaba tract, like many other similar ones in underdeveloped countries, had a persistently low rate of utilization of sites, lacked flexibility in plant expansion, and charged a rent substantially below average total costs (and probably even below average variable costs).[10] The Estate's

---

8. The large firms prefer to train their own personnel, and do not utilize extension training and consulting services, even when available. Nevertheless, those who do utilize the service, the small entrepreneurs, are still likely to have incomes higher than the average in Nigeria. My own view is, however, that the positive spillovers mentioned above outweigh the slightly negative effect on income distribution.

9. William Bredo, *Industrial Estates* (Glencoe, Ill.: Free Press, 1960), pp. 1-2.

10. A number of items - showers, toilets, garage, canteen facilities, and kitchen - which contributed to the high cost of construction of a single unit were required by Federal factory ordinances. The Yaba Estate might have reduced expenditures by heavy reliance on indigenous building materials, such as wood, bamboo, stabilized earth or thatch. Sayre P. Schatz, in his

engineering workshop was underutilized, primarily because the skills of the manager were not appropriate for the wide range of repair and service needs of the many types of enterprises.[11] Yet the unit cost per tenant in the Estate would have been prohibitively high if the Yaba unit had tried to hire personnel with the skills to service just a majority of the establishments of the tract.[12]

Despite the endeavor of the Industrial Officer at the Estate to provide technical aid, tenants complained about the lack of worthwhile advice and assistance.[13] The staffing of industrial estates is hindered by the shortage of persons with technical skills in Nigeria, and the expense of acquiring persons with ability in a wide range of industries.

Industrial estates are expected to be nurseries for the development of entrepreneurial talent in small industrial firms. Thus, except where there is a severe problem of an excess supply of plots, industrial estates seek to attract businessmen with new projects or with the potential to expand existing projects. The advantages of leasing property in an estate in comparison to the individual acquisition of plant sites include the reduction of initial capital requirements, the avoidance of delay due to land speculation and the problems of obtaining legal titles, rational location in terms of city planning (e.g., effluent removal, smoke dissipation, parking, and so forth), and economies of scale in the installation of utilities, the supply of services, and the provision of business assistance.[14]

The practice of compelling successful firms to leave the estate after three or four years, to be replaced by fledgling enterprises, is questionable. First, estates in Nigeria rarely ex-

---

thorough analysis of the Yaba case, doubts that these materials would have significantly reduced costs. "Aiding Nigerian Business: The Yaba Industrial Estate," *Nigerian Journal of Economic and Social Studies*, IV, No. 2 (July 1964), 199-217.

11. Engineering workshops are commonly underutilized in industrial estates in underdeveloped countries. See the author's "Entrepreneurship, Social Mobility and Income Redistribution: A Case Study of Industrialists in Visakhapatnam, South India" (unpublished manuscript, Honolulu, 1976), chapter 6.

12. Schatz, *Nigerian Journal*, IV, No. 2, 199-217.

13. Ibid.

14. Peter Kilby, *Industrialization in an Open Economy: Nigeria 1945-1966* (Cambridge: University Press, 1969), p. 316.

perience shortages of industrial plots. Furthermore, the policy discourages new investments in plant and equipment by the firms, and unduly disrupts well-established production lines and marketing nexi.

To combat the common problem of underutilization of an estate's engineering workshop, private businessmen might be encouraged to establish them, since they would have a strong incentive to serve the needs of as wide a number of estate tenants as possible, and inefficient machine shops would be eliminated through the market mechanism. Tenants also would be less hesitant about using a private workshop than that run by the estate's management, often linked in their minds with questions of rent arrears and firm assessment. There should, of course, be no restriction on sales of private workshops to firms within or outside the estate.

By and large, industrial estates should be planned in such a way that entrepreneurs, especially well-established businessmen, pay rent equivalent to the full cost of land, buildings, services, and other expenditures. In line with the objective of nursing new entrepreneurial talents, the estate might charge less than a full economic cost to fledgling entrepreneurs, e.g., those in the estate less than three years, in order to stimulate spillovers from learning management and technical skills.

More caution should be exercised in the establishment of industrial estates so as to reduce the excess of costs over revenues resulting from the over-building of factory units, especially those with expensive amenities. Except for a few standardized factory sites, buildings should be constructed only on the basis of a contract with an entrepreneur to lease or buy. Here the industrial estate might provide assistance to the businessman in arranging the dimensions and design of the building.

There may be some rationale for subsidizing the training components of the industrial estates, in order to give impetus to externalities from the development of the capabilities of the entrepreneurs.[15] However, it probably would not be possible for one or two industrial officers to provide assistance to a wide range of industries, except in accounting and management. The industrial estates should cooperate with other estates and I.D.C.s, especially those in their vicinity, to arrange for experts in various industries to render technical advice and as-

---

15. The same rationale indicated on p. 222, n. 8 applies here.

sistance for a few days. With cooperation between Departments of Commerce and Industry in the 19 states, it should be possible to arrange assistance for a specific industrial estate, or even a particular establishment, on a few days notice.

Small Loan Agencies

Most small industrialists mention a lack of capital as one of their major problems (chapter 8). Some prospective entrepreneurs with viable projects do not have access to the major source of funds, the resources of the extended family, for initial capital. Furthermore, some existing businessmen with profitable enterprises and high savings rates may lack retained earnings for expansion, because of short run liquidity problems or rapid rates of expansion of desired new industrial investment. Thus, there appears to be a *prima facie* case for the availability of more funds for small loans agencies. Although the Federal government has provided grants to match the expenditures by the states on the Small Industries Credit schemes (S.I.C.s) during the Second and Third National Development Plans (1970-80), only a small portion of these grants have been utilized by the states.

The high cost of lending by the Regional Loans Boards (R.L.B.s) in the 1950s and 1960s would suggest that the prospect for the successors of these boards, the S.I.C.s, is not favorable.[16] After eliminating costs due to corruption and political manipulation (e.g., bad-debt losses on politically inspired loans), Schatz computes the cost per loan of the R.L.B.s as £N842 plus two-thirds of the value of the loan which averaged £N1,500-2,000; this included senior staff time (for processing applications, assisting successful loan recipients, and collecting repayments), commercial and technical assistance to borrowers, the work of junior staff, general overhead costs, other administrative costs, and bad debts. Since on the average the total cost considerably exceeded the size of the loan, the R.L.B.s have given substantial subsidies to the private business sector.[17]

---

16. The activities of the R.L.B.s virtually ceased with the coup of January 1966. Sayre P. Schatz, *Economics, Politics and Administration in Government Lending: The Regional Loans Boards of Nigeria* (Ibadan: Oxford University Press, 1970), p. viii.

17. R.L.B. interest receipts are not considered in the calculation of net cost, since they are more than offset by the implicit interest costs of the funds devoted to the loans program. Schatz, "The High Cost of Aiding Business in Developing Economies: Nigeria's Loans Programmes," *Oxford Economic Papers*, XX, No. 3 (November 1968), 428-32.

Gerald Faust, Ford Foundation Advisor to the Small Industries Credit scheme in the Northern Region (now the ten northern states), contends that the "S.I.C. [in the North] has proved that supervised credit can work."[18] However, this view is not consistent with the experience of the R.L.B.s. Furthermore, his estimate of the success of S.I.C. loans is questionable. Of 69 ventures to which loans were issued or committed between 1 April 1966 and 1 April 1969, Faust finds that 19 (28%) were unsuccessful ("projects from which full repayment is expected although they have not performed as well as possible") and 13 (19%) were anticipated write-offs ("loans from which losses were expected"). The remaining 37 (54%) were considered successful. However, loan repayments by 41 (59%) of the ventures were already delinquent when Faust wrote. Thus, a number - at least nine - of the firms that Faust considered successful were delinquent. In addition, a number of the loans had no chance to become delinquent because no repayments had fallen due at the time of Faust's writing; grace periods before the first loan repayment was required ranged from three months to two years.[19]

The sanguine approach of Faust, who was apparently unaware of the previous experience of the Federal and Regional Loans Boards, was based less on the performance of the S.I.C.s than premises that "As a result of experience . . . perhaps most failures would be successes, . . . mistakes would not [be] repeated, . . . [and a] more rational approach would" be devised.[20] The statement by him that there has been "a complete absence of government policies and incentives [for] the development of small-scale industries"[21] suggests that his optimism results in part from a lack of knowledge of past efforts - tax relief, loans agencies, industrial extension centers, industrial estates, and technical and management training schemes.

Where small industry can be a nursery for the development of skills which generate external economies, there is a basis for a

---

18. Faust, "Small Industries Credit Scheme in Northern Nigeria: An Analysis of Operational and Lending Patterns," *Nigerian Journal of Economic and Social Studies*, XI, No. 2 (July 1969), 226.

19. Ibid. pp. 212, 217-8. Criticisms in the present and subsequent paragraphs borrow from the analysis of Sayre P. Schatz, "African Capitalism: Development Policy in Nigeria," chapter 12.

20. Faust, *Nigerian Journal*, XI, No. 2, 209, 213, 210.

21. Ibid. p. 205.

subsidy to the R.L.B.s and S.I.C.s.[22] Also, the development of small industrial enterprises (or in a few instances, prospective large-scale establishments) can help to provide economic and political competition and counter-weight to monopolistic or oligopolistic large-scale firms.

Training in Large Firms

As indicated above, a major barrier to the success of the firm is the lack of technical and managerial skills. However, post-primary training in Nigeria is often not adapted to the needs of large industry, and frequently produces manpower with attractive options in public agencies. Furthermore, official attempts to levy fees on private firms in order to establish training activities for large enterprises have had little positive impact on raising the level of competence. The major private firms - disproportionately foreign - have little incentive to assist in the dispersion of technical skills to potential competitors.

The primary training programs for prospective technicians and managers in all five large footwear firms have been conducted overseas, in management or technical schools or institutes, apprenticeships with European firms, or special arrangements with foreign collaborators or machinery dealers. It is still not economical for very many large Nigerian firms to invest in their own training centers for managers and technicians. In the first place, instructors are more expensive in Nigeria than in Europe, due to the large transfer inducement usually necessary. Secondly, a center for one firm would generally be too small to be efficient. Moreover, Nigerian large firms have a disincentive against training programs for managers.[23] If a trained indigenous

---

22. The beneficiaries of small loans boards, though less affluent than the average businessman, have incomes higher than the average in Nigeria. I think, though, that the positive externalities mentioned above exceed the modest negative impact on income distribution.

23. The more successful the training is, the higher the manager's alternative price is and the more expensive it is to retain him. See Schatz, "Economic Environment and Private Enterprise in West Africa," *Economic Bulletin*, VII, No. 4 (December 1965), 46. This difficulty can be countered only to a limited extent by long term contracts and restrictions on technology transfer. Although these might provide an inducement for the firm to invest more in training, it does hinder the dispersion of knowledge, techniques, and skills through the economy.

manager can only be retained for a year or two, employers may feel that it is more profitable to hire a foreign manager with comparable training and skill.

If the skills developed by a trainee are used outside the training firm in his lifetime, the benefit to the economy as a whole from training exceeds the benefit to the firm. The firm has no incentive to train high-level manpower to the point where the social cost of the program equals its social benefit. When the social benefit of training exceeds the benefit to the private firm, it might be argued that the government should give a partial subsidy to the training program of the firm.[24]

However, for several reasons, I do not think a subsidy is justified. First, the gains from the investment by other firms in training high-level personnel who transfer to the firm in question is often at least as great as the losses from training expenditures by the firm at hand on manpower moving to other enterprises. Secondly, in principle, a subsidy would only be appropriate for increases in the investment component of training over what it would have been without the government inducement. But it is difficult, if not impossible, to establish operational guidelines so as to identify the increment in investment in training which results from the subsidy. Furthermore, there are problems in distinguishing the "investment" component of training from the "current cost" component, on the one hand, and "learning by experience," on the other hand.[25] Thirdly, firms may adjust to their inability to capture the full benefits of training employees by breaking up the training over a longer period rather than by reducing its volume. Even though this would increase training costs at the margin, the dispersion of training might aid the retention of the skills transmitted, and might increase the two-way linkages between learning and doing. A final reason for not supporting the subsidy is the fact that the entrepreneurs and employees who benefit would have incomes, by and large, substantially above the average in Nigeria.

---

24. I have argued this way in "The Market for Nigerian Entrepreneurs" in *South of the Sahara: Development in African Economies*, ed. by Sayre P. Schatz (Philadelphia: Temple University Press, 1972), p. 72. However, for reasons indicated below, I no longer support a government subsidy.

25. See Fritz Machlup, *The Production and Distribution of Knowledge in the United States* (Princeton: Princeton University Press, 1962), pp. 58-60, 63-64.

Management Institutes and Schools for Large Firms

In the past, Nigeria has not placed enough emphasis on the development of management training institutions. In recent years, a few institutes and courses in Nigeria have been made available for the managers of large firms.[26] Some management training institutes have drawn up courses without sufficient knowledge of the problems encountered by entrepreneurs and the relevance of certain types of management techniques.[27] Instruction tends to be oriented toward the large foreign and parastatal enterprises. Furthermore, even Nigerian entrepreneurs and managers from establishments the size of the five large sample firms tend to be discouraged by the high fees set by those such as the Institute of Management (Lagos) and the Continuing Education Centre of the University of Lagos. A final weakness of the programs is the lack of stress on extension services for entrepreneurs and managers.

Technical Education

Most graduates of technical institutes and trade centers take government positions rather than jobs in private industry;[28] virtually all of the graduates in private industry are in large firms. A number of economists and policy-makers are concerned

---

26. Some of the management institutes and schools in Nigeria are the Centre for Management Development (Lagos); the Continuing Education Centre of the University of Lagos; Institute of Management (Lagos); Yaba College of Technology; the Institute of Administration's School of Management Development and Productivity (Enugu); and the Institute of Public Administration's Management Training Scheme (Zaria). In addition, there have been a number of short *ad hoc* management courses offered by departments and institutes of universities, and international and foreign agencies.

In 1970, the University of Nigeria, Nsukka, and the University of Lagos had the only business schools at a university level. As long as the opportunity price of the Nigerian university graduate is so high, it is unlikely that the graduates will enter many entrepreneurial positions. The author estimates that less than 10 percent of the (indigenous) entrepreneurs of Nigerian firms with more than fifty employed are university graduates.

27. De Wilde, *African Private Enterprise*, I, 39.

28. See Kilby, "Technical Education in Nigeria," *Bulletin of the Oxford University Institute of Economics and Statistics*, XXVI (May 1964), 190.

about the lack of these graduates in private industry, especially small industry.

Callaway, in emphasizing the merits of on-the-job training, contends that small entrepreneurs are not created by years of unbroken technical education.[29] The reason is not because the technical student is unprepared for entrepreneurial positions in small firms, as Callaway suggests, but because of the student's high opportunity cost. It is out of the question to expect a technical institute or trade center graduate to be utilized effectively in an entrepreneurial position in most small firms. The alternative price the graduate can command with public agencies or large private firms is too high.

The relative salaries of high-level manpower in the private and public sector may be difficult to change. But one step can be taken to insure that the employment of the technical graduates is commensurate with the purposes for which the center was established. Before training centers are established, there needs to be a systematic analysis of the agencies and firms demanding the type of skilled labor produced at the center. If the purpose of the training center is to provide technicians for small firms, the course will probably need to be much shorter than a year.[30]

Because the rapid aggregate and structural changes in Nigeria bring about changes in the type of technical skills demanded, the technical training should be more general. Highly specific training can more effectively be arranged by employing firms than by training centers.

Academic Education

With the low ratio of educated labor to other factors of production in the North, the social profitability of investment in primary education is very high.[31] The current expansion of primary education in the North, with its effect on literacy and

---

29. Archibald Callaway, "Nigeria's Indigenous Education: The Apprentice System," *Odu: University of Ife Journal of African Studies*, I, No. 1 (July 1964), 15.

30. Only a small fraction of the trainees at the Vocational Improvement Centres, in the North, designed to give technical training through ten-month courses held four evenings per week for persons already employed, were from small firms. De Wilde, *African Private Enterprise*, II, Annex VIII, 18.

31. Samuel Bowles, "The Efficient Allocation of Resources in Education: A Planning Model with Applications to Northern

basic computational skills, will probably provide a significant boost to the supply of entrepreneurial skills.

The high rate of unemployment, which accompanies a high primary age enrollment rate in the south,[32] suggests a labor imbalance, in which the marginal productivity of (primary) educated labor is low. The current expansion of primary education in the south will probably have only a modest impact on the development of industrial entrepreneurship. Investment in secondary education would probably have a greater impact on the supply of industrial entrepreneurship than investment in primary education.[33]

Apprentice Standards

I oppose the suggestion by some economists that the apprentice system could be strengthened by introducing trade testing and standardizing employment conditions.[34] With the present system, the supply of apprentice-trained entrepreneurs is regulated by market forces which eliminate inefficient firms. The exclusion of entrepreneurs from the industry who are poor craftsmen and technicians but economically efficient in producing the goods demanded by consumers, adds an unwarranted supply restriction. At the present level of per capita income in Nigeria, the demand for many low-quality handicrafts is brisk. The demand is being met, by and large, by producers who would be likely to fail a trade test. The opportunity cost of these producers, whose training is very narrow, is very low. However, the alternative cost of resources employed in administering the regulations would be high.

There should be no attempt to divert resources from indige-

Nigeria" (unpublished Ph.D. dissertation, Harvard University, 1965); and "The Efficient Allocation of Resources in Education," *Quarterly Journal of Economics*, LXXXI, No. 2 (May 1967), 189-219.

32. See Frederick Harbison, "Human Resources and Economic Development in Nigeria," in *The Nigerian Political Scene*, ed. by Robert O. Tilman and Taylor Cole (Durham, N.C.: Duke University Press, 1962), pp. 213-6; and Callaway, "School Leavers and the Developing Economy of Nigeria," in ibid., pp. 220-38.

33. Harbison, ibid., pp. 213-6; and Callaway, ibid., pp. 220-38.

34. Peter Kilby, *The Development of Small Industries in Eastern Nigeria* (Enugu: Eastern Ministry of Information, 1963), pp. 8, 43.

nous apprentice training to other forms of training, as the former is virtually a necessity for the success of Type II entrepreneurs. Yet there is some need for improving the quality of instruction in the apprentice course. This can best be accomplished by upgrading the managerial, technical and designing skills of the instructor-entrepreneurs at an industrial training center.

Economic Data and Their Utilization

Although Nigerians are very responsive to known economic incentives, they frequently lack the business and economic data needed for making decisions, and moving to new economic opportunities. It is often difficult to assess the prospective social or commercial profitability of an investment project because of insufficient data on: input-output relationships within the economy, the distribution and marketing of goods, aggregate and interregional employment data, changes in demand and supply of individual commodities, movements in aggregate demand and supply, costs and benefits of specific projects, and the nature of the labor market. More emphasis should be placed on centers engaged in the development of basic statistical gathering services.

In addition, the economic data procured have not been effectively disseminated to civil servants, institute advisors, and entrepreneurs. There needs to be more communication and coordination within the various government agencies and research and statistical institutes, and between them and industrial and management extension and training centers.[35] In turn, personnel in these centers could be instrumental in supplying existing and potential entrepreneurs with the relevant economic and business information. At present, extension centers focus their attention on conveying techniques and skills to the exclusion of communicating available business and economic information.

---

35. Like P.N.C. Okigbo, *Nigerian National Accounts, 1950-57* (Enugu: Federal Ministry of Economic Development, 1962), p. 82, and Kilby, *Development of Small Industries*, p. 45, the author, in collecting data, observed a duplication of effort and a lack of coordination between various government agencies. Duplication and lack of coordination were observed not only between different regions or between a region and the Federal government, but also between agencies within a region or within the Federal government itself.

Research and Development

One would expect that the returns on expenditures on research into new industrial processes and techniques appropriate to the factor proportions and cultural setting in Nigeria would be high. However, the results of about twenty years of research by the Federal Institute of Industrial Research, the major institute for research into new and adaptive technology in Nigeria, have been meager. First, research planning has been lacking, with no listing of topics to be dealt with or relative priorities to be assigned. Secondly, little attention has been paid to the economic, as opposed to the technical, aspects of the projects investigated. Only cursory attention has been given to: the size of the market in comparison to the optimal size of the plant; the impact of the implementation of the project on prices; and the effect of competition with small industry. In the third place, research in an individual field is rarely conducted in a systematic or comprehensive manner. Other major factors contributing to the meager returns have been severe staffing problems, inadequate government support, and insufficient coordination.[36]

The Third Development Plan provides that the Industrial Research Council of Nigeria should coordinate efforts in industrial research. This, together with a greater priority on research, more thorough planning, and increases in the number of Nigerian graduates in science and technology, should lead to an expansion of research output. The transfer of technology from foreigners, unconstrained by regulations on its use, would bring additional improvements (see below).

Banks

In recent years, the Federal government has placed pressure on the commercial banks to provide more credit to Nigerian firms. Even as late as 1970, less than one-third of the loans of foreign banks in the country were to Nigerian enterprises (including mixed enterprises with a majority Nigerian ownership) and about one-half of the loans of indigenous banks were to indigenous enterprises. However, the Central Bank issued a directive that 35 percent of loans (a figure higher than the percentage of loans by several foreign banks) should be to Nigerian enterprises.[37] The recent move by the Federal government to acquire 40 percent of the equity in three major commercial banks (Standard Bank,

---

36. Kilby, *Industrialization in an Open Economy*, pp. 182-98.
37. De Wilde, *African Private Enterprise*, II, Annex VIII, 25-6.

Barclay's Bank and United Bank for Africa) has enhanced the prospect of an increase in the proportion of loans going to the indigenous private sector.[38]

The Central Bank of Nigeria and the International Finance Corporation each have one-fourth of the ordinary share capital in the Nigerian Industrial Development Bank, a Federal bank which makes loans and equity investments primarily in large enterprises. Although most of the financial commitments from its beginning, 1964, through 1969, were to foreign enterprises, in the 1970s a majority of the commitments were to indigenous firms.[39]

Another Federal bank, the Nigerian Bank for Commerce and Industry, went into operation in October 1973 to help finance indigenous businessmen acquiring foreign shares under the Nigerian Enterprises Promotion Decree[40] (discussed below).

The government can play a major role in insuring that the indigenous sector receives a larger share of loans from banks. There are, of course, limits to the extent to which banks will be able to find viable projects in the small industrial sector which have not had access to credit from other sources. However, there would appear to be substantial opportunities available for the commercial and Federal industrial banks to influence the domination of the industrial sector from foreign to indigenous, and to lessen concentration in the manufacturing industries.

Nigerianization of Foreign Firms

A major argument for the indigenization of the equity ownership and management structure of a firm is that it facilitates the transfer of technical knowledge from abroad.[41] Aside from its economic advantages, native control of local industry is usually considered desirable for political reasons also.

---

38. Nigeria, *Third Plan*, pp. 183, 196.
39. De Wilde, *African Private Enterprise*, II, Annex VIII, 27.
40. Nigeria, *Third Plan*, p. 183; and V.I. Bello, "The Intentions, Implementation Processes and Problems of the Nigerian Enterprises Promotion Decree (No. 4) 1972," in *Nigeria's Indigenisation Policy*, ed. by the Nigerian Economic Society (Ibadan: Caxton Press, 1975), p. 15.
41. See chapter 2 for a discussion of the extent of concentration of industrial technology in the west and Japan.

The official policy of the Federal government is to set quotas on the amount of foreign managerial and technical personnel brought in by a firm.[42] However, because the quotas have not been vigorously applied, many foreign firms with several managers have failed to prepare a single Nigerian for management positions. For example, in 1965 only one of the nineteen management officials, in the four foreign footwear firms that had been established for at least three years, was a Nigerian. The official, a personnel manager, although involved in routine matters of hiring, dismissal, and discipline of workers, had no major decision-making responsibility. Only two of the twelve foreign footwear firms indicated any concrete plan for recruiting and/or training Nigerians for eventual management positions.[43] Five of the twelve top managers even refused to give lip service to the idea of Nigerianization of a management post, on the ground that they could not find Nigerians who could be trusted with decision-making authority. Frequently, where a Nigerian is in a management position, the appointment may be, as one Nigerian official charged, "window dressing," with the Nigerian enjoying the trappings of power - a good salary, an office, a title, a staff, a telephone and a personal automobile - without exercising any real authority.

In the short term Nigerian government officials need to be stricter in their use of the "expatriate quota system" (i.e. system for restricting the amount of foreign personnel) as a tool to induce Nigerianization. The policy toward a specific foreign firm should be determined by an assessment of the success of the firm in transferring technical knowledge to indigenous personnel.

Policies toward Multinational Corporations

There are, however, substantial limitations to the use of Nigerianization of foreign firms as an instrument to accelerate the transfer of technology to locals. It would be incorrect to assume that the appointment of Nigerians to a substantial majority of the managerial positions in multinational corporations

---

42. Nigeria, Ministry of Information, *Statement of Industrial Policy*, Sessional Paper No. 6 (Lagos, 1964), pp. 4-5.

43. *Inter alia*, the following questions were asked. Are there any plans for training and educating Nigerian personnel for management positions? What are these plans?

Any misrepresentation on the part of respondents would be more likely to be in the direction of an overstatement of the extent of the program to train Nigerians.

means that indigenes have significant control in the firm, even when they have been entrusted with day-to-day decision-making. Overseas enterprises are unlikely to establish and retain subsidiary or branch plants in Nigeria unless major control and decision-making remain centered abroad. The maintenance of the international market position of the parent company usually requires that it restrain the dispersion of information about manufacturing processes, and the expansion of output of subsidiary enterprises. Multinational corporations restrict the use of technology and output in Nigeria, and other less developed countries, by, e.g., banning exports, limiting technology to the period of agreement, preventing modification of a technology, requiring purchase of intermediate inputs into the technology from the country of the foreign company, and forbidding former employees to transfer techniques and information (some of which are patented) from the branch establishment to other enterprises in the country.[44] Restrictions of this type decrease the contribution of foreign firms to the transfer of industrial technology in Nigeria.

One implication of this is that multinational corporations, by virtue of their concern for control by the parent company, only train and prepare indigenous management personnel to operate efficiently within the limits of directives set abroad. Although local personnel may be hired as production, sales or branch managers, they acquire little experience and training in dealing with top-management problems which are crucial to the long term success of an establishment, such as the level of capital investment, the expansion of output, the range of products produced, the setting of prices, and the nature of the organization of the firm.[45]

Joint Foreign-Indigenous Enterprises

A potential vehicle for the acquisition of new skills by indigenous persons would be a joint venture between a Nigerian party with capital, and a foreign group with capital, and technical and managerial expertness. In time, after the Nigerian part-

---

44. Robert L. Curry, Jr., "Technology Transfer to Africa: The Role of Multinational Corporations," (paper presented at the African Studies Association meeting, Syracuse, 31 October-3 November 1973).

45. Cf. Murray D. Bryce, *Industrial Development: A Guide for Accelerating Economic Growth* (New York: McGraw-Hill, 1960), p. 159.

ner or partners have obtained the essential skills to manage the enterprise by themselves, they might be expected to buy out the shares of the foreign participants.

Although this arrangement would frequently appear attractive to the Nigerian, it would only rarely appeal to the established foreign business group. In the first place, foreign investors usually have an international market position to protect, which they fear would be jeopardized by sharing company information on process and techniques with local partners. Secondly, unless the terms are lucrative, the foreign interests are likely to hesitate to accede to an arrangement that would later result in the selling of their shares to indigenous partners. Thirdly, joint ventures frequently are plagued by a problem similar to that of the Southeastern Shoe Company (chapter 6), the lack of clarity concerning where responsibility and authority resided.[46]

Where foreigners have sought or accepted joint ventures in Nigeria, it has usually been to seek long run political protection by cooperation with a public firm or prominent political figure. Only rarely have foreigners been induced to form joint enterprises with small indigenous businessmen seeking an opportunity for the development of entrepreneurial, managerial, and technical skills.

The Reservation of Industrial Sectors for Nigerians

Schedule I of the Nigerian Enterprises Promotion Decree of February 1972 listed twenty-eight industrial and commercial ventures which were reserved exclusively for Nigerian citizens and associations. Some of these activities included newspaper publishing and printing, radio and television broadcasting, non-departmental retail trading, rice milling, bottling of soft drinks, hairdressing, and road haulage. The decree indicated in Schedule II twenty-five activities in which Nigerians must have an equity participation of not less than 40 percent. Notable among these were beer brewing, manufacture of soaps and detergents, paper conversion, fish and shrimp trawling and processing, and wholesale distribution.[47] Gradually, as Nigerians acquire

---

46. Southeastern Shoe cannot be considered a joint venture, since the indigenous and foreign partners did not hold equal shares of 50 percent. The Nigerian party, E.N.D.C., provided 80 percent of the initial capital, and the foreign company 20 percent.

47. Nigeria, *Third Plan*, I, 19.

skills and experience in industrial and commercial activities, the government should increase the number of activities encompassed by the two schedules, especially those in Schedule I. Doubtless a policy which increases over time the number of economic sectors reserved for indigenes will seriously discourage new foreign investment. However, the marginal benefits from new investment from abroad need to be weighed against the extra benefits derived from greater experience in and control of domestic manufacturing industry by Nigerians.

It would be ironic if the Nigerian government, in the promulgation of an indigenization decree instituted in part to reduce foreign concentration, should in the process create widespread native monopolies and oligopolies that would be difficult to dislodge in the future. Persons with more extensive holdings in commerce, finance, and manufacturing, and greater political power can more readily obtain the financial resources and the government aid that expedites the purchase of shares of foreign enterprises. To counteract the economic strength of existing major Nigerian entrepreneurs, the government needs an explicit program for industrial extension centers to provide training and technical assistance, and lend capital to less established businessmen to acquire firms from foreigners. Even some delay in the sale of equity shares from foreigners to Nigerians might be tolerated where haste would greatly increase the long term concentration of business power.[48]

Foreign Managers and Consultants

Because of the reluctance of foreign managers and consultants to move to Nigeria, some large Nigerian firms have made arrangements with foreign firms to supply personnel. However, it is unlikely that a foreign firm would send promising managerial material abroad, unless there were a major financial inducement, as when the foreign firm's assistance is tied to the supplying of machinery. However, there are obvious drawbacks for the Nigerian firm in such an arrangement; for example, the foreign firm's personnel might have an interest in advising the Nigerian firm to acquire more machinery than is optimal.

The use of "turnkey" projects, in which the seller of ma-

---

48. "It was suspected by many ... that the ... transfers of shares went to a very limited number of people," although evidence on the distribution of holdings is not yet available. P.C. Asiodu, "Closing Remarks," in *Nigeria's Indigenisation Policy*, ed. by the Nigerian Economic Society, p. 51.

chinery arranges to have the plant built and management provided "so that the factory is ready to come into operation at the turn of a key," has been fairly widespread in the public sector in Nigeria. Kilby suggests a political explanation for this: "prestigious capital-intensive projects can be achieved quickly, they provide well paid directorships for politicians as well as jobs for the unemployed, they are an important source of party finance via the 'kick-back', and they do not require any money down - they are financed on the basis of supplier credit." However, he asserts that, as of December 1966, not a single "turnkey" project in Nigeria was earning a profit. Furthermore, sizable deferred foreign exchange costs had a substantial negative impact on the balance of payments. Some of the reasons for the lack of viability of these projects were the extensive corruption of the political leadership, the poor matching of machinery and equipment in the production process, the excessive charges for capital costs, and the over-staffing and poor quality of management and technical personnel.[49]

Another option is for the Nigerian firm to obtain the services of personnel from a western consulting firm.[50] The consulting firm might make a feasibility study, carry out the initial decisions, find a management staff for the first few years, assist in training it and begin a program to improve the entrepreneurial, managerial and technical skills of the initiating entrepreneurs and high-level Nigerians in the firm. Although their cost is high, professional consultants would have a greater motivation than personnel of machinery firms to act in the interest of the Nigerian firm. For the Nigerian businessman, however, the problem remains of evaluating the consulting firm - especially with respect to its ability to handle problems requiring knowledge of the Nigerian culture and economy.[51] Furthermore, con-

---

49. Peter Kilby, *Industrialization in an Open Economy: Nigeria 1945-1966* (Cambridge: University Press, 1969), pp. 78-9.

50. This would not be an appropriate option if, as in a majority of the cases in the United Kingdom, the consulting firm concentrates on analysis at the shop level rather than on the broader perspective of the management of the firm. David Granick, *The European Executive* (Garden City, N.Y.: Doubleday and Co., Inc., 1962), pp. 255-6.

51. Some consulting firms do have personnel who are specialists in management problems in West Africa, or even Nigeria specifically.

See also J.M. Paton, "Management Consulting in Developing Countries," *Management in Nigeria*, II, No. 3 (September-October 1966), 112-5, 128.

sulting services are not likely to be effective unless the initial entrepreneur has defined objectives, indicated problems, and outlined options with some clarity. Finally, this entrepreneur will probably need his own experts to protect his interest, and review what the consultants propose to do and then how they do it. To be able to utilize experts and consultants effectively requires a minimal amount of entrepreneurial competence.

Government Assistance in Obtaining Foreigners

The economics ministries or statutory development corporations can have a major role in evaluating foreign entrepreneurs or consultants. For example, there are foreign consultants to government who are able to give advice to Nigerian firms on the procurement of foreign entrepreneurs.

In addition, the Nigerian government might arrange with some foreign governments to compile a register of foreign managerial personnel interested in work in Nigeria. Foreigners listed in the register would need to be screened before their names were made available to Nigerian firms. For each foreigner, Nigerian officials would, if possible, obtain an evaluation from some person acquainted with the problems of foreign managers in less developed economies.

Foreign Experience

Since the control of industrial technology has been concentrated in the developed economies of North America, Western Europe, and Japan (see chapter 2), it is not surprising that countries like Nigeria that wish to industrialize attempt to borrow this technology from abroad. Because of the barriers to the dispersion of technology from foreign firms to indigenous firms within Nigeria,[52] there is much merit in prospective entrepreneurs and managers trying to acquire this technology by short

---

52. Representatives of the parent company fear that high-level native employees might use any company secrets revealed to them in the establishment of rival enterprises in the domestic economy. Even though local contracts might limit the company's technology to the subsidiary firm for the period of agreement and prevent the modification of this technology, representatives of the parent company may still hesitate to allow indigenous managers to be privy to company secrets, since the foreigners are very dubious about the possibility of using local law courts to enforce contractual provisions.

term employment in factories overseas. For example, Samuel Slater and Francis Lowell, separately instrumental in launching the two first ventures in the New England (U.S.) cotton textile manufacturing industry around the turn of the nineteenth century, cracked the British monopoly on textile techniques by acquiring information on machine design, installation, and operation while working in English textile mills.[53] Sample businessmen with foreign experience include Messrs. M.E. Akitoye and M.W. Ejor, the entrepreneurs of the two large firms with the highest profit rates, and Mallam M.D. Sanusi, entrepreneur of the largest Northern footwear producer among firms with less than £N5,000 net worth. Mr. Akintoye held a sub-management position in a plastic footwear manufacturing firm for twelve months in England in 1959-60; Mr. Ejor spent four years studying management and business administration while training with a foreign footwear firm in Europe; and Mallam Sanusi received practical training on machines while being an apprentice in a London shoe factory for two years in 1955-7. It is difficult, especially for large entrepreneurs, to acquire experience at home as valuable as that acquired abroad in firms at the forefront of generating new industrial knowledge and techniques.

Although the primary initiative for obtaining practical industrial experience abroad needs to come from prospective businessmen, the Nigerian government can facilitate this by relaxing barriers to the migration of private individuals for industrial experience and training. A second step which the government can take is to sponsor traineeships, apprenticeships, and work ex-

---

53. Both men used surreptitious means to circumvent English laws against the export of machine blueprints or the emigration of expert mechanics. In 1789, "Slater sewed his apprentice papers, which he needed to prove he was no imposter, in his clothing, but carried all other information [on textile machines] in his head and, disguised as a farm boy," emigrated from England to the United States. Within a year, Slater became the production expert and manager in a partnership formed with William Almy and Moses Brown in Pawtucket, Rhode Island. Lowell went to England in 1810, "allegedly for a rest cure, but his relaxation took the form of visiting textile factories which he regarded as the secret of Britain's industrial supremacy." Upon his return to the U.S., Lowell, in partnership with his brother-in-law, designed and constructed the machines essential for a cotton cloth factory. Donald L. Kemmerer and C. Clyde Jones, *American Economic History* (New York: McGraw-Hill Book Company, 1959), pp. 158-9.

perience abroad in areas of industrial endeavors where indigenous skills are scarce.

There are of course difficulties in obtaining employment or admittance abroad; but a further problem of a policy encouraging foreign experience is that in many instances, especially where small-scale entrepreneurs are involved, this is not relevant or transferrable to the Nigerian industrial environment. The case of Mallam M.D. Sanusi is an illustration of this, for he claimed that his scholarship at an English college was of no value, although his extracurricular activity in a London shoe factory, was of considerable benefit.[54] The potential permanent emigration of skilled personnel (or "brain drain"), the probability of which is enhanced as a result of exposure to educational facilities and work opportunities in developed countries, is another problem which the government should consider when pre-evaluating the costs and benefits of a foreign training program. But permanent emigration is likely to be less where the trainee has an entrepreneurial position to return to.

Tax-Subsidy Policies

As indicated above, a number of entrepreneurs complained about steep excise tax rates, frequent and substantial changes in the rates, and arbitrary differential inter-industry and intra-industry rates. To many, the pattern of tax rates and their changes appeared to benefit high government officials with business interests. For example, the structure of the April-August 1965 excise tax levies were highly favorable to the footwear firm of a Federal minister. The excise tax structure, regardless of the motivation, undermined the confidence of entrepreneurs in the soundness and fairness of government policy, and made it difficult for entrepreneurs to plan investment projects and firm policy rationally.

Another inequality in tax policy, as perceived by some of the entrepreneurs, resulted from the fact that only a few (five out of about 3,000) small footwear firms were subject to excise duty, since these were the only ones identified by the Federal Board of Customs and Excise.[55] There were a number of parallels

---

54. See above, chapter 6. Mr. C.S. Akpabio, whose enterprise incurred persistent losses, was also disillusioned by the lack of relevance of the training at the same college. See chapter 9.

55. See the discussion in the appendix to chapter 6.

to this discrimination against excisable firms in other manufacturing industries.

The awarding of tax concessions and inducements to stimulate new and expanded industrial output tended to discriminate in favor of foreign firms. In fact, fiscal incentive legislation - such as The Aid to Pioneer Industries Ordinance, 1952; the Industrial Development (Import Duties Relief) Act, 1957; The Industrial Development (Income Tax Relief) Act, 1958; the Customs (Drawback) Regulations, 1958; and the Income Tax (Amendment) Act, 1958 - passed during the period of British decolonization but in effect even during the Independence era, was designed with the purpose of attracting foreign industry. A new enterprise considered to be of high priority was given a "pioneer certificate," which entitled it to an income-tax holiday from two to five years. Of the 145 designated as "pioneer" companies between 1952 and 1966, only six were exclusively Nigerian holdings. Foreign firms (and to a lesser extent, large indigenous and public enterprises) benefited disproportionately from many other governmental concessions, such as preferred purchases by government departments, accelerated depreciation allowances, import duty relief, and equity and loan finance.[56]

The effect of substantial differentials in fiscal concessions and inducements was not only to distort resource allocation, but also to distribute benefits capriciously. In some cases, resources were reallocated away from low-cost producers with no fiscal concessions to higher-cost producers with tax inducements or subsidies. Those benefiting from even one type of fiscal incentive frequently acquired a substantial edge over their competitors in the industry. For example, the onerous excise taxes on a number of manufacturing products which were repealed in August 1965 were replaced by increases in tariffs on material inputs. Where import duties consisted of one-half of the cost of a raw material which comprised a large portion of the unit cost of a product, the receipt of tariff relief could make the difference between substantial profits and substantial losses.[57]

---

56. Samuel A. Aluko, *Fiscal Incentives for Industrial Development in Nigeria* (New York: United Nations Department of Economic and Social Affairs, 1967), pp. iii, 49-65; and Ola Oni, "Development and Features of the Nigerian Financial System - A Marxist Approach," *Nigerian Journal of Economic and Social Studies*, VIII, No. 3 (November 1966), 386-91.

57. Of course, import duty relief would be less important

Distortion in the social equity and rationality of the fiscal incentive system result from the divergence between the economic interests of the political elite, on the one hand, and society as a whole, on the other. As suggested in chapter 2, a large part of the Nigerian political leadership is intent on the widening of its own income and patronage, through the award of fiscal concessions and the encouragement of foreign investment, to the detriment of overall economic growth and social progress. The change in economic policy necessary to curtail the capricious and arbitrary use of tax power and to obtain the confidence of businessmen may require substantial political change, or even revolution.

Tariff Policy

Evidence from both longitudinal and cross-sectional data indicate that the share of GNP originating in the manufacturing sector increases as economic growth takes place.[58] The Nigerian government has tried to accelerate this structural change by a long term increase in the height of the tariff on imported manufactured goods.

Chapter 1 indicates some of the arguments in favor of a country encouraging (through tariff protection) specialization in the production of manufacturing goods in which it has a static comparative disadvantage.[59] The increase in the protection of domestically manufactured goods has contributed to more industrial entrepreneurship. For example, in the case of the Nigerian footwear industry, higher tariffs enhanced the attractiveness of manufacturing entrepreneurship relative to entrepreneurial activity in trade. As indicated in chapter 7, a major catalyst for the shift by Messrs. M.E. Akitoye and M.W. Ejor from trade to industry was deliberate post-Independence government policy encouraging import substitution in manufacturing through higher tariffs and tighter import quotas.

However, although high tariffs have favored manufacturing entrepreneurship, the adverse effects of increased tariffs on

---

where domestic materials were readily substitutable for imported materials.

58. Simon Kuznets, *Modern Economic Growth: Rate, Structure and Spread* (New Haven: Yale University Press, 1966), pp. 86-143.

59. These arguments are discussed in connection with the question as to why countries aspiring for rapid economic development might want to place a high priority upon industrialization.

those traders, consumers, and buyers of inputs protected by import duties cannot be overlooked. Ideally, each industry needs to be examined to ascertain the optimal tariff rate, but a discussion of import duties in detail is beyond the scope of this study.

Government Attitudes and Capabilities

A large proportion of Nigerian entrepreneurs described government officials as frequently indifferent, inefficient, obstructionist, discriminatory, and corrupt in their dealings with business. According to Schatz, the following response by one entrepreneur reflects a view widely held in the Nigerian business community.

> Both internal and external business would be much facilitated if departmental staffs (particularly those junior grades with whom the public has most contact) were to be made to understand the importance of business to the life of the country. The usual attitude at present varies between disinterestedness and deliberate obstruction. The question seems to be not "How can I help this person?" but "What can I do (exceeding the limits of my authority if necessary) to hold up this transaction?"
>
> As a result, the simplest piece of business takes more time and trouble than it should and frequently requires the attention of a senior instead of a junior employee before it can be done at all. This adds considerably to the actual cost of operating a business and involves uneconomic use of manpower.[60]

Although I would not concur with the view that government officials are deliberately obstructionist, there is little doubt that senior civil servants, government administrators, and high-ranking politicians, a part of the dominant elite in Nigeria, used a broad range of political favors and economic sanctions to retain and enhance their position and power, and to widen their

---

60. Sayre P. Schatz, "Economic Environment and Private Enterprise in West Africa," *The Economic Bulletin*, VII, No. 4 (1963), 48-9; and Schatz, "African Capitalism: Development Policy in Nigeria," chapter 5.

own income and patronage. The lack of decision-making on the part of junior personnel may result from the reluctance of political leaders and senior government servants to share the prerogatives, patronage, and power associated with their offices.

The ability of government officials to provide business assistance was limited. Some shortages of technical and administrative skills are to be expected in a newly industrializing country which is only recently free from colonial rule, and which lacks a population with experience in the modern sector and adequate levels of education and training. However, as indicated in chapter 2, the political and bureaucratic leadership has been slow to encourage the development of planning and administrative skills and initiatives by subordinates capable of posing a threat to the security of their positions. Lush vegetation does not flower beneath the huge banyon tree; analagously, new administrative and managerial talent does not readily develop in a government bureaucracy like Nigeria's where high-level officers tend to maintain patron-client relationships with their subordinates.

Implicit in this discussion is the necessity to restructure the civil service to give more decision-making responsibility to junior officers, to provide more in-service training to government officials to acquaint them with the role of business in the modernization of the Nigerian economy, and to reduce the concentration of political power in government. However, since these are less techno-economic problems than political problems, their resolution requires fundamental change in the political sphere.

Entrepreneurship in Government

Nevertheless, as a result of the relatively high salaries and attractive allowances, fringe benefits, and working conditions in the civil service, there are probably more high-level organizational and managerial skills in the public sector than the private sector. Where the talent is available, there is much rationale for officials in the ministries and statutory corporations frequently serving as the initial entrepreneur for a private enterprise - originating the idea for the firm, finding local initiative to establish it, and arranging to obtain the proper skills. In some cases, civil servants can exercise a useful restraining influence on an ill-conceived firm. Frequently, government agencies withhold a land title, rent permit, pioneer firm certificate and/or capital until the firm has made arrangements to obtain the necessary technical and managerial skills. Needless to say, this power should be used with discretion.[61]

---

61. Obviously, the power to preclude the establishment of a

In some instances, the government agency or official that perceives the need for a new enterprise may try to get a public firm established.

Anti-monopoly Measures

Table 2.9 indicates that the total value-added of the largest four establishments in thirty-one selected manufacturing industries as a percentage of the total value-added in the thirty-one industries was 69.0 in Nigeria in 1965 in comparison to 3.7 in the same industries in the U.S. in 1947. The dominance of foreign private ownership, which, according to the 1965 *Industrial Survey*, comprised 62 percent of the total ownership of manufacturing establishments with ten or more employed, was a major factor associated with the high rates of industrial concentration (chapter 2). The barriers to the viability and expansion of small-scale indigenous enterprises can be explained partly in terms of their weakness and vulnerability in an economy with a high degree of concentration of power (by foreign firms, and large public establishments), and a policy with few effective measures to lessen the concentration.

Joseph Schumpeter argued that economic concentration may be associated with large-scale economies and technological innovation.[62] Despite the fact that the largest firms in Nigeria are substantially smaller than the largest in the West, my view is that concentration in Nigerian manufacturing is higher than optimal. In chapter 2, I suggested that large firms inhibit technological dispersion within Nigeria. Furthermore, the distribution of manufacturing output by product is skewed in the direction of industries which have a low optimal size of firm (e.g., light and consumer goods industries tend to be disproportionately represented) (see table 2.8). Finally, it is clear from table 2.9 that the concentration rates in Nigeria are much higher than U.S. rates, which some economists consider higher than optimal.[63] Ac-

---

firm until it acquires high-level skills can also be used to prevent the setting up of the unit for more capricious reasons. Corruption and arbitrariness are probably more likely to flourish where civil servants have this type of authority. A discussion of the political reform and administrative reorganization needed to reduce these problems are, however, beyond the scope of this study.

62. *Capitalism, Socialism and Democracy* (New York: Harper and Row, 1942), pp. 87-106.

63. E.g., Gardiner Means, "Economic Concentration," from

cordingly, one can expect that restraints on free entry and exit of firms, and competition in pricing and output are more severe in Nigeria than in the U.S. Although more research is needed on industrial concentration in Nigeria before definitive conclusions can be reached, I will assume here that the disadvantages of industrial concentration in Nigeria outweigh the advantages.

A high degree of concentration in manufacturing was not something that was inevitable, but was a by-product of official government policy - especially fiscal incentive legislation and strategy towards foreign investment. Nigeria's economic policymakers, in the attempt to emulate the process of large-scale, capital-intensive industrialization in the west, surmised that advanced technology could only be acquired through opening the economy to foreign investment. Also, as indicated above, foreign firms and public establishments benefited disproportionately from the granting of fiscal concessions and inducements. On the other hand, small indigenous private enterprises received virtually no tax or subsidy benefits. Controls, restrictions, and licenses tended to favor sizable (and existing) firms, which benefit from large-scale economies, more experience, and greater political leverage in dealing with the public bureaucracy.

Ideally, there would be merit in the creation of a department, perhaps within the Federal Ministry of Industries, to engage in trust-busting and monopoly dissolution. In practice, though, it is difficult to conceive of a unit with the political strength and skill able to avoid using arbitrarily the power to dissect companies, and to divest foreign oligopolistic firms of some of their industrial holdings. Furthermore, breaking up monopoly power may involve an abrogation of an agreement with foreign companies, which has international policy implications, such as the possible use of economic sanctions by major capitalist countries.

Foreign and public firms are at the root of the problem of oligopolistic power, and there are several tactics less drastic than confiscation which could be used to reduce the relative, and even absolute, size of the foreign industrial sector. Tax incentives and subsidies, which almost always benefit large establishments, could be eliminated or substantially curtailed. If used,

---

U.S., Congress, Senate, Committee on the Judiciary, *Antitrust and Monopoly: Overall and Conglomerate Aspects, Hearings*, before a subcommittee of the Committee on the Judiciary, Senate, on S. 262, 88th Cong., 2nd sess., 1964.

they could serve as an instrument to decrease concentration, or perhaps even be reserved only for the small-scale sector. Other measures that could be taken are restrictions on the expansion (including vertical growth) of foreign firms, requirements that foreign companies divest themselves of ancillary production units[64] and/or marketing and distribution channels, and the promulgation of indigenization regulations which increase the number of industries reserved for Nigerians and raise the requirements for local equity participation in a number of enterprises. Also, in theory, the government could use its control over statutory corporations to restrain their size and expansion.

The reduction of monopoly power involves much more than a recognition of the possible policy prescriptions. It is also necessary to identify and create interests in government which will attempt to curtail the oligopolistic strength that official policy previously encouraged or tolerated.

Achievement Motivation Training

The evidence is strong that a person learns unconsciously in his early childhood the patterns of behavior that are safest and most rewarding, and that this learning substantially influences his adult behavior. For example, the individual who is expected and encouraged to be curious, creative, and independent as a child is more likely to engage in innovative and entrepreneurial activity as an adult. Although a society might consciously attempt to nurture imagination, self-reliance, and achievement orientation in the socialization and education of children, this process has been considered by scholars to be at best slow and uncertain, and to take at least a generation before deliberate efforts at improvement affect entrepreneurial and innovative activity, and economic growth.[65] David C. McClelland and several associates, who hypothesized that the fundamental

---

64. The Indian government not only bars large foreign enterprises from certain ancillary output that can be carried on by small-scale units. It also requires the large enterprises to provide technical assistance to their ancillary suppliers. See E. Wayne Nafziger, "Entrepreneurship, Social Mobility and Income Redistribution," chapter 6.

65. Everett E. Hagen, *The Economics of Development* (Homewood: Richard D. Irwin, Inc., 1975), pp. 282-3; and David C. McClelland and David G. Winter, *Motivating Economic Achievement - Accelerating Economic Development Through Psychological Training* (New York: Free Press, 1971), pp. 39-41.

behavior patterns of adults could be altered in a short period of time, tried to test whether the achievement motive could be inculcated in businessmen in southern and central India through motivational training courses in small groups, and whether the training would result in heightened business activity. Even though it varies greatly from other strategies discussed, I consider an examination of the psychological approach to the development of entrepreneurship essential, not only because of the importance of the pioneering studies of Professor McClelland, but because of the widespread use of achievement motivation training in programs to engender entrepreneurs and managers in poor countries and the controversy over their use. In the appendix to this chapter, I attempt to appraise the most ambitious project in underdeveloped countries so far reported: an "intervention effort" by alien "change agents" in southern and central India.[66] On the basis of the Indian experience, I do not recommend the use of this type of training in Nigeria.

Concluding Remarks

Nigeria's post-Independence strategy has been to try to emulate the process of large-scale, capital-intensive industrialization in the West. This type of approach has necessitated the attempt to acquire advanced technology abroad. The prime vehicle envisioned for the transfer of techniques of modern manufacturing production to Nigeria has been foreign industrial investment. However, the protection of the international market position of the parent company precluded the transmission to domestic counterparts of the technical information or industrial secrets upon which commercial success is based.

Domestic interests have profited from foreign investment during the Independence era. In some cases, overseas capitalists formed partnerships with members of the governing elite or their business constituents, or with the parastatal corporations, which widened the patronage and income base of this elite. Frequently, political leaders benefited from foreign firms through "rake-offs" on their contracts, intermediary roles in land deals, sales of inputs and services, and positions on the boards of directors.

Since 1970 the government has instituted policies to reduce the relative size of the foreign sector. Among the reasons for its actions are: the lukewarm support of a number of countries

66. McClelland and Winter, *Motivating Economic Achievement*, pp. 362, 159.

for the Federal government during the civil war; the decline of the civilian politicians and indigenous high-level personnel who gained from the presence of foreign capitalists; the enhanced power of the civil servants, intelligentsia, and local industrialists, especially from the south, who favor a de-emphasis on foreign investment; and the increased international legitimacy and reduced economic sanctions associated with measures to weaken the position of existing foreign capital.

One advantage of this shift in strategy will be the increasing indigenous control over the direction of the economy. Furthermore, despite transitional problems, I would expect Nigeria to benefit from the process of technological learning, and the development of techniques more appropriate to the local culture and factor proportions. Nevertheless, the government may need some restraint in the process of indigenization in order to assist less established businessmen, and to prevent the creation of widespread native monopolies and oligopolies that would be difficult to dislodge in the future.

This chapter has attempted to sketch some of the approaches that might be taken to develop indigenous entrepreneurship in Nigeria. However, more study is essential in order to ascertain what policy measures are feasible. Future research needs to consider not only what is technically feasible, but the political steps essential for the policies to be undertaken.

Appendix: A Note on Achievement Motivation Training in Underdeveloped Countries

David C. McClelland, in *The Achieving Society*, contends that a society with a generally high need for achievement or "urge to improve" (n Ach) produces more energetic entrepreneurs who, in turn, bring about more rapid economic development. As a first step, he establishes a significant positive relationship between n Ach scores (in children's readers) and subsequent rates of growth in electrical output (a proxy for economic growth) in a cross-national sample from the twentieth century. Then McClelland finds that those persons with a high n Ach are more likely to behave like an entrepreneur, i.e. (1) take personal responsibility for decisions, (2) prefer decisions involving a moderate degree of risk, and (3) evince interest in concrete knowledge of the results of decisions. Furthermore, his empirical evidence suggests that persons with high n Ach tend to be attracted into entrepreneurial positions (when society places a high prestige upon these occupations).[67]

The Achieving Society is pessimistic about the possibility of policy measures to induce substantial increase in n Ach, as this is dependent upon child-rearing techniques and parental attitudes. But even if these could be changed, there would be a delay before the children grew up to have an impact upon entrepreneurial activity and economic growth. A logical next step for McClelland was to restate his theory and to test whether n Ach might be increased among adults to enhance development.[68]

His laboratory for this "intervention effort" was southern and central India. Businessmen from Kakinada and Rajahmundry,

---

67. Princeton: D. Van Nostrand Company, 1961. I make no attempt to undertake a comprehensive evaluation, as the work has been widely reviewed and criticized. Economists who have reviewed the McClelland theses include Sayre P. Schatz, "n Achievement and Economic Growth: A Critical Appraisal," *Quarterly Journal of Economics*, LXXIX, No. 2 (May 1965), 234-41; Benjamin Higgins, *Economic Development: Problems, Principles, and Policies* (New York: W.W. Norton, 1968), pp. 241-9; Peter Kilby, ed., *Entrepreneurship and Economic Development* (New York: Free Press, 1971), pp. 7-11, 15-21, and Fritz Redlich, "Economic Development, Entrepreneurship, and Psychologism," *Explorations in Entrepreneurial History/Second Series*, I, No. 1 (Fall 1963), 10-35.

68. McClelland and Winter, *Motivating Economic Achievement*, p. 2.

Andhra Pradesh, and Vellore, Tamil Nadu, travelled to Hyderabad, Andhra Pradesh in 1964-65 to take a ten-day course at the Small Industries Extension Training Institute, an institute of the government of India which collaborated in the undertaking. The purpose of the experiment was to investigate whether the achievement motivation could be inculcated in businessmen through motivational training courses in small groups, and whether the training would result in heightened business activity. In the course, students were to acquire a higher need to achieve through (1) learning to recognize and produce achievement-related fantasies; (2) self-study to ascertain how the achievement syndrome relates to their lives, careers, goals and values; (3) attempts to define more precisely their basic goals, the blocks to these, methods to overcome blocks, and ways to measure progress towards these goals; and (4) the development of new interpersonal supports and reference groups to reinforce values associated with the urge to improve.[69]

I would argue that a program of n Ach acquisition for entrepreneurs, while it may very well be suitable to Western societies, is less likely to be appropriate for underdeveloped countries like Nigeria. First, in a society with substantial limitations on resource availability, high n Ach, associated with a competitive spirit, "becomes a sin against one's fellows." When available resources are scarce, persons with a high need for cooperation will produce more than those with high n Ach.[70] Secondly, high n Ach may be appropriate where an individual can control his activity, but not where he faces substantial restraints on decision-making.[71] Persons with a high n Ach may be frustrated and counter-productive in a society which places an emphasis upon decision-making in the public sector. Thirdly, a "course [which] is basically one of self-development" and which emphasizes "a personal decision" with regard to life goals[72] may have merit in the U.S., where independence and self-reliance is emphasized, but not in India and Nigeria where the communal and family nexus is important in choices. In these two countries, where the extended family is the basic unit for individual identification and orientation, and frequently for business ventures,

---

69. Ibid., pp. 39-175.

70. Jai B.P. Sinha, "The n-Ach/n-Cooperation under Limited/Unlimited Resource Conditions," *Journal of Experimental Social Psychology*, IV (1968), 233-46.

71. McClelland and Winter, *Motivating Economic Achievement*, pp. 123-5, 250-1.

72. Ibid. pp. 150, 60, 71-2.

n Ach, a measure of individual achievement motivation, does not explain entrepreneurial behavior.[73]

The authors seem to be unaware of the moral ambiguities which arise when "change agents," primarily from an alien culture, embark on "personality change" and behavior modification in a society of which, by their own admission, they had little understanding.[74] Ashis Nandy puts it this way:

> One must . . . recognize that something more than mere achievement training was involved. What these quasi-therapeutic interventions tried to do could be crudely summed up as an attempt to generate personality vectors functional to modern economic behavior and help individuals to integrate these vectors in their personality system by altering, among other things, self-image, significant others, access to the relevant aspects of their own phantasy life, and sense of efficacy vis-à-vis the external world. The inputs package represented, in this sense, more nearly a program of total personality change. Such a program of intervention demands some awareness of the cultural forces which shape a person's behaviour and with which he has to cope at so many levels as well as sectors of social living.[75]

One problem in interpreting the authors' findings is the lack of a genuine control group to compare with those entrepreneurs given the achievement motivation course. Given the claims of the course, the prestige of sponsorship by a Harvard Center, and the support of the District Collector, Chamber of Commerce, and leading local officials, e.g., in Kakinada,[76] it would not be surprising if the course had attracted a select group of entre-

---

73. Gloria V. Javillonar and George R. Peters, "Sociological and Social Psychological Aspects of Indian Entrepreneurship," *British Journal of Sociology*, XXIV, No. 3 (September 1973), 314-28.

74. McClelland and Winter, *Motivating Economic Achievement*, pp. 26, 154-5, 159, 337.

75. Nandy, review of *Motivating Economic Achievement*, by McClelland and Winter, in *Economic Development and Cultural Change*, XX, No. 3 (April 1972), 578.

76. McClelland and Winter, *Motivating Economic Achievement*, pp. 66, 117-37.

preneurs, especially interested in personal and business development. Among other things, the high level of personal capital and subsequent business activity of participants from Kakinada in the first two courses, in comparison to the last two courses, would suggest that the attempt, especially in early courses, to attract leading businessmen with a substantial interest in self-improvement, was successful.[77] A group of businessmen who did not participate in the course are labelled "Kakinada controls" by the authors. However, this group is not really a control group, because of the fact that they could have taken the course, but did not. Neither is the group of businessmen from another coastal Andhra city, Rajahmundry, who never had the opportunity to sign up for the course, a "control group." To obtain a *bona fide* control group - i.e. to control for the variable of desire to seek self- and business improvement - it would have been essential to prevent some who sought to enroll in the course - perhaps systematically paired with those who did participate - from taking it.[78]

There is no information presented on the relationship between n Ach and entrepreneurial activity prior to training. Naturally, n Ach scores for participants increased after training, since they were guided in practice sessions to obtain higher scores than they did at first.[79] Otherwise, the only data available on n Ach scores is a comparison between participants who were active in expanding their business and those who were inactive. "For all practical purposes the *n* Ach acquisition and retention [scores for those active and those inactive] are iden-

---

77. Ibid. pp. 126-8, 313-9.

78. It is possible that this could not have been done without misunderstanding, harmful to the overall program.

79. The participants "first take a form of the Thematic Apperception Test in which they write imaginative stories about a series of pictures. They then learn how to code what they have written according to the standard system for identifying *n* Achievement. . . . They then rewrite the stories at various times, trying to maximize the number of scoring categories they can introduce. . . . Few can [obtain a maximum score] without considerable practice, but most are able after a few lessons to get much higher scores than they did at first."

"The idea behind this training is very simple. It is to form the associative network, which in a certain sense could be considered the motive itself." McClelland and Winter, *Motivating Economic Achievement*, pp. 46-7.

tical."[80] On the other hand, other variables measured - the number of mutual friendship bonds with other participants, scores with regard to efficacy of thinking, and observations by the chief architect of the course regarding the probability of change by various participants - proved to be more powerful in predicting business activity than n Ach.[81]

The authors contend that the courses, as intended, had a number of benefits besides raising the participants' n Ach. Yet they present no hypothesis on the relationship between n Ach, economic opportunities, and social structure, and between these variables and entrepreneurial activity. Nandy contends that the authors' approach "still is not a comprehensive theory of personality which considers personality as an open system and individual motive structure as an interface between personal and community pasts."[82]

How does the performance of the course participants compare to what the authors considered a control group? Given the fact that the data on firm performance - employment, investment, sales, and so forth - over a five-year period were oral, and "given the continuous and apparently successful attempts to generate a 'Hawthorne effect' (which also tends to obscure any personality change), there is a strong presumptive bias favoring positive results for the training."[83] Towards the end of the course, the staff of the training unit, through their help in preparing businessmen for future contacts and surveys by the sponsors, may have inadvertently reinforced a positive bias. Course participants were told that they "would keep in touch with them not only informally over [the two-year] time period but would be back every six months to find out how they were doing in terms of their personal and group plan and in terms of such general business criteria as gross income, capital invested, profit, etc. They practiced filling out the forms they would be asked to return in six months' time so that they would be guided in their actions by the thoughts of how they would be evaluated later."[84]

---

80. Ibid. pp. 324-8.
81. Ibid. pp. 258, 268, 271-2.
82. *Economic Development and Cultural Change*, XX, 578.
83. Kilby, ed., *Entrepreneurship and Economic Development*, p. 21.
84. A.D. Pabaney, Elliot Danzig, M.S. Nadkarni, Udai Pareek, and David C. McClelland, "Developing the Entrepreneurial Spirit in the Indian Community," Small Industries Extension Training Institute and Harvard University, Working Report, Hyderabad, India, 20 September 1964.

Reports from visitors who evaluated the entrepreneurs after the course suggest embarrassment by some respondents as a result of the lack of business progress, and "an occasional guilt feeling."[85] In view of this, it would not be surprising if the entrepreneurs overstated their progress, or understated their setbacks.

Yet despite the predilection for favorable reports on growth and performance, there are no significant differential percentage increases in gross incomes by the course participants, although there are significant differential percentage increases in the entrepreneurs' time input, attempts to start new businesses, labor employed, and capital invested, when compared to those considered controls.[86] "Thus, if the test were to be treated as valid, it would indicate that motivational training engenders a willingness to increase inputs while at the same time it reduces entrepreneurial efficiency and, thereby, the returns to entrepreneurial effort."[87]

There is an alternative hypothesis to explain the association between n Ach and entrepreneurship. McClelland's data indicate that in the U.S., there is a positive correlation between social class and n Ach ($p < 0.001$). Black Americans, particularly those from the lower classes, score especially low in n Ach.[88] Robert A. LeVine's study of achievement motivation in Nigeria indicates a significant positive correlation between n Ach, on the one hand, and paternal class and education, on the other.[89] However, because McClelland and LeVine's conceptual matrix is not oriented to deal with class analysis, they do not pursue the implications of these findings. Upper-class individuals, who encounter fewer blocks (i.e. deficiencies in education, training,

---

85. McClelland and Winter, *Motivating Economic Achievement*, pp. 189, 297.

86. Ibid. pp. 215, 217, 221, 226.

87. Kilby, ed., *Entrepreneurship*, p. 21.

Although Pabaney, et al., "Developing the Entrepreneurial Spirit," suggest that the entrepreneurs were to report profits, the book provides no information on these data. The decrease in entrepreneurial efficiency and returns suggests the possibility that profits increased less among course participants than in the "control groups."

88. McClelland, *Achieving Society*, p. 362, based on Bernard C. Rosen, "Race, Ethnicity and the Achievement Syndrome," *American Sociological Review*, XXIV, No. 1 (February 1959), 51-2.

89. *Dreams and Deeds: Achievement Motivation in Nigeria* (Chicago: The University of Chicago Press, 1966), pp. 48, 56-7.

experience, and skills, and lack of capital and contacts), are more likely to be achievement oriented, and to be able to take advantage of entrepreneurial and other economic opportunities. On the other hand, for those members of underprivileged classes who live in a "subculture of poverty," low n Ach and low aspirations are an adaptation to the low probability of economic success resulting from blocks in society, educational institutions, and the family milieu.[90] McClelland and Winter are correct when they contend that "energetic striving to improve one's lot may seem rational enough to a man with high *n* Achievement, but not to a man with low *n* Achievement." However, they attribute this lack of striving by those with low n Ach to a lack of sensitivity to changes in economic opportunities and incentives,[91] whereas in the alternative scheme it appears to result from blocks to class mobility.

My hypothesis is that n Ach is not a primary variable, but merely a correlate of socio-economic class, which is significantly related to entrepreneurial activity through differential provision of economic opportunity. The basis for the hypothesis is not only the positive correlation between class and n Ach discussed in the preceding paragraph, but also the positive relationships I find between socio-economic class and entrepreneurship in chapter 7, and in a study of South Indian industrialists.[92]

Unfortunately, McClelland and Winter have no data on the relationships between caste or class, on the one hand, and n Ach, on the other,[93] and I have access to no other information on

---

90. See Oscar Lewis, *La Vida: A Puerto Rican Family in the Culture of Poverty - San Juan and New York* (New York: Vintage Books, 1968), pp. xlii-lii, and William H. Grier and Price M. Cobbs, *Black Rage* (New York: Bantam Books, 1968).

91. *Motivating Economic Achievement*, p. 9.

92. E. Wayne Nafziger, "Class, Caste and Community of South Indian Industrialists: An Examination of the Horatio Alger Model," *Journal of Development Studies*, XI, No. 2 (January 1975), 131-48. See a summary of the findings of this study in chapter 1.

93. Ironically, the only references to a measure of n Ach among Indian entrepreneurs who were trained are in the context of a comparison of the pre-course scores of entrepreneurs who were active and those inactive after the course, and the aggregate trend in n Ach scores of participants from before the training to two to three years later. *Motivating Economic Achievement*, pp. 270, 324-30.

this relationship. Thus, one can only suggest by inference that all cross-relationships between n Ach, socio-economic class, and entrepreneurial activity are positive. In the future, scholars might wish to investigate more explicitly the relationship between n Ach and socio-economic class in samples of entrepreneurs.

Whatever the differences between the McClelland approach and my alternative approach in terms of explanatory variables, there is an equally important implication in terms of the legitimacy of the position of the dominant elites in society. For example, McClelland and Winter indicate that in Pennsylvania, unemployed workers with high n Ach were more likely to seek and find jobs than those with low n Ach, although a critic might suggest that those most unemployable adapt to this state by keeping their achievement expectations low. The McClelland paradigm, with its premise that n Ach can be changed, suggests that the individual bears responsibility for unemployment or for lack of entrepreneurial activity. The alternative approach implies that the fault may lie, in part, with the impediments that society and its dominant classes place in the road to upward mobility in jobs and business activity. To what extent are the economically weak responsible for poverty, unemployment, and a lack of entrepreneurial activity, and to what extent is their class mobility impeded by the cumulative advantages of the prevailing economic elite? The data in chapters 1 and 7 indicate that economic success is significantly related to paternal economic class standing.

Policy-makers should surely be cautious before introducing an "intervention effort" by alien "change agents" to undertake substantial personality changes to key individuals within a country. The evidence available from the underdeveloped world gives little indication that the benefits of achievement motivation training would outweigh the costs. Thus, this training would not seem to be applicable in Nigeria.

Appendix

A Brief Elaboration of Sources, Procedures and Methods of the Study

Sources of Information on Sample Firms

The major sources of information were interviews with entrepreneurs and other representatives of the twenty-five sample firms. Independent sources included officers in the Federal and regional ministries, industrial extension centers, and loan agencies; bankers, suppliers, customers, competitors and employees. Elsewhere I have indicated in more detail the frequency distribution of hours of interview in sample firms, the time spent with different independent sources, the written sources pursued, and the degree of confidence in the various sources consulted.[1]

Sources for Quantitative Data

In December 1965, output, net worth, employment and profit for eight firms were obtained from the files of loan applicants of the Fund for Agricultural and Industrial Development (the Eastern Region small loan board). *Inter alia*, a balance sheet

---

1. E. Wayne Nafziger, "Nigerian Entrepreneurship: A Study of Indigenous Businessmen in the Footwear Industry" (unpublished Ph.D. dissertation, University of Illinois, 1967), pp. 192-7. See ibid. pp. 205-20, 254-82, for non-sample firms in which interviews were conducted, the nature of the interview, the complete questionnaire, problems with the interview schedule, the position of the entrepreneur in sample firms, the methods and assumptions used to obtain the regional distribution of indigenous firms by employment size, the presentation and discussion of time-series data on output, imports, and consumption of footwear, and the basis of estimates of aggregate employment, net worth, and value of output in the footwear manufacturing industry.

and a profit and loss statement were available for each firm.

In five firms, the author was allowed to obtain the profit and loss statements and balance sheets,[2] which formed a basis for data on profit, output and net worth.[3] A technical advisor at the Federal Ministry of Commerce and Industry provided detailed cost and revenue data and figures on net worth for one firm. Figures on cost, revenue and net worth for another firm were acquired from Jerome N. Afuba.[4] In three firms, the entrepreneurs themselves had, in the author's judgment, sufficient understanding of the concepts to provide quantitative data on the questionnaire,[5] which were evaluated by outside sources.[6] For seven other establishments, information from representatives of the firm, and independent sources was sufficient to obtain data on

---

2. For two large firms, statements were certified by a chartered accountant.

The reason for the willingness of the two large firms to show profit and loss data is probably due to the fact that both had losses exceeding 50 percent. In one of the firms, the top manager was not reluctant to release data from the previous period, since he had only recently joined the firm.

Because of their small size, the other three firms were not reluctant to show data on profits and losses.

3. In the fiscal year, 1963-64, Northern Leather Works kept only cursory records of cost and revenue. Since no new capital was issued in the fiscal year, (business) losses equalled the decrease in net worth shown in the balance sheet.

4. "A Feasibility Study of an Eastern Shoe Firm" (Economic Development Institute Working Paper No. 1, University of Nigeria, Enugu, March 1965).

5. Answers were checked for internal consistency. The author acquired information on the state of bookkeeping, including methods and concepts used in computing profit and depreciation and the relationship to methods and concepts of the study. By asking specific questions on assets and liabilities, the author obtained figures on net worth.

6. The International Labour Organisation Footwear Expert at the Industrial Development Centre in Owerri had worked closely with the entrepreneurs of the three firms. He was helpful in assessing the credibility of data supplied by the entrepreneurs and responding to specific questions about the bookkeeping of the firm, the concept of depreciation used and the concept of profit used.

output, net worth, and employment, but not on profits or losses.[7]

Major Adjustments to the Data

Original firm data frequently had to be adjusted, so that the figures in table 6.1 would be comparable. First, for seven small firms adjustments were made for inadequate or nonexistent depreciation figures for buildings, equipment and machines.[8] To facilitate computation, the straight-line method of depreciation was used. Secondly, as discussed above, in order to compute profits, implicit costs of the businessman's own factor resources were calculated.

Sample Bias

There was no sample bias among large indigenous footwear firms (i.e., those with a 1964 net worth of £N5,000 or more), since all firms were in the sample.

Since only thirty-six out of eighty-two small urban indigenous firms with eight or more persons employed were listed in the ten 1964-5 firm directories, information based on a probability sample of firms listed in the directories need not be valid for the statistical universe of urban footwear firms. Even if it were possible to obtain a probability sample of urban footwear firms, however, it would not be possible to acquire reliable figures from most of the firms.[9]

Table A.1, p. 263, indicates that when distribution of firms by employment size is considered, sample firms with eight or more employed and less than £N5,000 net worth were fairly representative both of footwear firms in the ten directories and of all indigenous urban footwear firms in Nigeria.

---

7. I estimate that one or two more firms in the universe had records from which it would have been possible to obtain data on output, net worth and employment, if I could have had access to them.

8. The lack of depreciation figures is quite common among small firms. Peter Kilby, in his study of small manufacturing firms in the Eastern Region in 1960, found that no more than 10 percent of the firms had a minimally adequate bookkeeping system. Included in the concept of a minimally adequate system were ample depreciation figures. *The Development of Small Industries in Eastern Nigeria* (Enugu: Eastern Ministry of Information, 1963), p. 15.

9. The directories are listed in n. 4, p. 100.

Table A.1

Distribution of Various Groupings of Firms by Employment Size, 1964

Average Employment and Average Net Worth, 1964	(1) Indigenous Footwear Firms in the Sample		(2) Indigenous Urban Footwear firms in Universe of 10 Firm Directories		(3[a]) Indigenous Urban Footwear Firms in Nigeria	
	No.	%	No.	%	No.	%
£N5,000 or more net worth:						
100 or more employed	2	40	2	40	2	40
25-99 employed	3	60	3	60	3	60
TOTAL	5	100	5	100	5	100
less than £N5,000 net worth:						
25-99 employed	2	15	3	8	3	3
10-24 employed	8	62	27	75	49[b]	60
8-9 employed	3	23	6	17	30[b]	37
TOTAL	13	100	36	100	82	100

a. Figures in column (3) do not correspond exactly to figures in table 5.1, which is dated at a later time.

b. Estimates.

There were other sample biases.

(1) Since only firms with fairly reliable data on net worth, employment, and value of output were included in the sample, the sample was significantly biased in favor of firms with good bookkeeping systems. The businessmen of firms with good records would be expected to have a higher level of education and a greater fluency in English than the businessmen of other firms.

(2) Since regional and federal captial cities and other large urban areas were more likely to be enumerated, there were a disproportionate number of firms from large cities in the universe of eleven directories and the sample.

Bibliography

Books and Monographs

Adedeji, Adebayo. *Nigerian Federal Finance: Its Development, Problems, and Prospects.* London: Hutchinson, 1969.

Aitken, Hugh G.J., ed. *Explorations in Enterprise.* Cambridge, Mass.: Harvard University Press, 1965.

Akeredolu-Ale, E.O. *The Underdevelopment of Indigenous Entrepreneurship in Nigeria.* Ibadan: Ibadan University Press, 1975.

Alexander, Alec P. *Greek Industrialists: An Economic and Social Analysis.* Athens: Center of Planning and Economic Research, 1964.

Aluko, Samuel A. *Fiscal Incentives for Industrial Development in Nigeria.* New York: United Nations Department of Economic and Social Affairs, 1967.

Ashton, T.S. *The Industrial Revolution.* New York: Oxford University Press, 1948.

Awa, Eme O. *Federal Government in Nigeria.* Berkeley and Los Angeles: University of California Press, 1964.

Bain, Joe S. *International Differences in Industrial Structure: Eight Nations in the 1950's.* New Haven: Yale University Press, 1966.

Baran, Paul A. *The Political Economy of Growth.* New York: Monthly Review Press, 1957.

Bauer, Peter T. *West African Trade: A Study of Competition, Oligopoly and Monopoly in a Changing Economy.* Cambridge: Cambridge University Press, 1954.

Berna, James J. *Industrial Entrepreneurship in Madras State*. London: Asia Publishing House, 1960.

Bowman, Mary Jean; and Anderson, C. Arnold. *Development of Emerging Countries: An Agenda for Research*. Washington, D.C.: The Brookings Institution, 1962.

Bryce, Murray D. *Industrial Development: A Guide for Accelerating Economic Growth*. New York: McCraw-Hill Book Company, Inc., 1960.

Buchanan, K.M.; and Pugh, J.C. *Land and People in Nigeria*. London: University of London Press, 1965.

Callaway, Archibald. "Nigerian Enterprise and the Employment of Youth: Study of 225 Businesses in Ibadan." Nigerian Institute of Social and Economic Research Monograph Series No. 2. Ibadan, March 1973.

Cantillon, Richard. *Essai sur la Nature du Commerce en General*. Edited and translated by Henry Higgs. London: Frank Cass and Co., Ltd., 1959.

Carroll, John J. *The Filipino Manufacturing Entrepreneur: Agent and Product of Change*. Ithaca: Cornell University Press, 1965.

Clark, Colin. *The Conditions of Economic Progress*. London: Macmillan, 1951.

Clemence, Richard V.; and Doody, Francis S. *The Schumpeterian System*. Cambridge, Mass.: Addison-Wesley Press, Inc., 1950.

Cohen, Robin. *Labour and Politics in Nigeria, 1945-71*. New York: Africana Publishing Co., 1974.

Cole, Arthur H. *Business Enterprise in its Social Setting*. Cambridge, Mass.: Harvard University Press, 1959.

Coleman, James S. *Nigeria: Background to Nationalism*. Berkeley and Los Angeles: University of California Press, 1958.

Collins, Orvis F.; Moore, David G.; and Unwalla, Darab B. *The Enterprising Man*. East Lansing: MSU Business Studies, 1964.

Crowder, Michael. *The Story of Nigeria*. London: Faber, 1962.

Diamond, Stanley. *Nigeria: Model of a Colonial Failure*. New York: American Committee on Africa, 1966.

Dobb, Maurice. *Capitalist Enterprise and Social Progress.* London: Routledge, 1926.

Dudley, B.J. *Parties and Politics in Northern Nigeria.* London: Frank Cass and Co., Ltd., 1968.

Dupriez, L. *Economic Progress: Papers and Proceedings of a Round Table Held by the International Economic Association.* Louvain: Institut de Recherches Economiques et Sociales, 1955.

Enke, Stephen. *Economics for Development.* Englewood Cliffs, N.J.: Prentice-Hall, Inc., 1963.

Frank, André Gunder. *Capitalism and Underdevelopment in Latin America: Historical Studies of Chile and Brazil.* New York: Monthly Review Press, 1969.

Geiger, Theodore; and Armstrong, Winifred. *The Development of African Private Enterprise.* Washington, D.C.: National Planning Association, 1964.

Granick, David. *The European Executive.* Garden City, N.Y.: Doubleday and Co., Inc., 1962.

Grier, William H.; and Cobbs, Price M. *Black Rage.* New York: Bantam Books, 1968.

Hagen, Everett E. *The Economics of Development.* Homewood, Ill.: Richard D. Irwin, 1968, 1975.

Harbison, Frederick; and Myers, Charles A. *Management in the Industrial World: An International Analysis.* New York: McGraw-Hill Book Company, Inc., 1959.

Hay, A.M.; and Smith, R.H.T. *Interregional Trade and Money Flows in Nigeria, 1964.* Ibadan: Oxford University Press, 1970.

Helleiner, Gerald K. *Peasant Agriculture, Government and Economic Growth in Nigeria.* Homewood, Ill.: Richard D. Irwin, Inc., 1966.

Higgins, Benjamin. *Economic Development - Problems, Principles, and Policies.* New York: W.W. Norton and Company, 1968.

Hirschman, Albert O. *The Strategy of Economic Development.* New Haven: Yale University Press, 1958.

Kemmerer, Donald L.; and Jones, C. Clyde. *American Economic*

History. New York: McGraw-Hill Book Company, 1959.

Kilby, Peter. *African Enterprise: The Nigerian Bread Industry*. Stanford: Hoover Institution, 1965.

__________. *The Development of Small Industry in Eastern Nigeria*. Enugu: Eastern Region Ministry of Information, 1963.

__________, ed. *Entrepreneurship and Economic Development*. New York: Free Press, 1971.

__________. *Industrialization in an Open Economy: Nigeria, 1945-1966*. Cambridge: Cambridge University Press, 1969.

Kindleberger, Charles P. *Economic Development: Principles, Problems and Policies*. New York: McGraw-Hill Book Company, 1965.

Knight, Frank. *Risk, Uncertainty and Profit*. Boston: Houghton Mifflin Co., 1921.

Kuznets, Simon. *Modern Economic Growth: Rate, Structure and Spread*. New Haven: Yale University Press, 1966.

__________. *National Product in Wartime*. New York: National Bureau of Economic Research, 1945.

LeVine, Robert A.; and others. *Dreams and Deeds: Achievement Motivation in Nigeria*. Chicago: University of Chicago Press, 1966.

Lewis, Oscar. *La Vida: A Puerto Rican Family in the Culture of Poverty - San Juan and New York*. New York: Vintage Books, 1968.

Lewis, W. Arthur. *Reflections on Nigeria's Economic Growth*. Paris: Organisation for Economic Cooperation and Development, 1967.

Luckham, Robin. *The Nigerian Military - A Sociological Analysis of Authority and Revolt, 1960-67*. Cambridge: Cambridge University Press, 1971.

McClelland, David C. *The Achieving Society*. Princeton: D. Van Nostrand Company, 1961.

__________; and Winter, David G. *Motivating Economic Achievement - Accelerating Economic Development Through Psychological Training*. New York: Free Press, 1971.

McConnell, Campbell R. *Economics: Principles, Problems, and Policies*. 5th ed. New York: McGraw-Hill Book Company, Inc., 1972.

McCrory, James. *Case Studies in Latent Industrial Potential: Small Industry in a North Indian Town*. Delhi: Government of India, Ministry of Commerce and Industry, 1956.

Mackintosh, John P. *Nigerian Government and Politics*. Evanston: Northwestern University Press, 1966.

Machlup, Fritz. *The Production and Distribution of Knowledge in the United States*. Princeton: Princeton University Press, 1962.

Marshall, Alfred. *Principles of Economics*. 1st ed. London: Macmillan, 1890.

Marx, Karl. *Capital*. Edited by F. Engels. 3 vols. Moscow: Progress Publishers, 1966.

Meier, Gerald M.; and Baldwin, Robert E. *Economic Development: Theory, History, Policy*. New York: John Wiley and Sons, Inc., 1957.

Meier, Gerald M. *Leading Issues in Economic Development: Studies in International Poverty*. Stanford: Oxford University Press, 1970.

Merett, A.J.; and Monk, D.A.G. *Inflation, Taxation and Executive Remuneration*. London: Hallam Press Limited, 1967.

Myint, Hla. *The Economics of the Developing Countries*. New York: Frederick A. Praeger, Publishers, 1966.

Newcomer, Mable. *The Big Business Executive: The Factors that Made Him, 1900-1950*. New York: Columbia University Press, 1955.

Nichols, Fred Hammond, compiler. *The Building of a Shoe*. Lynn, Mass.: The Nichols Press, 1912.

Nimhoff, M.F. *Comparative Family Systems*. Boston: Houghton Mifflin Co., 1965.

Okigbo, P.N.C. *Nigerian National Accounts, 1950-57*. Enugu: Federal Ministry of Economic Development, 1962.

Papanek, Gustav F. *Pakistan's Development: Social Goals and*

Private Incentives. Cambridge, Mass.: Harvard University Press, 1967.

Papelasis, Adamantios; Mears, Leon; and Adelman, Irma. *Economic Development: Analysis and Case Studies*. New York: Harper and Brothers, Publishers, 1961.

Perham, Margery. *Native Administration in Nigeria*. London: Oxford University Press, 1962.

Post, K.W.J. *The Nigerian Federal Election of 1959: Politics and Administration in a Developing Political System*. London: Oxford University Press, 1963.

Prasad, S.B.; and Negandhi, A.R. *Managerialism for Economic Development: Essays on India*. The Hague: Martinue Nijhoff, 1968.

Roper, J.I. *Labour Problems in West Africa*. London: Penguin Books Ltd., 1958.

Rostow, Walter W. *The Stages of Economic Growth: A Non-Communist Manifesto*. 2nd ed. Cambridge: Cambridge University Press, 1971.

Rusinoff, S.E. *Manufacturing Processes*. Chicago: American Technological Society, 1949.

Sasso, John, ed. *Plastics Handbook for Product Engineers*. New York: McGraw-Hill Book Company, Inc., 1946.

Say, J.B. *A Treatise on Political Economy*. 2 vols. Translated by C.R. Prinsap. 4th ed. Boston: Wells and Lilly, 1824.

Sayigh, Yusif A. *Entrepreneurs of Lebanon: The Role of the Business Leader in a Developing Economy*. Cambridge, Mass.: Harvard University Press, 1962.

Schatz, Sayre P. *Development Bank Lending in Nigeria*. London: Oxford University Press, 1964.

__________. *Economics, Politics and Administration in Government Lending: The Regional Loans Boards of Nigeria*. Ibadan: Oxford University Press, 1970.

Schumpeter, Joseph A. *Business Cycles*. 2 vols. New York: McGraw-Hill Book Company, Inc., 1939.

Schumpeter, Joseph A. *Capitalism, Socialism and Democracy.* New York: Harper and Row, 1942.

__________. *The Theory of Economic Development: An Inquiry into Profits, Capital, Credit, Interest, and the Business Cycle.* Translated by Redvers Opie. New York: Oxford University Press, 1961.

Simonds, Herbert R. *Industrial Plastics.* New York: Pitman Publishing Co., 1941.

Sklar, Richard L. *Nigerian Political Parties: Power in an Emergent Nation.* Princeton: Princeton University Press, 1963.

Smelser, Neil J.; and Lipset, Seymour Martin; ed. *Social Structure and Mobility in Economic Development.* Chicago: Aldine Publishing Company, 1966.

Smith, Adam. *An Enquiry into the Nature and Causes of the Wealth of Nations.* 2 vols. London: G. Bell and Sons, Ltd., 1912.

Smythe, Hugh H.; and Smythe, Mable M. *The New Nigerian Elite.* Stanford: Stanford University Press, 1960.

Stolper, Wolfgang F. *Planning Without Facts: Lessons in Resource Allocation from Nigeria's Development.* Cambridge, Mass.: Harvard University Press, 1966.

Uchendu, Victor C. *The Igbo of Southeast Nigeria.* New York: Holt, Rinehart and Winston, 1966.

United Shoe Machinery Corporation. *How American Shoes Are Made.* Boston: By the Author, 1961.

Viner, Jacob. *International Trade and Economic Development.* Glencoe, Ill.: Free Press, 1952.

Walras, Leon. *Elements of Pure Economics or the Theory of Social Wealth.* London: George Allen and Unwin, Ltd., 1954.

Warner, W. Lloyd; and Abegglen, James C. *Occupational Mobility in American Business and Industry.* Minneapolis: University of Minnesota Press, 1955.

Wells, F.A.; and Warmington, W.A. *Studies in Industrialization: Nigeria and The Cameroons.* London: Oxford University Press,

1962.

West Africa Directory. London: Thomas Skinner and Co., 1965.

Whitaker, C.S., Jr. *The Politics of Tradition: Continuity and Change in Northern Nigeria, 1946-1966*. Princeton: Princeton University Press, 1970.

Articles

Aboyade, O.; and Ayida, A. "The War Economy in Perspective." *Nigerian Journal of Economic and Social Studies*, XIII, No. 1 (March 1971), 13-37.

Akeredolu-Ale, E.O. "A Sociohistorical Study of the Development of Entrepreneurship among the Ijebu of Western Nigeria." *African Studies Review*, XVI, No. 3 (December 1973), 347-65.

Alexander, Alec P. "Industrial Entrepreneurship in Turkey: Origins and Growth." *Economic Development and Cultural Change*, VIII, No. 4, Part I (July 1960), 349-65.

Aluko, Samuel A. "Displaced Nigerians." *West Africa* (15 April 1967), pp. 495, 497-8.

__________. "The Educated in Business: The Calabar Home Farm - A Case Study." *Nigerian Journal of Economic and Social Studies*, VIII, No. 2 (July 1966), 195-208.

__________. "Wages, Costs and Prices." Conference on National Reconstruction and Development in Nigeria, University of Ibadan, Ibadan, 24-29 March 1969.

Asiodu, P.C. "Closing Remarks." *Nigeria's Indigenisation Policy*. Edited by the Nigerian Economic Society. Ibadan: Caxton Press, 1975.

Aubrey, Henry G. "Industrial Investment Decisions." *Journal of Economic History*, XV (December 1955), 335-51.

Ayida, A. Akene. "Development Objectives." Conference on National Reconstruction and Development in Nigeria, University of Ibadan, Ibadan, 24-29 March 1969.

Baker, Pauline H. "The Politics of Nigerian Military Rule." *Africa Report*, XVI, No. 2 (February 1971), 18-21.

Balassa, Bela A. "An Abstract Model of Capitalism." *Capitalism, Market Socialism and Central Planning*. Edited by Wayne A.

Leeman. Boston: Houghton Mifflin Company, 1963.

Bello, V.I. "The Intentions, Implementation Processes and Problems of the Nigerian Enterprises Promotion Decree (No. 4) 1972." *Nigeria's Indigenisation Decree*. Edited by the Nigerian Economic Society. Ibadan: Caxton Press, 1975.

Bernstein, Henry. "Modernization Theory and the Sociological Study of Development." *Journal of Development Studies*, VII, No. 2 (January 1971), 141-60.

Bohr, Kenneth A. "Investment Criteria for Manufacturing Industries in Underdeveloped Countries." *Review of Economics and Statistics*, XXXVI, No. 2 (May 1954), 157-66.

Bowles, Samuel. "The Efficient Allocation of Resources in Education." *Quarterly Journal of Economics*, LXXXI, No. 2 (May 1967), 189-219.

Burghart, Richard. "Ministerial Emoluments in Nigeria." *Nigerian Opinion*, I, No. 8 (August 1965), 10-12.

Callaway, Archibald. "Creating Employment for Nigeria's School Leavers." *Administration: The Quarterly Review of the Institute of Administration, University of Ife*, III, No. 1 (October 1969), 1-11.

__________. "Educational Expansion and the Rise of Youth Unemployment." *The City of Ibadan*. Edited by P.C. Lloyd, A.L. Mabogunje and B. Awe. London: Cambridge University Press, 1967.

__________. "From Traditional Crafts to Modern Industries." *Odu: University of Ife Journal of African Studies*, II, No. 1 (July 1965), 35-51.

__________. "Nigeria's Indigenous Education: The Apprentice System." *Odu: University of Ife Journal of African Studies*, I, No. 1 (July 1964), 1-18.

__________. "School Leavers and the Developing Economy of Nigeria." *The Nigerian Political Scene*. Edited by Robert O. Tilman and Taylor Cole. Durham, N.C.: Duke University Commonwealth Studies Center, 1962.

"The Civil Service." *Nigerian Opinion*, I, No. 8 (August 1965), 3-4.

Cole, Arthur H. "An Approach to the Study of Entrepreneurship:

A Tribute to Edwin F. Gay." *Explorations in Enterprise*. Edited by Hugh G.J. Aitken. Cambridge, Mass.: Harvard University Press, 1965.

Dudley, B.J. "The Military and Development." *Nigerian Journal of Economic and Social Studies*, XIII, No. 2 (July 1971), 163-74.

Eke, Ifagun I.U. "Population of Nigeria, 1952-1965." *Nigerian Journal of Economic and Social Studies*, VIII, No. 3 (November 1966), 289-309.

Ekukinam, A.E. "Main Trends in Banking and Monetary Policy to 1968." *Reconstruction and Development in Nigeria: Proceedings of a National Conference*. Edited by A.A. Ayida and H.M.A. Onitiri. Ibadan: Oxford University Press, 1971.

Faust, Gerald. "Small Industries Credit Scheme in Northern Nigeria: An Analysis of Operational and Lending Patterns." *Nigerian Journal of Economic and Social Studies*, XI, No. 2 (July 1969), 205-27.

Friedland, William H. "Paradoxes of African Trade Unionism: Organizational Chaos and Political Potential." *Africa Report*, X, No. 6 (June 1965), 6-13.

Green, Reginald H. "Four African Development Plans: Ghana, Kenya, Nigeria, and Tanzania." *The Journal of Modern African Studies*, III, No. 2 (1965), 253-74.

Hagen, Everett E. "Discussion." *American Economic Review*, LII, No. 2 (May 1962), 59-61.

Hakam, A.N. "The Motivation to Invest and the Locational Pattern of Foreign Private Industrial Investments in Nigeria." *Nigerian Journal of Economic and Social Studies*, VIII, No. 1 (March 1966), 49-65.

Hansen, A.H. "Public Enterprise in Nigeria." *Public Administration*, XXXV (Winter 1958), 371-82, and XXXVI (Spring 1959), 32-45.

Harbison, Frederick. "Human Resources and Economic Development in Nigeria." *The Nigerian Political Scene*. Edited by Robert O. Tilman and Taylor Cole. Durham, N.C.: Duke University Press, 1962.

__________. "The Prime Movers of Innovation." *Education and Economic Development*. Edited by C. Arnold Anderson and Mary

Jean Bowman. Chicago: Aldine Publishing Co., 1965.

Harris, John R.; and Rowe, Mary P. "Entrepreneurial Patterns in the Nigerian Sawmilling Industry." *Nigerian Journal of Economic and Social Studies*, VIII, No. 1 (March 1966), 67-95.

Harris, John R. "Nigerian Entrepreneurship in Industry." *Entrepreneurship and Economic Development*. Edited by Peter Kilby. New York: Free Press, 1971.

Hay, A.M.; and Smith, R.H.T. "Preliminary Estimates of Nigeria's Interregional Trade and Associated Money Flows." *Nigerian Journal of Economic and Social Studies*, VIII, No. 1 (March 1966), 9-35.

Hill, Polly. "The Myth of the Amorphous Peasantry: A Northern Nigerian Case Study." *Nigerian Journal of Economic and Social Studies*, X, No. 2 (July 1968), 239-60.

Hoselitz, Bert F. "Entrepreneurship and Traditional Elites." *Explorations in Entrepreneurial History/Second Series*, I (Fall 1963), 36-49.

Javillonar, Gloria V.; and Peters, George R. "Sociological and Social Psychological Aspects of Indian Entrepreneurship." *British Journal of Sociology*, XXIV, No. 3 (September 1973), 314-28.

Katzin, Margaret. "The Role of the Small Entrepreneur." *Economic Transition in Africa*. Edited by Melville J. Herskovits and Mitchell Harwitz. Evanston, Ill.: Northwestern University Press, 1964.

Kilby, Peter. "African Labour Productivity Reconsidered." *Economic Journal*, LXXI (June 1961), 273-91.

__________. "Technical Education in Nigeria." *Bulletin of the Oxford University Institute of Economics and Statistics*, XXVI, No. 2 (May 1964), 181-9.

Kuznets, Simon S. "Industrial Distribution of National Product and Labor Force." *Economic Development and Cultural Change*, V, No. 4 (July 1957), 3-111.

__________. "Levels and Variability of Growth Rates." *Economic Development and Cultural Change*, V, No. 1 (October 1956), 5-94.

Lagos Chamber of Commerce. Economic Sub-committee. "The Morgan

Report and its Aftermath." *Economic Trends in Nigeria*, 4th issue (August 1964), pp. 8-12.

Leibenstein, Harvey. "Entrepreneurship and Development." *American Economic Review*, LVIII, No. 2 (May 1968), 72-83.

__________. "Shortages and Surpluses in Education in Underdeveloped Countries: A Theoretical Foray." *Education and Economic Development*. Edited by C. Arnold Anderson and Mary Jean Bowman. Chicago: Aldine Publishing Co., 1965.

Lewis, W. Arthur. "Aspects of Industrialization." *Nigerian Trade Journal*, II, No. 4 (October-December 1954), 11-2.

Means, Gardiner. "Economic Concentration." U.S. Congress. Senate. Committee on the Judiciary. *Antitrust and Monopoly: Overall and Conglomerate Aspects*. *Hearings* before a subcommittee of the Committee on the Judiciary, Senate, on S. 262, 88th Cong., 2nd sess., 1964.

Morgen, Robert W., Jr. "Occupational Prestige Ratings by Nigerian Students." *Nigerian Journal of Economic and Social Studies*, VII, No. 3 (November 1965), 325-32.

Müller, Ronald. "The Multinational Corporation and the Underdevelopment of the Third World." *The Political Economy of Development and Underdevelopment*. Edited by Charles K. Wilber. New York: Random House, 1973.

Nafziger, E. Wayne; and Richter, William L. "Biafra and Bangladesh: The Political Economy of Secessionist Conflict." *Jour- of Peace Research*, XIII, No. 2 (1976), 91-109.

Nafziger, E. Wayne. "Class, Caste and Community of South Indian Industrialists: An Examination of the Horatio Alger Model." *Journal of Development Studies*, XI, No. 2 (January 1975), 131-48.

__________. "Economic Aspects of the Nigerian Civil War." *Civil Wars in the Twentieth Century*. Edited by Robin Higham. Lexington: University of Kentucky Press, 1972.

__________. "The Economic Impact of the Nigerian Civil War." *The Journal of Modern African Studies*, X, No. 2 (1972), 223-45.

__________. "The Economic Impact of the Nigerian Civil War: a Reply." *The Journal of Modern African Studies*, XI, No. 3 (1973), 463-5.

Nafziger, E. Wayne. "Inter-regional Economic Relations in the Nigerian Footwear Industry." *The Journal of Modern African Studies*, VI, No. 4 (1968), 531-42.

__________. "The Market for Nigerian Entrepreneurs." *South of the Sahara: Development in African Economies*. Edited by Sayre P. Schatz. Philadelphia: Temple University Press, 1972.

__________. "The Mennonite Ethic in the Weberian Framework." *Explorations in Entrepreneurial History/Second Series*, II, No. 1 (Spring-Summer 1965), 187-204.

__________. "The Political Economy of Disintegration in Nigeria." *The Journal of Modern African Studies*, XI, No. 4 (1973), 505-36.

__________. "A Reconsideration of 'Capital Surplus' in Nigeria." *Nigerian Journal of Economic and Social Studies*, X, No. 1 (March 1968), 111-6.

__________. Review of *Interregional Trade and Money Flows in Nigeria, 1964*, by A.M. Hay and R.H.T. Smith. *The Journal of Modern African Studies*, X, No. 1 (1972), 162-3.

Nandy, Ashis. Review of *Motivating Economic Achievement - Accelerating Economic Development Through Psychological Training*, by David C. McClelland and David G. Winter. *Economic Development and Cultural Change*, XX, No. 3 (April 1972), 575-81.

O'Connell, James. "Authority and Community in Nigeria." *Nigeria: Modernization and the Politics of Communalism*. Edited by Robert Melson and Howard Wolpe. East Lansing: Michigan State University Press, 1968.

__________. "Political Integration: The Nigerian Case." *African Integration and Disintegration: Case Studies in Economic and Political Integration*. Edited by Arthur Hazlewood. London: Oxford University Press, 1967.

Odufalu, J.O. "Indigenous Enterprise in Nigerian Manufacturing." *The Journal of Modern African Studies*, IX, No. 4 (1971), 593-607.

Oni, Ola. "Development and Features of the Nigerian Financial System - A Marxist Approach." *Nigerian Journal of Economic and Social Studies*, VIII, No. 3 (November 1966), 383-402.

Onitiri, H.M.A. "Nigeria's International Economic Relations: A

Survey." *Nigerian Journal of Economic and Social Studies*, III, No. 3 (November 1961), 13-38.

Ottenberg, Phoebe. "The Afikpo Ibo of Eastern Nigeria." *Peoples of Africa*. Edited by James L. Gibbs, Jr. New York: Holt, Rinehart and Winston, Inc., 1965.

Packard, Philip C. "The Need for Product Market Analysis: A Case Study of the Feasibility of Import Substitution in Nigeria. *Journal of Industrial Economics*, XVI, No. 1 (November 1967), 63-72.

__________. "A Note on Concentration and Profit Rates within the Manufacturing Sector 1963 and 1965." *Nigerian Journal of Economic and Social Studies*, XI, No. 3 (November 1969), 379-95.

Paden, John N. "Communal Competition, Conflict and Violence in Kano." *Nigeria: Modernization and the Politics of Communalism*. Edited by Robert Melson and Howard Wolpe. East Lansing: Michigan State University Press, 1971.

Papanek, Gustav F. "The Development of Entrepreneurship." *American Economic Review*, LII, No. 2 (May 1962), 46-58.

Patel, Surendra J. "The Economic Distance Between Nations: Its Origins, Measurement and Outlook." *Economic Journal*, LXXIV (March 1964), 122-9.

Paton, J.M. "Management Consulting in Developing Countries." *Management in Nigeria*, II, No. 3 (September-October 1966), 112-28.

Pearson, Scott R. "Nigerian Petroleum: Implications for Medium-Term Planning." *Growth and Development of the Nigerian Economy*. Edited by Carl K. Eicher and Carl Liedholm. East Lansing: Michigan State University, 1970.

Redlich, Fritz. "Economic Development, Entrepreneurship, and Psychologism." *Explorations in Entrepreneurial History/Second Series*, I, No. 1 (Fall 1963), 10-35.

Rimmer, Douglas. "Schumpeter and the Underdeveloped Countries." *Quarterly Journal of Economics*, LXXV (August 1961), 433-50.

Rosen, Bernard C. "Race, Ethnicity and the Achievement Syndrome." *American Sociological Review*, XXIV, No. 1 (February 1959), 47-60.

Schatz, Sayre P. "Aiding Nigerian Business: The Yaba Industrial

Estate." *Nigerian Journal of Economic and Social Studies*, IV, No. 2 (July 1964), 199-217.

__________. "The Capital Shortage Illusion: Government Lending in Nigeria." *Oxford Economic Papers*, XVII, No. 2 (July 1965), 309-16.

__________. "Economic Environment and Private Enterprise in West Africa." *Economic Bulletin*, VII, No. 4 (December 1963), 42-56.

__________. "The High Cost of Aiding Business in Developing Economies: Nigeria's Loans Programmes." *Oxford Economic Papers*, XX, No. 3 (November 1968), 428-32.

__________. "n Achievement and Economic Growth: A Critical Appraisal." *Quarterly Journal of Economics*, LXXIX, No. 2 (May 1965), 234-41.

__________. "Nigeria's First National Development Plan (1962-68): An Appraisal." *Nigerian Journal of Economic and Social Studies*, V, No. 2 (July 1963), 221-35.

__________; and Edokpayi, S.I. "Economic Attitudes of Nigerian Businessmen." *Nigerian Journal of Economic and Social Studies*, IV, No. 3 (November 1962), 257-68.

Schumpeter, Joseph A. "Economic Theory and Entrepreneurial History." *Change and the Entrepreneur: Postulates and Patterns for Entrepreneurial History*. Harvard University Center in Entrepreneurial History. Cambridge, Mass.: Harvard University Press, 1949.

Scitovsky, Tibor. "Two Concepts of External Economies." *Journal of Political Economy*, LXII (April 1954), 143-51.

Sinha, Jai B.P. "The n-Ach/n-Cooperation under Limited/Unlimited Resource Conditions." *Journal of Experimental Social Psychology*, IV (1968), 233-46.

Sklar, Richard L. "Nigerian Politics: The Ordeal of Chief Awolowo, 1960-65." *Politics in Africa: Seven Cases*. Edited by Gwendolen M. Carter. New York: Harcourt, Brace, and World, Inc., 1966.

Solow, Robert. "Technical Change and the Aggregate Production Function." *Review of Economics and Statistics*, XXXIX (August 1957), 312-20.

Stolper, Wolfgang F. "The Main Features of the 1962-68 National

Plan." *Nigerian Journal of Economic and Social Studies*, IV, No. 2 (July 1962), 85-91.

Teriba, O.; and Philips, O.A. "Income Distribution and National Integration." *Nigerian Journal of Economic and Social Studies*, XIII, No. 1 (March 1971), 77-122.

Tyagarajan, Meenakshi. "The Development of the Theory of Entrepreneurship." *Indian Economic Review*, IV, No. 4 (August 1959), 135-50.

"Vinyl Polymers and Copolymers." *Modern Plastics Encyclopedia, 1965*, XLII, No. 1a. Edited by Joel Frados. New York: B.F. Goodrich Chemical Co., 1964.

Warren, W.M. "Urban Real Wages and the Nigerian Trade Union Movement, 1939-1960." *Economic Development and Cultural Change*, XV, No. 1 (October 1966), 21-36.

Weisbrod, Burton A. "Education and Investment in Human Capital." *Journal of Political Economy*, LXXX, No. 5, Part 2 (October 1962), 105-13.

Wolf, Charles, Jr. "Institutions and Economic Development." *American Economic Review*, XLV (December 1955), 867-83.

Yesufu, T.M. "Manpower and Educational Objectives for Nigeria's Reconstruction and Development." Conference on National Reconstruction and Development in Nigeria, University of Ibadan, Ibadan, 24-29 March 1969.

Official Publications and Documents

Central Bank of Nigeria. *Annual Report and Statement of Accounts*. Lagos, 1960-1975.

Central Bank of Nigeria. *Monthly Report*. Lagos, 1960-1975.

Eastern Nigeria. *Approved Estimates of Eastern Nigeria, 1965-66*. Enugu, 1965.

Eastern Nigeria. Ministry of Economic Planning. *Eastern Nigeria Industrial Directory*. Enugu, 1963.

Mid-Western Nigeria. Ministry of Internal Affairs. *Mid-Western Nigeria Estimates, 1965-66 (Approved)*. Benin City, 1965.

Mid-Western Nigeria. Mid-Western Nigeria Industrial Directory, 1964. Unpublished document, Benin City, 1964.

Nigeria. *Supplement to Official Gazette Extraordinary, L.N. 46*, Vol. LII, No. 29 (1 April 1965).

Nigeria. *Supplement to Official Gazette Extraordinary, L.N. 92*, Vol. LII, No. 65 (18 April 1965).

Nigeria. Ministry of Commerce and Industry. *Handbook of Commerce and Industry in Nigeria*. Lagos, 1962.

Nigeria. Ministry of Commerce and Industry. *Industrial Directory, 1964*. Lagos, 1964.

Nigeria. Ministry of Commerce and Industry. Quantitative Information on the Footwear Industry. Lagos, May 1965.

Nigeria. Ministry of Commerce and Industry. Registration of Business Names. Lagos, 1965.

Nigeria. Ministry of Economic Development. *Guidelines for the Third National Development Plan, 1975-80*. Lagos, n.d.

Nigeria. Ministry of Economic Development. *Guideposts for Second National Development Plan*. Lagos, June 1966.

Nigeria. Ministry of Economic Development. *National Development Plan, 1962-68*. Lagos, n.d.

Nigeria. Ministry of Economic Development. *Second National Development Plan, 1970-74: First Progress Report*. Lagos, 1972.

Nigeria. Ministry of Economic Development. *Third National Development Plan, 1975-80*. 2 vols. Lagos: Central Planning Office, 1975.

Nigeria. Ministry of Education. *Investment in Education: The Report of the Commission on Post-School Certificate and Higher Education in Nigeria*. Lagos, 1960.

Nigeria. Ministry of Finance. *The Six Budget Speeches, 1958-1963*. Presented to the Federal House of Representatives. Lagos, n.d.

Nigeria. Ministry of Information. *Economic and Statistical Review*. Lagos, 1960-1973.

Nigeria. Ministry of Information. *Estimates of the Government of the Federal Republic of Nigeria, 1965-66 (Approved)*. Lagos, 1965.

Nigeria. Ministry of Information. *Second National Development Plan, 1970-74*. Lagos, 1971.

Nigeria. Ministry of Information. *Statement on Industrial Policy*, Sessional Paper No. 6. Lagos, 1964.

Nigeria. Ministry of Labour. Registration of Businesses. Lagos, 1965.

Nigeria. Office of Statistics. *Annual Abstract of Statistics: Nigeria*. Lagos, 1962-1973.

Nigeria. Office of Statistics. *Digest of Statistics*. Lagos, 1962-1972.

Nigeria. Office of Statistics. *Economic Indicators*. Lagos, 1960-1972.

Nigeria. Office of Statistics. *Gross Domestic Product of Nigeria, 1958/59-1966/67*. Lagos, August 1968.

Nigeria. Office of Statistics. *Nigeria Trade Summary*. Lagos, 1960-1972.

Nigeria. Office of Statistics. *Industrial Survey of Nigeria, 1964 and 1965*. Lagos, 1968.

Nigeria. Office of Statistics. *Population Census of Nigeria, 1963*. III vols. Lagos, 1968.

Nigeria. Office of Statistics. Supplement to the Industrial Directory, 1965. Lagos, 1965.

Nigeria. Office of Statistics. *Survey of Rural Household Enterprises*. Lagos, 1965.

Nigeria. Parliament. *Parliamentary Debates* (House of Representatives), Vol. XVIII, No. 10 (5 April 1965).

Northern Nigeria. *Estimates of the Government of Northern Nigeria, 1965-66 (Approved)*. Kaduna: Government Printer, 1965.

Northern Nigeria. Ministry of Economic Planning. *Northern Nigeria Industrial Directory*. Kaduna, 1965.

United Nations. Statistical Office. Department of Economic and Social Affairs. *Statistical Yearbook, 1964*. New York, 1965.

United States. Department of Commerce. Bureau of the Census.

Census of Manufacturers: 1947, Vol. II. *Statistics by Industry*. Washington D.C.: U.S. Government Printing Office, 1949.

United States. Department of Commerce. Bureau of the Census. *Sixteenth Census of the United States: 1940*, Vol. III. *The Labor Force: Occupation, Industry, Employment and Income*, Part I. *U.S. Summary*. Washington, D.C.: Government Printing Office, 1943.

Western Nigeria. *Western Nigeria Estimates, 1965-66 (Approved)*. Ibadan, 1965.

Unpublished Sources

Afuba, Jerome N. "A Feasibility Study of an Eastern Shoe Firm." Economic Development Institute Working Paper No. 1, University of Nigeria, Enugu, March 1965.

Bowles, Samuel. "The Efficient Allocation of Resources in Education: A Planning Model with Application to Northern Nigeria." Unpublished Ph.D. dissertation, Harvard University, 1965.

Curry, Robert L., Jr. "Technology Transfers to Africa: The Role of Multinational Corporations." Paper presented at the African Studies Association meeting, Syracuse, 31 October-3 November 1973.

DeWilde, John C. *The Development of African Private Enterprise*. II vols. International Bank for Reconstruction and Development, and International Development Association Report No. AW-31, Washington, D.C., 10 December 1971.

Harris, John R. "Industrial Entrepreneurship in Nigeria." Unpublished Ph.D. dissertation, Northwestern University, 1967.

Henderson, John P. "Wage Policy in Africa." Paper presented to the Conference on African Economic Development, Temple University, Philadelphia, 18-19 April 1968.

Kilby, Peter. "Nigerian Industry in the Northern Region." Unpublished report submitted to the United States International Cooperation Administration, April 1961.

Melson, Robert. "Marxists in the Nigerian Labor Movement." Unpublished Ph.D. dissertation, Massachusetts Institute of Technology, 1967.

Miller, Joseph C. "Nigerian Tax Legislation: An Outline." Report to the Economic Development Institute, University of Nigeria, Enugu, 1965.

Nafziger, E. Wayne. "Entrepreneurship, Social Mobility and Income Redistribution: A Case Study of Industrialists in Visakhapatnam, South India." Unpublished manuscript, Honolulu, 1976.

Nafziger, E. Wayne. "Nigerian Entrepreneurship: A Study of Indigenous Businessmen in the Footwear Industry." Unpublished Ph.D. dissertation, University of Illinois, 1967.

Pabaney, A.D., Danzig, Elliot; Nadkarni, M.S.; Pareek, Udai; and McClelland, David C. "Developing the Entrepreneurial Spirit in the Indian Community." Small Industries Extension Training Institute and Harvard University, Working Report, Hyderabad, India, 20 September 1964.

Schatz, Sayre P. "African Capitalism: Development Policy in Nigeria." Unpublished manuscript, Berkeley, Calif., 1976.

Soyade, A.; and Oyejide, A. "Market Share and Profitability in Commercial Banking: The Case of Nigeria." Discussion paper 75-02, Department of Economics, University of Ibadan, 1975.

Periodicals

Standard Bank Review. London, 1960-1975.

West Africa. London, 1960-1976.

Index

ABOUT THE AUTHOR

E. Wayne Nafziger is an associate professor of economics at Kansas State University. His studies of the economics of Nigeria as a developing country, focused in this book on the successes and weaknesses of the capitalist class, have taken him several times to West Africa. He conducted research in Nigeria while based at Ahmadu Bello University in 1969 and at the University of Ibadan in 1970. Later a visiting scholar at the African Studies Center at Boston University, he continued his studies of Nigerian economics there and subsequently in the United Kingdom, where he was an honorary research fellow at the Centre of West African Studies, University of Birmingham, and a visiting scholar at the African Studies Centre, University of Cambridge.

Professor Nafziger is the author of numerous articles which have appeared in books and in such journals as the *American Economic Review*, *Journal of Modern African Studies*, *Journal of Development Studies*, *Nigerian Journal of Economic and Social Studies*, and *Explorations in Entrepreneurial History*. In addition to his work on African capitalism, he has written several studies dealing with entrepreneurship in South India.